MICHAEL YARDNEY's

GUIDE TO INVESTING SUCCESSFULLY

Published by:
Wilkinson Publishing Pty Ltd
ACN 006 042 173
PO Box 24135
Melbourne, VIC 3001
Ph: 03 9654 5446
enquiries@wilkinsonpublishing.com.au
www.wilkinsonpublishing.com.au

A catalogue record for this book is available from the National Library of Australia

NATIONAL LIBRARY OF AUSTRALIA

Title: Michael Yardney's Guide to Investing Successfully
ISBN(s): 9781925927931 : Printed - Paperback

Printed and bound in Australia by Ligare Pty Ltd
Design by Spike Creative
www.spikecreative.com.au

WilkinsonPublishing

wilkinsonpublishinghouse

WPBooks

Note to reader

This publication contains the opinions and ideas of the author. It is sold with the understanding that neither the author nor the publisher is engaged in rendering legal, tax, investment, insurance, financial, accounting, or other professional advice or services. If the reader requires such advice or services, a competent professional should be consulted. Relevant laws vary from state to state and from country to country.

Additionally, it is important to note that Australian laws and regulations are subject to constant revision and amendment and as such, some of those mentioned in this book may now be out of date. Any opinions, conclusions or recommendations set forth in this book are subject to change without notice.

The strategies outlined in this book may not be suitable for every individual and are not guaranteed or warranted to produce any particular results. Past performance may not be a reliable indicator of future performance.

This book has been written without taking into account the objectives, financial situation or needs of any specific person who may read this book, which means that before acting on the information in this book, the reader should seek appropriate professional or financial advice.

No warranty is made with respect to the accuracy or completeness of the information contained herein, and both the author and publisher specifically disclaim any responsibility for any liability, loss or risk, personal or otherwise which is incurred as a consequence, directly or indirectly, of the use and application of any of the contents within this book.

Acknowledgements

In early 2006 I approached publisher Michael Wilkinson with the manuscript for my first book.

He was initially courteous and polite, but not overly enthusiastic — until he read the manuscript. Then his gut feel gave a new, and then unknown, author (me) a chance.

Since then Michael Wilkinson has published my nine books and he regularly encourages me to update my books for the current economic climate, which is the reason you are holding this current edition of my bestselling book in your hands.

Many people have influenced my life, my thoughts, my values and my business and investment success. Creating wealth is never a solo effort. Similarly, this book would not have been possible without the support and encouragement of certain people who have contributed to my life in many ways.

Achieving this was far from a solo effort. Similarly, this book would not have been possible without the support and encouragement of certain people who have contributed to my life in many ways.

In particular, my wife Pam for encouraging me, supporting me in every way and putting up with all my late nights and weekends on the computer. She endures my almost fanatical attitude to business and property and continually encourages me through the good times and through all the things I still need to learn. I am humbled by her love and devotion, which I try hard but never quite succeed to match.

Special thanks go to my family, including our children and grandchildren for their love and encouragement.

Further thanks to my partners and leadership team at Metropole including, Ken Raiss, Mark Creedon, Brett Warren, Kate Forbes, Greg Hankinson, Leanne Jopson, Bryce Yardney, Arthur Kallos and the whole team of property professionals at Metropole. And thanks also to our many clients whose collective inspiration has given me strength.

Over the years I have read almost every book about wealth creation and investment ever written. I have learned a lot along the way and there are many ideas sprinkled throughout this book that I have learned from others. I guess I had to learn everything from someone at one stage, so I am sorry I cannot acknowledge everyone — I really can't remember where I first came across many of my strategies.

Where I recollect first hearing about an idea I try to give credit where it is due, but if I have omitted mentioning your name, please excuse me as I shamelessly acknowledge borrowing other people's good ideas picked up from observation or from conversation, books, CDs, DVDs, podcasts and seminars. As knowledge about negotiation, influence and persuasion isn't one individual's sole domain and there are really no secrets, I can only assume that these people also learned from and copied other people's ideas, books, CDs, DVDs, podcasts and seminars.

I must make special mention of Robert Kiyosaki who contributed to some of my concepts about wealth discussed in this book; Pete Wargent, some of whose thoughts on share investments I've included, and Morgan Housel, previously a columnist for Fool.com and now for the Collaborative Find — you really must read his witty investment wisdom.

I have also learned from the many successes, and also the failures, of the more than 3,000 property investors and businesspeople I have personally mentored through my 12-month mentorship program over the last 16 years. I am very proud of your successes.

And finally, to you the reader — thank you for choosing to invest in this book. Please take advantage of the information I have to offer by using it to become a better persuader so you can achieve more of what you want in life, by obtaining the financial independence you deserve.

Michael Yardney

Contents

INTRODUCTION

The fact is: money is central to our lives — we make tons of financial decisions every day. Wouldn't it feel good to make those choices with confidence?

So are you satisfied with your financial situation? Most people are not!

Maybe you've dreamt of retiring early, or of being able to retire at all? Maybe you're wanting to become rich so you're wondering how the rich got their wealth and then kept it growing?

Well … the one thing the rich have in common is this: they all invest.

Investing is the act of committing to an endeavour (a business, stocks, real estate, etc.) with the expectation of obtaining an additional income or profit.

Most people who want to change their financial circumstances know they should invest, but don't know where to start.

For many, it's a trip into the unknown and investing in our changing markets today is harder than ever because as well as the abundant investment advice and information available, there is all the noise, fake news and complexity to filter out.

Want proof? Not that long ago the Royal Commission into Banking made it very clear that the banks and many financial planners (especially those that work for financial institutions) really didn't have their clients' best interests at heart and many investors paid fees they didn't have to pay for services they often did not receive, while others achieved suboptimal investment returns.

But with us living longer, spending more years in retirement, and having to fund our golden years the need for the average Australian to invest is more important than ever.

However, I want you to see this book as investing in your future self, not your retirement. By the way, you can't rely on the government to fund your retirement. Currently the annual pension for a couple is around $36,000 a year and who knows what the government will be able to afford in the future.

So the aim of the third edition of this book is to help give you the financial education they didn't teach you in school, so you can learn to invest successfully.

I realise the world of investing can be awfully intimidating, but the financial world won't seem so complicated once you learn some of the lessons in this book.

I know this because for the past 21 years I have educated thousands and thousands of people from all walks of life in the fields of money management, personal finance and investment through my books, blogs, videos, seminars and podcasts.

In fact, I've been voted Australia's leading property educator and mentor, and one of Australia's 50 most influential thought leaders and it really makes my day when I get an email from somebody I've never met who credits my teachings to helping their financial success.

I've now written this book to help a whole group of new readers (and some who I have had the pleasure of working with before). There will be something in this book for you whether you have very little money to invest or a lot, whether you know very little about investing or whether you're an experienced investor.

I have written it for anyone who wants to be a better informed investor and secure their financial freedom, no matter how much money they have today.

While this book won't give you specific investment advice, my intention is to give you an insight into how successful investors invest, what they do differently to the average investor, how they make money and how they develop financial freedom.

If you want a really short answer to the above questions here it is … find out what the average person is doing and do the exact opposite.

For a more detailed answer, you'll have to read on, but don't worry if you don't understand some parts of this book at first. While I'm going to try and keep things simple, I'm obviously going to have to introduce you to new concepts, jargon and even some technical stuff. Take what you can out of it as you keep reading and I have extra resources for you when you register your book at www.InvestingSuccessfully.today.

You'll notice I'm not going to offer you any hot investment tips or "get rich quick schemes", but by the time you finish reading, you will know more about investing than the average person. Then with the extra resources you will receive when registering your book and ongoing support by listening to **The Michael Yardney Podcast** and reading my blog at www.PropertyUpdate.com.au, which is where a group of experts give daily success, money and investing advice, you'll be well on your way to investment success.

So, let me ask you …

How do you really feel about your financial future? Are you a little scared?

That's OK. Sometimes fear can be good because when you're afraid about your financial future it can prompt you to change your ways.

But I also know that for others, fear can paralyse them, forcing them to remain locked in their unproductive ways.

What I hope to do in this book is give you a different way of looking at money, your finances and wealth creation, and teach you the fundamentals of investing that the wealthy people already know.

If you don't learn to become financially fluent you will always be a slave to money rather than having money working for you.

You see … your current financial situation is the accumulation of all the things you've chosen to do and all the things you've chosen not to do about money.

But how do you decide what to do — or what not to do? The problem is that we seem to receive an overwhelming amount of frequently contradictory information about money, finance and wealth creation — often from people with vested interests. You know what I mean … the latest investment guru who offers a sure-fire way to make high returns with low risks in the areas of stocks, real estate or investing.

Let me be clear … what I'm going to discuss with you is not theory, but has worked personally in my life, for my family and for many thousands of my clients.

Becoming financially independent may be simple but it's not easy — and that's not a play on words.

Why listen to me?

I don't claim I know everything about money and personal finances — I only know what has worked for me (and what hasn't), and what has worked for the more than 3,000 people I have personally mentored over the years and the many more thousands of clients my team at Metropole has assisted.

And over the years my team and I have been involved in well over $4.5 billion worth of property transactions and currently my company Metropole Property Management manages over $2 billion worth of property assets for our clients.

And while I'm not a financial planner I'm a partner in licensed financial advisory and planning firm Metropole Financial Planning and I've learned a lot over the years from Ken Raiss my business partner in this company. I also have an interest in a second financial planning company—— Spark Private Wealth — with leading financial advisor Arthur Kallos.

Why invest?

When most people answer this question, they would say it's for the money, but in fact money isn't really what you're after, is it?

Most people are after choices in life — time choices, work choices, the feeling of freedom and security as well as the ability to contribute to your family and those less fortunate.

How would you feel if you woke up each morning knowing there was enough money coming in to cover not only your basic needs, but also your dreams? Well … learning to invest and building yourself a substantial "Cash Machine" of assets will give you the ability to turn your dreams into reality.

Once we achieve this, the truth is a lot of us will keep working. I know I have, but I'm doing it because I want to work, not because I have to work.

However, for most Australians maintaining the purchasing power (the ability to continue to fund their lifestyle as prices continue to rise) of their financial investments is their real challenge. Crafting a portfolio that will beat inflation over their decades of retirement is their second big financial challenge.

Most people don't think about how the spending power of their retirement income or pension will erode in the 20–30 years they spend in retirement. They don't realise that inflation is the cruellest tax of all, because it doesn't hurt the rich, but boy does it hurt poor people.

That because the wealthy are both owners and users. So, as the price of goods and services increase, the rich people who own property and shares are increasing their net worth and income in sync with (or usually greater than) what they use. Conversely, the poor could be classed as only users, subject to buying all the same goods and services at higher prices, while their lack of investments and ownership leaves their net worth and incomes stagnant and in reality falling behind in real terms.

Fortunately this book is about helping you get from where you are today to where you want to be financially in the future — it's about teaching you an important skill that most people have never learned, which is the ability to invest successfully.

The lockdowns and financial challenges caused by the COVID-19 pandemic reminded many Australians that they must take care of their own financial futures. They realised they couldn't rely on their job or their employer for security and even though the government did provide assistance and support, most of us understood that this was just temporary.

Interestingly, according to a report by Canstar, 2021 was the year when one in five Australians invested for the first time. Some in shares, others in property and yet others in cryptocurrency (I'll talk about this later in the book — but while they thought they were investing, in my mind this was speculation).

The same Canstar report showed that 22% of Australians think they'll need $1 million or more to retire comfortably. By the way … I don't think this is anywhere near enough, especially as we are living longer.

I also found it scary that 55% of the respondents to the survey felt they could enjoy a comfortable retirement on less than $1 million and that almost 25% of Australians had no idea how much they need to retire.

If you think about it, because of inflation, being a millionaire in 10 years' time will mean you are only middle class and by the time you retire being a millionaire will put you in the lower rungs of wealth in Australia.

The problem is most Australians don't have any investment plan, and this is much the same all around the world.

Studies show that three out of four Americans say they have financial worries but less than half report having any investment plan to solve their financial woes. In Australia, one in four people are in financial trouble, while in the UK it's one in five people, who say they have serious financial difficulties.

While the Australian Bureau of Statistics shows that overall Australians are wealthier than they ever have been, partly due to the increased value of their homes and their superannuation funds, clearly the current economic climate is still challenging for many Australian families.

Moving forward many Australian families will find themselves in financial difficulty as inflation creeps in, the cost of living increases, and interest rates rise more than their wages meaning their mortgage or their rent will eat up a bigger proportion of their pay packet.

That's why investing is important

One of the benefits of investing is that it helps your money grow faster than inflation, which as you now know will slowly erode the purchasing power of your dollar, making everything from bread to cars a little more expensive each year.

To understand this better, let me give you a couple of examples.

I bought my first investment property in 1971 — it cost $18,000 and I took a 30-year loan, not having any idea how I'd ever pay that off. And my tenant paid me $12 a week rent (and I was excited!).

Today, because of inflation, that same house would cost around $1.5 million and the tenant would pay $900 a week rent, but they would be able to afford to do so because their wages had gone up by the same proportion.

Similarly, my first car — a new Toyota Corona — cost $3,000 in the 1970s and today the equivalent would cost over $30,000. That's what inflation does — it decreases your purchasing power.

And this is unlikely to change in the future. In fact, after many years of low inflation, inflation is increasing around the world. Every year goods and services will get more expensive — things like your grocery and utility bills as well as clothing.

If you do nothing with your money, your purchasing power diminishes.

Imagine if you had $10,000 today — what could you do with it? Now ... what would it be worth in 10 years' time?

Of course you could put it in a savings account earning one or two per cent interest per year. Your account would now be worth around $11–$12,000 in 10 years. The problem is that inflation over the next 10 years will likely mean that it will cost you around $15–$16,000 then to buy what would cost you $10,000 today.

So inflation on the price of goods outpaced the interest rate in your savings account. And I haven't even considered the tax you'd pay on the interest.

While Australia's Reserve Bank is trying to increase the rate of inflation a little because a small amount of inflation is good for the economy, they're going to try hard to keep it within the 2–3% per annum band. What this means is you, as a consumer, are going to face higher prices on almost everything moving forward.

Now this will be a new concept to some because we have been in a low inflationary environment for the last decade, but most commentators agree that we're heading into a period of much higher inflation.

If you think about it, money is future purchasing power and one of your biggest financial threats is inflation. Another is outliving your money.

However, investing your money in assets that grow in value helps you beat inflation, and if you get it right it could outpace it a lot, which makes investing a crucial part of saving for your retirement.

You see ... an investment makes you money in one of two ways: by paying out income or by increasing in value over time.

Why saving doesn't work

I've just explained why saving your money doesn't work as a financial plan — your savings will lose money through inflation and tax.

In fact, the vast majority of what you will own when you retire will not be your savings; it will be the compounding effect of the growth in value of your home and your investments.

INVESTMENT SUCCESS FACT

The truth is, you'll never earn or save your way to wealth.

So for you to get a different financial result to the average person, or to those millions of baby boomers who sadly can't afford to retire, and to the younger generations who'll have the same problem when their turn comes around; you'll have to learn to master money, otherwise the lack of money will always master you!

You need to learn, and know, the rules of investing and understand the strategies used by those who have already achieved what you want to achieve. The good news is that you can save years of time and much heartache by simply learning the pitfalls to avoid and the successful strategies used to make the incredibly complex world of investing relatively simple.

Just in case you didn't realise, many of us are already investors. In Australia, your employer is contributing to your superannuation, socking away 10 per cent of your weekly pay packet for your financial future. In the United States, your employer may have enrolled you in the company's 401(k) and in the UK you're probably part of an occupational pension fund, which both you and your employer contribute too.

But, trust me on this, these compulsory pension or superannuation savings won't be enough!

In the past, life was much simpler — you'd get a decent education, a good job, work hard and eventually retire with the pension. Sometimes this was supplied by the government (depending on which country you lived in) and sometimes this was provided by your employer.

But I don't have to tell you that times have changed — you can't count on your job for life (most people have many different careers and jobs in their working life today), you can't count on the government to give you a pension, and you can't count on your automatic savings account, pension fund or superannuation to make you financially free.

And just to make things even more interesting, the choices seem more complicated today, too!

Sure you could invest in real estate or shares. But which property is "investment grade" and which stock should you buy? There are hundreds of global stock exchanges to choose from, tens of thousands of different stocks and thousands upon thousands of mutual funds. Plus there's a whole lot of instruments, some quite obscure, with clever acronyms like REITs, CDOs, $PCRs, CSCEs and HIBORs.

Today, we have so much information available (and even more misinformation) that even the most experienced investors can feel overwhelmed — especially when you realise that much of this information comes from people with a vested interest.

Isn't that where the financial services industry can help us? Not really.

Surveys show that less than one in four people trust the financial system, financial planners or brokers — and generally with good reason. While there are some great financial planners in Australia, unfortunately there has been a lot of questionable, self-serving advice given to many naïve investors over the years.

To counter this our financial regulators are making it harder to become a financial adviser and those remaining in the industry have become more regulated. This has resulted in many older planners leaving the industry as higher professional standards come into effect.

The big problem is that there is hardly any new advisers coming into the industry to replace them and those who are staying have increased their fees, in large part due to the extra cost of compliance and professional indemnity insurance. It has been estimated that advice fees at skyrocketed more than 28% in the past two years alone.

The result is those with significant assets can afford to and are prepared to pay the higher fees-for-service now demanded. But that can leave those who want simple advice or those who are just starting their investment journey (and really need help) left out in the cold.

The right advice

You may have noticed that when it comes to money, and particularly investing yours, *everyone* seems to have an opinion, but don't be misled because they rarely have one that will really help you. Opinions are a bit like belly buttons — everyone has one but they're rarely useful!

On the other hand, some people have got it right in the world of investing and their successes leave clues, which you can benefit from. Your job is to learn how they did it and my job in this book is to teach you how they did it.

By the way, they weren't lucky, they just did things differently to everyone else. Remember that it's your money, so it's time for you to learn how to control it and make it work for you.

And what I'll be discussing is not just theory — I've invested successfully since the early 1970s.

Well, let me be honest, that's actually not true. I've invested for five decades, and successfully for the past 25 to 30 years, but in the first 20 years I made a heap of mistakes. I got scammed by investing in a goldmine, hoping I would "get rich quick" overnight. I invested in shares, not really knowing what I was doing, made money during a mining boom in the 1960s and then lost all of my profits and more when the boom ended. I lost more than $500,000 handing over my money to a financial planner, someone supposedly qualified to manage my assets for me. But then slowly but surely I learned the right way to invest.

This book is to help you avoid the pain I went through and the "learning fees" I had to pay the market. What I'm going to share in this book could save you 15 to 20 years of heartache — it's what I would have liked to have known way back when I started.

Today I'm financially free and, while I live in Australia, I'm an international bestselling author on the psychology of success and wealth creation but as I mentioned I'm not a theorist. Remember … I bought that first investment property in the early 1970s for $18,000 and proceeded to turn a $2,000 personal loan into a very, very substantial multimillion-dollar property portfolio … in my spare time.

Today I am CEO of the Metropole Group of Companies, with a team of over 85 property and wealth professionals across our Australian offices in Melbourne, Sydney and Brisbane.

I've written nine books, four of them bestsellers, and two have consistently been #1 bestsellers on Amazon. Two of these have been translated into foreign languages and are bestsellers overseas. I've been voted Australia's leading property investment advisor or property educator and mentor five times in the last seven years, plus I'm frequently quoted in newspapers, magazines, on TV and on the radio.

My investment success has given me the time to contribute back to the community, including writing books like this one, to help others learn how to invest successfully.

I've been honoured to have great relationships with some of the most successful investors in Australia, both in real estate and the share market, and with successful investors around the world.

The purpose of this book is to teach you to become a successful investor and set up your own Cash Machine so you have an income for life without ever having to work for it — that's what I call financial freedom!

A difficult question

Before we begin your journey to investment success, however, we need to consider a difficult question, which none of us really likes to think about.

That question is: How long do you think you'll live?

Advances in medicine mean that we're all living much longer than our forefathers. In the UK, the average life expectancy is 81, in the US it's 79, and in Australia it's 83. Women generally live longer as well, with at least one spouse likely to live well into their 80s or beyond. So, with these long lives, we're going to enjoy (or not) a long retirement of 20 or more years, but the problem is most people aren't financially prepared for it.

No matter where you live, if you don't have another source of income, you will find your latter years to be very lean indeed. After working hard all of your life, who wants to just "survive" in our twilight years? No one does, of course, so you need to learn how to prevent such a terrible turn of events.

An important fact to consider is that your future is coming — whether you like it or not — but how much have you saved or accumulated for retirement? How are you going to survive? The answer, of course, is you have to save more (not that this will ever make you rich), so that you can invest your money successfully.

Why don't we do it? What is holding you back?

I'll discuss this in more detail throughout the book, but for many they just haven't thought about it. For others, it's just that they don't know what to do. To them, it just seems too complicated, or they lack financial fluency. But for most of us, it's just human nature; we're "too busy" living in the present to save and to make long-term investment commitments.

So what does your future look like?

Have you ever stopped to consider what you will be doing when you retire?

How you spend your money is entirely up to you. You deserve to be happy and enjoy a long and satisfying retirement. After all, haven't you worked for the majority of your life, earning money and paying taxes? Why shouldn't you finally enjoy the fruits of your labour?

So what do you want to do?

No more getting up because the alarm goes off. You get to choose what you will do each day. Maybe a round of golf? That's what my wife Pam does and she chooses to get up earlier than me two or three mornings a week to enjoy her golf.

Maybe you'll travel? Pam and I enjoy two extended overseas vacations a year (well that was before Covid locked the borders) and manage to fit in a few shorter local ones also.

Perhaps you'll give back to the community by volunteering your time and expertise?

You can do anything you want as long as you have enough money.

That's the kicker. You can do almost anything you want, but only if you have the financial means to do so.

So what's the solution?

What you do today will determine your tomorrow. You will have to look after your own retirement years by building a Cash Machine of investment assets that will create income without you having to work.

By the way ... I'm not suggesting that you should want to stop working once you build your Cash Machine — retirement is a middle-class concept and I've found that most wealthy people want to keep working. Consider these older people who still love what they do:

1. Rolling Stones' front man Mick Jagger (age 78 and with a net worth estimated to be over US$360 million) and the Beatles' Ringo Starr (age 81 and with a net worth estimated to be over

US$350 million) are still touring and entertaining audiences and they certainly don't need the money.

2. Warren Buffett remains the world's most successful investor, busily working at Berkshire Hathaway at 91.

3. Rupert Murdoch is still running his empire at age 90 — in fact, he's got married again recently.

4. Morgan Freeman continues to be an in-demand actor at age 84 and still loves his "job".

5. Yoko Ono, at 88, continues to hold successful art shows — and probably annoy Paul McCartney.

The point I'm trying to make is that life is for living, at any age, but we need the financial resources and knowhow to achieve our dreams and goals. I'm confident this book will provide you with the insight, knowledge and motivation to help you achieve a successful and fulfilling life — for today and for your many tomorrows — by teaching you how to invest successfully.

What is investing?

Just to make sure we're on the same page, in my mind investing is the act of committing money to an endeavour with the expectation of obtaining an additional income or profit.

In other words, investing means putting your money to work for you, which is different to what most people do — they work for money. The big problem with this is that if you want more money, you have to work more hours and there is a limit to how many hours you can work.

What investing is not

Most people who say they are investors are not. Sure, they think they are, but in my mind they're speculators or gamblers.

You may have heard that investing is about a "buy and hold" mentality but most investors have a "buy and hope" mentality. They buy and hope that the location of their property will be the next "hotspot" or they buy a stock and hope the market rises.

That's not what successful investors do. They make money regardless of the general movements in the market. I've noticed that successful investors make money in good times and just as much during bad times. On the other hand, average investors do poorly in good times and even worse during bad times. Interesting, isn't it? What this means is that it's something inside that makes investors successful, they're not dependent on the outside world.

Long-term investing success has very little to do with investment returns, but a lot to do with investor behaviour. Investing is more emotional than intellectual. In fact I've co-authored a book all about this — *Rich Habits, Poor Habits* (www.RichHabitsPoorHabits.com), which you will find in excellent adjunct to the information you learn in this book.

So, as I started to explain, investing is not speculating, gambling or a "get rich quick scheme". Sure you'll occasionally hear the story of somebody who invested in Apple years ago and made a killing, but that's a rarity.

If you try to pick the next Facebook, Google or Amazon today, I'd call that speculating. Just like those who look for the next real estate "hotspot". This is really just gambling, putting your money at risk by betting on an uncertain outcome with the hope that you might win money.

Taking control of your personal finances will take work, and, for some readers, a steep learning curve. But the rewards will far outweigh the effort required, with the benefit being that you won't have to let banks, your boss or investment professionals push your money in directions that you don't understand. You will be in control.

So what are you doing right now to invest in your future?

The fact is we should invest in the future all the time.

Some people are already doing that by planning now. They are making sure that today looks after tomorrow.

Every successful investor continuously works on their financial plan, every failed investor continuously reacts to the market and current events.

Of course, some people don't even bother investing for their future and as I've already explained there are many reasons for this. But the fact that you've picked up this book and are reading these words suggests that you're ready to invest ... so let's get started!

CHAPTER 1.
7 NUMBERS YOU NEED TO KNOW IF YOU WANT TO BECOME FINANCIALLY INDEPENDENT

When you first start considering investing it seems like there are so many things you need to understand to become financially successful that it can be difficult trying to keep on top of it all.

While there seems to be an overwhelming number of things to get your head around, the good news is the most important things you need to know about your personal finances can be summed up in a few simple numbers.

And by knowing these numbers you can track your wealth journey, make sure you're on target to become financially independent and it can help you plan how to get there.

So, in this chapter I'd like to make you aware of seven key numbers you need to know about your personal finances, and how to calculate them.

But before I do, I'd like to ask you a question ...

Where are you headed?

If you're like me you believe you have a future waiting for you, so what is store for you financially? If you think about it, it's likely to be one of four possible financial outcomes.

The following model should bring this home to you, so look at the following graphic and please work through this exercise with me.

What's your future?

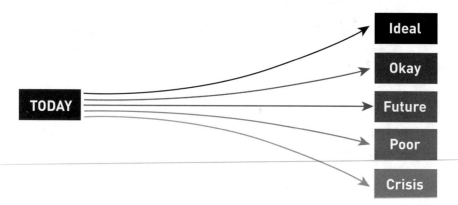

How long till you want to reach financial independence? 10 years? 15 years? Maybe longer?

If you don't invest wisely you'll run out of money before you run out of life.

Let's face it ... it's likely you're facing one of these four possible financial futures:

1. **An ideal future** where your Cash Machine will pour out so much money that you'll have the financial freedom to choose to work or not. You'll also have a sufficiently large asset base to live off the funds that it is generating and there will be a sufficient surplus to keep growing your assets so you'll be able to leave a legacy.

2. **An OK future** where you'll have reasonable income and limited choices, and on retirement you'll probably have to slowly eat away at your asset base and hope you don't live longer than your income.

3. **A poor future** where you'll still need to keep working.

4. **A crisis future** where you hope there will still be a pension to help you survive.

Looking at the above graphic, which trajectory are you on? Sometimes it's hard to know because at the beginning of the journey the four paths look much the same, but the further along your wealth creation journey you have travelled the further part the lines become.

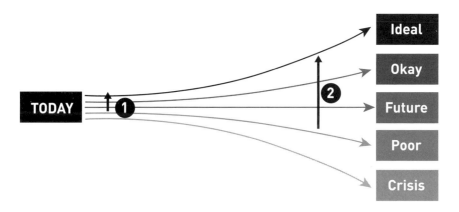

Looking at the graphic above if you are point 1 it won't take much to move you up a line or two onto a better trajectory and towards a better financial future. However, if you're at point 2 along your financial journey it will be much harder to get you to the financial future you desire.

If you think about it, the difference between the line you are on today and the line you want to be on in the future will only get larger. The gap between where you are now and the trajectory you want to be on will never be so small — this gap will only get larger — that's why it's time to take action.

And if you're already on your way to an ideal future — congratulations! The aim of this book is to give you the information to help get you there faster and safer.

So here's 7 numbers you need to understand to help you attain your ideal future ...

1. Your wealth window

One of the first personal finance numbers you need to know is how many months until you want to develop financial independence?

This is what I call your "wealth window".

Given the choice, we'd all like to stop working when we're good and ready. Or just work only because we want to, not because we have to.

So in order to plan for this, it's vital to know how many months or years you want, or have, to wait until you can stop working.

Once you know how much time you have left before reaching your goal of financial independence, you'll know how long you have for your investments to grow sufficiently to be able to either replace or contribute to your personal income.

How to calculate your wealth window:

- Decide when you plan to gain financial independence.

- Calculate how much time between now and then.

- That gives you your wealth window.

2. Your current net worth

You need to know where you're at now along your wealth journey which means you need to calculate your net worth.

Start by adding up the value of everything you own. Things like your savings accounts, cars, investments, any equity in a business, valuable items around your home, and obviously any investment properties you own.

While doing this it's also very important to note how much you have invested in appreciating assets like real estate, and how much of your money is tied up in depreciating assets such as a car or computer or any other high-value items which will only decline in value.

Remember, your returns will come from investing in or owning assets that appreciate in value, so this is where you want to ensure you invest your money.

Next, find out the amount you owe on each of your debts and add them up. The total number equals your total liabilities. This is everything from your home loan to personal loans, car loans, student loans, credit card balances, business loans, and any other type of debt you might have.

It might be a painful process to add these all up but how do you improve on your financial position if you don't know what position you're currently in?

It's important to remember here that not all debt is "bad debt".

Bad debt refers to where you've put money into something which is going to depreciate in value — such as cars and doodads. On the other hand, good debt can improve your financial position because you're using it to buy appreciating assets like residential real estate.

How to calculate your net worth:

- Take the value of all the things you own which have any value, add them up. This equals your total assets.

- Find out the amount you owe on each of your debts and add them up. The total number equals your total liabilities.

- Subtract your liabilities from your assets and that's your net worth.

3. *Your debt-to-income ratio*

Apart from understanding what you have in terms of assets and liabilities, it's important to figure out your debt-to-income ratio.

This is how much you owe relative to your income.

It's vital to know this because it shows you how much debt you have versus how much income you're bringing in. It is also an influencing factor when you apply for a home loan because many lenders want to see a lower debt-to-income ratio to be satisfied that you're not overstretching yourself.

But as a general rule of thumb, a debt/income ratio of 10% or less is outstanding.

If it's between 10–20%, your credit is good, and you can probably borrow more.

But once you hit 20% or above it's time to take a serious look at your debt load.

How to calculate your debt-to-income ratio:

  • Divide your total monthly debt payments by your income.

4. *Your rate of savings*

Every dollar from your monthly wage that you are able to put aside into savings is another dollar you are investing into yourself and your future.

So how much of your net income are you using to invest in your future self?

The rule of thumb is that we should all be saving 15–20% of everything we earn. Because the reality is, the more disciplined you are, the more you can save, the more you can invest and therefore the sooner you will be able to retire.

I've found you need to do the hard things now so that you have an easier life later, however, most people do the easy things now and have a hard life later. But most people don't learn to delay gratification, spend less than they earn, save, invest and keep re-investing till they have a substantial asset base.

That's the trick: Spend less than you earn, save and invest and earn some more of your investment.

It's a no-brainer.

How to calculate your rate of savings:

- Take the amount you save per month, divide it by your total income for the month then times by 100. This will give your rate of savings.

5. *Your financial independence value*

So now you understand your current financial position and you know when you want to become financially independent, and how much time you have left in your wealth window, but do you know how much money you need when that time comes?

It's worth thinking about how big your required asset bases will be right now.

How much do you need in property, shares, and superannuation to be able to provide the income you require to give you the type of lifestyle you want to live?

How much are you short?

How much do you need to add to your asset base in the remainder of your wealth window to be able to achieve this goal?

Once you've worked out how much you'll need per year to live the life you want, you can easily work out how to get to that number.

How to calculate your independence value:

- Calculate your expected monthly outgoings for when you reach that period of your life. That's your big number.

- Minus any investment income, you may have access to at the time and that gives you the shortfall you need to make up between now and then.

6. Your health disaster fund sum

How much have you put aside for a health disaster?

If something happens tomorrow, are your finances protected or insured? It doesn't matter whether or not you have children or other dependents – if illness would mean you couldn't pay the bills, you should consider income protection insurance.

But you're most likely to need it if you're self-employed or employed and you don't have sick pay to fall back on.

With average monthly premiums in the hundreds, it's easy to see why people don't want to pay for, or even claim on, income protection insurance. But it's a critical part of structuring and protecting your wealth creation for the long term.

How to calculate your health disaster fund:

- Calculate how much money you'd need to live on a monthly basis if you were incapacitated tomorrow and unable to earn your usual income.

7. Your credit score

It's vital that everyone checks their credit score at least once per year.

As a reflection of your past financial decisions, like your ability to pay bills on time, and how much debt you have in your name, it's a very important tool to show you how easy it'll be for you to make future financial decisions like buying a home or investment property.

Banks want to see a high credit score and will reward those who have it with the best rates. If you have a bad credit score it can make things much more difficult, and costly, in the long run.

You also want to look at your credit report to make sure nothing seems out of place.

It's a great way to discover fraudulent accounts in your name or pick up on mistakes that could have been made by companies with which you have loans.

It's been said there are only two types of people …

Those who outlive their money and those who don't.

Of course everyone wants to be in the latter group but most don't fall into that category.

However those that do develop financial independence tend to live their lives by design — they know the financial goals, they know what they want to achieve and by when, and then by understanding their financial numbers they do what they have to do to get there.

The longer your time frame between now and when you want to leave the rat race the easier it's going to be for you to build a substantial asset base to provide the retirement income you can't outlive.

Think about it … currently your life expectancy is likely to be in the 80s, yet with advances in medical science it's likely that many people reading this book will live to be 100 years old or more. In other words, their investment "cash machine" will need to fund 30 or even 40 years of retirement.

OK, now that you understand these financial numbers, you're starting to understand what you need to do to become financially free and enjoy your golden years, so let's move on with my framework of the 5 Levels of Investor.

CHAPTER 2:
THE FIVE LEVELS OF INVESTOR

Over the 50 or so years I have been investing I have had the privilege of working with many successful investors along the way.

In that time I have seen some who I thought were smarter than me fall by the wayside when their decisions proved to be wrong and I have carefully observed those who have maintained and grown their long-term wealth and investment success.

And in the past, when I was presenting at seminars throughout Australia and South East Asia, I had many lengthy discussions with successful investors to look for characteristics they had in common.

Interestingly, but probably not surprisingly, I discovered they had very similar habits and attributes which contributed to their ongoing success.

Throughout this book I'm going to share the top ideas and concepts that I've learned along the way to help you on the path to investment success. They have worked for others and they've worked for me, so they should work for you, too!

By the way … if in this book I talk about average returns on investments, even though these are based on past historical returns, please don't get bogged down in complexities.

I'm not suggesting, for example, that real estate will increase in value seven per cent each and every year however for the sake of illustrating a relevant point or principle I will assume a constant rate of return because over time things do average out.

So I'm not giving specific investment advice about the returns you'll receive — I'm just trying to illustrate a principle.

You can't get this by becoming a lender — you must become a borrower and use other people's money wisely. People have borrowed other people's money in return for interest payments for centuries but if you look back you'll find it was always the bankers who became wealthy, not the depositors putting money into their accounts.

So, if diligently saving your money in a bank isn't going to increase your wealth, how do you become a successful investor?

Models of success

As part of my mentoring of investors, I've created a number of models to allow them to understand where they're heading financially, what stage they are along the way and what the key focus areas and leverage points are that they can use to fast-track their journey to success.

In this and the next chapter, I'll explain the Five Levels of Investor and my Wealth Pyramid to help you see where you fit in and what you need to do to become a successful investor.

In my experience, while a few people will move up the rungs of these models and make it to the top, and some will drift a little from one level to the other, unfortunately most people will *safely* sit at one level for their entire life and never move anywhere at all!

These people become "stuck" because of their mindset, which is their programming about how they deal with money and the concept of success, and this stymies their potentially stellar financial and investment outcomes.

INVESTMENT SUCCESS FACT

Despite living in the some of the most affluent countries in the world, most people never achieve financial independence or investment success.

However, let's first start with a life-changing conversation I around 40 years ago.

Success concepts

Way back in the early 1980s my business partner at the time, Brian, came up to me and said, "Michael — I want a Cash Machine!"

"What?" I responded.

Brian explained, "You know, a Cash Machine. I'd like to come to work in the morning, flick the switch and the machine would start working and churn out money. At the end of the day I'd flick off the switch and go home to my family and then come back tomorrow and flick on the switch once more. And the machine would again start working and churn out more money."

As you can imagine I replied: "Sure, I'd like a Cash Machine, too." I mean — who wouldn't want one?

And even though at the time it seemed like a rather absurd pipedream, over the years I actually created exactly that — a substantial property investment portfolio that spits out cash week after week.

It has allowed me the opportunity to take two extended holidays per year with my family, to work because I want to work not because I have to work, and the ability to contribute back to the community, charities and my family.

I guess you also want a Cash Machine, don't you? And why not? Well, that's what this book is about; if you invest wisely over time you will be able to build your own substantial asset base that will become your Cash Machine.

This will take time, effort, moving out of your comfort zone and a little risk, and it has nothing to do with how much you earn in your day job. I've seen many people who earn hundreds of thousands of dollars a year, yet by spending most of it on a flashy lifestyle they fail to become wealthy.

Having said that, I've also seen successful investors build a substantial property investment or share portfolio while working at what some would call menial day jobs, earning relatively little in their pay packet. In other words, their job becomes something they choose to do, not something they have to do for their primary source of income. Yes, to build our own Cash Machine.

But they haven't done it by saving — it's too hard to do it that way, they've done it by becoming investors. So, let's look at the five levels of investors that I've come across, so you can work out where you are along your journey to success.

Level 0 — The Spender

Level 0 are really not investors — they tend to be spenders and borrowers and as a result they end up with a high level of debt. They spend everything they earn and often more. Their money runs out before the month does. They usually survive from pay packet to pay packet, using credit cards and store credit where they can.

The Level 0 investor lives for today. If they have some money they spend it, if they don't have money, they borrow it.

These are the people who when they need some cash go to the ATM and pay a fee to collect an advance on their own money and then pay interest for the privilege of using it. Their solution to financial issues that arise is to spend their way out of it or to take on more debt.

Do you know any Level 0 investors? A large part of our adult population falls into this category, and they will never become wealthy unless they do something radically different.

Level 1 — The Saver

The vast majority of people who aren't spenders will generally be what I call savers. Their main investment is their home, which they aim to pay off over time. Sometimes they squirrel away a few dollars of what's left over after paying tax but in general they save to consume, not to invest.

Savers tend to be afraid of financial matters and are generally unwilling to take risks. They're following the plan their parents and grandparents followed, which was to get a steady job, buy a house, pay it off and save a nest egg for retirement. The problem is savings, or even owning your home outright, doesn't make you rich and is not a strategy for investment success.

What usually happens is that they work hard over their lifetime, diligently save or pay off their home and are left with what will be a modest, and most likely an old and tired, house.

Savers are what I would call *financially illiterate*. They need to focus their efforts on building a solid base of financial and investment skills upon which they can grow their financial future. They will get the most leverage by investing in themselves and getting a quality financial education and beginning to build a network of peers that they can make the journey to success with.

Level 2 — The Passive Investor

Level 2 investors have become aware of the need to invest. They realise their superannuation or pension plan won't get them through retirement, so they start learning about investment and begin accumulating assets.

While they are generally intelligent people, they are still what I would call financially illiterate — they don't really understand the rules of money. But remember it's not their fault — nobody taught them. If anything, their parents taught them old fashioned, out-dated concepts about money.

Rather than taking responsibility for their financial education themselves, Level 2 investors tend to look for answers to their investment needs from outside sources or "experts". This makes them easy prey for the newest "get rich quick scheme" advertised in magazines or the latest flash-in-the-pan investment strategies spruiked by telemarketers.

Instead, they should refine their financial and investing education and focus their efforts on choosing a specific wealth vehicle that they are going to master on their journey to investment success. They must unlearn the flawed, incorrect and misguided lessons they have learned about money and wealth from unqualified teachers.

Level 3 — The Active Investor

Level 3 investors realise they must take responsibility for their financial future and become actively involved in their investment decisions to achieve success. They become financially literate by building a knowledge base of investment strategies and techniques, and they are starting to get their money working for them.

These investors *actively* participate in the management of their investments and concentrate on building their net worth. Their main focus is on growing their asset base by building a share or property portfolio.

As this is the asset accumulation stage of their investment life, these investors have in general moved to high growth, low yield investments to grow their wealth. This is where residential real estate really shines — it's the best asset class I know for growing your wealth safely and investing successfully.

Level 3 investors usually leverage the time and expertise of a network of industry professionals as they realise that they can't do it all themselves. They also upgrade their network of advisors and peers, often joining a "mastermind" group of like-minded people.

Level 4 — The Professional Investor

A very small group of investors move to the top rung of the ladder and become a Level 4 "professional" investor who has built, and now manages, a true investment business.

A Level 4 investor's property investment business has a substantial asset base that generates sufficient recurring passive income to pay for their lifestyle costs, plus they keep growing their investment portfolio whether they work in a real job or not.

They are well-educated, financially fluent, comfortable with the language of money and understand how the game is played. They understand the "system" of finance, tax and the law and use them to their advantage.

These investors tend to concentrate on optimising the performance of their properties, whilst at the same time minimising their risks to optimise their chances of investment success. While they are still accumulating assets, they are now more interested in cash flow that will allow them to gain the most out of life.

Rather than investing what is left after they have spent their money, they have the correct tax structures in place that enable them to spend what is left over after their money-making investment machine ploughs more cash back into further investments.

They have a finance strategy and financial buffers to buy themselves time and see themselves through the ups and downs of the economic and property cycles. And they understand the law as it relates to property so that they don't make the mistakes many beginning investors do.

These professional investors don't hand control of their investments over to others; they retain control while employing a proficient team of accountants, finance brokers, property managers, solicitors and property strategists who have great systems that achieve repeated and consistent results, which are reliable and predictable.

This gives Level 4 investors the freedom to choose whether they get up in the morning to go to work or not. Many still continue working because they enjoy it, but now they go to work because they choose to, not because they have to. Others find the time to contribute more to their community or to charities.

Neither the state of the economy nor the stage of the property cycle seems to affect the professional investor who makes money in good economic times as well as bad.

INVESTMENT SUCCESS FACT

Level 4 investors rarely stop educating themselves. They read, still attend seminars and webinars and surround themselves with a team of advisors and mentors. They're prepared to pay for solid advice — not only to increase their wealth but also to protect their assets from opportunistic family members, lawsuits and the government.

You will find that these investors personally own very little in their own names. But even though they "own nothing", they control everything through companies and trusts. By controlling the legal entities that own their assets, these investors gain considerable legal tax benefits and asset protection.

And a final point about Level 4 investors is that they teach their financial knowledge to their children and pass on their family fortune to future generations as their companies and trusts endure after they have departed this life.

So, where do you fit in? Are you a Level 0 or a Level 1 investor like so many people across the world? If so, don't lose heart, there is still time to learn how to invest successfully.

We'll start your journey in the next chapter as I outline how you can commit to your goals, understand where you sit on the Wealth Pyramid and most importantly how to move up it, so you are on the right path to financial freedom and investment success.

CHAPTER 3:
WHERE DO YOU WANT TO BE?

How are you going financially?

Are you where you want to be? Have you thought about retirement and what you would need to live out your days comfortably?

Interestingly, most people never get around to planning their retirement, but having clear, compelling goals and a plan to get there mobilises your focus toward actionable behaviour to achieve your dreams.

By the way ... plan on your plan never going to plan! Trouble happens to nearly everyone, but if you don't have a plan how will you know what to do or if you're heading in the right direction financially.

Many don't plan because life's too busy or they're not really even sure how to work out how much is "enough" so they never start the process of investing.

Of course, what is "enough" for one person may not be for another, depending on the lifestyle that you enjoy now, and the one you aspire to enjoy throughout your life and in retirement.

I've found many people want to end up with their home paid off with no mortgage plus a nest egg to live off. But they've never really thought about how big the nest egg should be or what they'd do if they outlive their nest egg.

That's why I started off by asking you to get a handle on seven financial numbers that's you'll need to understand to start planning to build your Cash Machine.

INVESTMENT SUCCESS FACT

Wealth creation is rarely an overnight success — it's a long-term strategy that requires ongoing attention and energy.

So how much is enough?

The question of what amount of money is "enough" is a very personal one — only you know the answer (actually maybe you don't!).

As you move through your life, working your way towards financial freedom, there will be bills that need to be paid and you'll need to put food on the table for your family.

Then there will be all those "things" you need to buy and fees you need to pay that will make life easier or better.

But once those needs are met, then what? How do you calculate the number that will be enough for you to live comfortably for the rest of your days?

Just so we're clear, this baseline number will be different for every reader of this book because what feels good to you is likely to be completely different from your neighbour.

Once you decide how much you'll need to live off, and it's best to do it in today's dollar value — it's just too hard to do it any other way — you'll then have to work out how big an asset base you need, so how many properties (actually the total value of your portfolio more than how many properties) or how big a share portfolio you will require to produce the Cash Machine you desire.

Then you have to devise a plan to build a Cash Machine. Don't think it's possible?

It may surprise you how much you'll earn over your lifetime. Working 40 years earning an average wage you're likely to earn $4 million in today's currency. Don't believe me? Just do the sums yourself.

The trick is not to spend it all, but to save some and invest it so it grows and multiplies. The trouble, in today's consumer-focused world, is that most of us have personal finances and an investment plan that resembles a hole-filled bucket! By the time the end of the month comes around, most people don't seem to have enough money left to do anything at all, let alone invest in a portfolio of wealth-producing assets.

If you want to see how productive your investment plan has been to date, first calculate your net worth (all assets minus all debts and liabilities). Then divide that number by the number of years you have been in the workforce. If the number is substantially less than your salary, where did the rest go? Tax would be some but what about the rest?

I've read some fascinating case studies where effective investors have used the power of compound growth (which I'll explain in detail later) to earn more money from investment in a few years than what they did during their entire working lives.

INVESTMENT SUCCESS FACT

The great challenge today is to maintain the discipline to invest a healthy portion of earnings into assets that produce a wealth-producing rate of return before you spend, which will underpin longstanding investment success.

And one of the first places to begin is with understanding where you fit into the Wealth Pyramid so you can start working towards your financial goals.

The Wealth Pyramid

Not too long ago the Great Australian Dream of home ownership was considered a way to fund retirement.

Ask any Baby Boomer and they'll tell you their parents taught them to get a good education, get a secure job, buy a home, pay it off and voila! You'll be set for your golden years!

Well … it's not really as simple as that — it takes more than just one house to fund retirement, especially as you can't count on the government or pension plans to look after you.

Of course owning your home free and clear in your latter years is certainly a good start, however, you will also need to set some investment goals and timelines.

To help you understand what's ahead let's look at one of my other models — my Wealth Pyramid. This shows what level you are at on your way to financial independence and what the key focus areas and leverage points are to speed up your journey.

It allows you to take stock of where you are now and where you want to be.

LEVEL 4
FINANCIAL
ABUNDANCE

LEVEL 3
FINANCIAL FREEDOM

LEVEL 2
FINANCIAL SECURITY

LEVEL 1
FINANCIAL STABILITY

LEVEL 0
FINANCIAL INSTABILITY

Like all pyramids it has a wide base and tapers towards the top — in other words, most people are at the lower levels of the wealth spectrum and fewer reach the top. Hopefully the knowledge and skills you'll learn from this guide will help you work your way up the pyramid, but the solutions you'll need to move from one level to the next will vary depending on where you are on the pyramid.

Unfortunately, most people don't really have any wealth and therefore are stuck at the first level.

Wealth Level 0 — Financial Instability

Since most people live from one pay day to the next, they're what I call *financially unstable.*

If they lose their job, or if they have an emergency (you know how these keep cropping up — an illness, the car breaks down, the refrigerator packs up), they have no financial reserves to cope.

Since they have no spare financial capacity, the only way to cope with these burdens is for people at Level 0 to borrow more (and get further into debt) and this only creates more financial hardship. They live their lives with their heads buried in the sand, not really conscious about money and their spending habits.

If they have money, they'll spend it, if they don't, they'll borrow it because their favourite pastime is shopping and buying "stuff" they don't really need. This means much of what they own has debt attached to it. They keep doing this and fooling themselves that they'll just work harder and pay off their debt some day.

If you ask them what their problem is, they'll tell you they don't make enough money. They think more money will solve their problems. But that's not right.

Their biggest problem is their money habits, which has nothing to do with how much they earn. It's what they do with the money they earn. As they move on in their lives and earn more, they just spend more. Today, they can't survive on the type of income they would have only dreamed they could achieve five years ago.

There are many high-income earners who fall into this category because they spend as much, or more, than they make. Sure some people at Level 0 Wealth can look rich — they may even have big homes or fancy cars, but they also have huge loans that they struggle to repay.

Unfortunately they often argue with their spouses about money, being in financial denial and justifying why they bought this or that.

In my experience, Level 0 Wealth can really be divided into two subgroups:

1. Casualties — I call those at the lowest level of the pyramid this because they're casualties of the money game. Each month they seem to find themselves in a worse place than they were the month before — getting themselves deeper and deeper in debt, usually through credit cards. They're paying high interest rates today to use tomorrow's money now. Of course they blame others for their problems — it's never their "fault".

They've often read books about budgeting or been told the trick of cutting up credit cards, but that just doesn't work. They don't know how to "do" money. Then half a level up the pyramid are the ...

2. Survivors — these are the employees, self-employed or even business people who seem to make just enough money each month to have nothing. And, if by accident, they end up with some money in the bank they spend it or take a holiday. They are just surviving.

While the fact is that at Level 0 people simply live beyond their means, the real cause of their problems is denial of this fact. Unless they are prepared to change, their financial future is bleak.

INVESTMENT SUCCESS FACT

The fundamental key to getting out of this level is mindset, education and taking financial responsibility.

Wealth Level 1 — Financial Stability

This is the most basic level of wealth and gives you some level of financial security or stability, which is when:

1. You have accumulated sufficient liquid assets (such as money in an offset account, line of credit or savings) to cover your current living expenses for a minimum of six months.

2. You have private medical insurance and some life insurance to protect you and your family's lifestyle should you become permanently ill, disabled, unable to work or if worst comes to worst — you suddenly die. I know that's an unpleasant thought, but in the past year, two of my own acquaintances died leaving their families in financial trouble.

At this level you will have the peace of mind that should any unexpected challenges come your way, such as retrenchment, a business failure, illness or disability, you and your family's lifestyle will not be unduly compromised. You will have adequate time to look for new sources of income to put you back on track.

The problem at this level is that your cash flow is being controlled by others — your boss who pays your salary or your clients who pay for your services. This means you're still on a treadmill and you don't have the ability to increase your cash flow without working more and that has its limits. Sure you've got a bit of a financial buffer, but if you stop working for a while you slip back to Level 0.

If you're at Level 1 your goal should be to move more of your cash flow into assets and build that Cash Machine so your income does not depend on you putting in more effort.

At this level your biggest leverage comes from investing in yourself and becoming financially savvy, building a solid base of financial and investment skills upon which you can grow your financial future, as well as beginning to build a network of peers you can make your journey with.

You'll also have to choose the first investment vehicle you are committed to master and become a devoted student, learning all you can about this niche wealth vehicle. In my opinion the best place for most people to start is residential real estate investing.

In making the decision on which wealth vehicle to go after, you must cultivate the discipline to say no to the pull of other "great opportunities" and methods.

INVESTMENT SUCCESS FACT

I've made more money by saying no to second-rate investment opportunities than I've made by saying yes to them.

Then carefully choose who you'll study with. Contrary to popular belief, the most expensive education isn't "graduate school" like an MBA. The most expensive education is one based on a flawed model and incorrect information. The hardest form of learning is unwinding all the wrong, mistaken, and flawed things you "learned" from unqualified teachers. So choose to learn from the best. It will save you years of frustration following defective models.

Wealth Level 2 — Financial Security

You achieve *financial security* when you have accumulated sufficient assets to generate enough passive income to cover your most basic expenses. These would include not more than the following:

- Your home mortgage and all home-related expenses such as your utilities, rates and taxes.

- All your tax payments plus the interest payments on your loans and debts.

- Your car expenses.

- Your grocery bills and minimal living expenses.

- Any insurance premiums including medical, life, disability and your house.

When you reach the level of financial security you will be able to stop working and still be able to maintain a simple, basic lifestyle. Of course you'll want more than that.

At Level 2 you will be an investor focused on building your net worth by owning assets that appreciate in value and ideally you'll accelerate the process by "manufacturing" capital growth through renovating or developing residential real estate, which I'll cover in a later chapter.

At the advanced stage of Level 2 you are beginning to make the transition from capital gains investing to investing for passive, residual cash flow. This means you've got to master a whole new skill-set.

You'll also have to radically upgrade your advisor network and peer group. Being the big fish in a small pond no longer serves you. You need to begin playing with people better than yourself.

Wealth Level 3 — Financial Freedom

You know you have achieved *financial freedom* when you have accumulated sufficient assets to generate enough passive income to pay for the lifestyle you desire (not necessarily your current lifestyle) and all of your expenses, without ever having to work again.

Having first built a substantial asset base (of properties, shares or businesses), now you are using your assets to create cash flow, which doesn't mean you *won't* go to work again, but you will now be able to make the choices you want because you have freedom.

At Level 3 your focus should be on stabilising your passive income streams and fine-tuning your estate planning and asset protection. Now is also a great time to grow your service to the world by finding ways to expand your contribution.

Level 3 is NOT about "retirement", it's about regeneration and contribution.

Wealth Level 4 — Financial Abundance

A small group of people around the world achieve *financial abundance* when their Cash Machine works overtime. Not only are they free of financial pressures, but they have so much surplus income after paying for their lifestyle, all of their expenses and their contributions to the community (often through charity work or donations) that their asset base just keeps growing and growing.

A couple of last thoughts about the Wealth Pyramid. There is nothing new about this hierarchy of wealth — it's always been there and we're all part of it. Complaining about where you are won't help. However, your level of wealth is your choice. Despite that, most people get stuck at a particular level and never achieve investment success.

INVESTMENT SUCCESS FACT

The main question you need to ask yourself is this: "Are you planning on getting rich and being an investment success or are you planning on being poor?"

Steps to investment success

As I've already explained, the rich keep getting richer — there's no denying that. They get a lot richer. And the poor get — well, what do they get? Too often, they get ignored. Or we don't even know who they are.

Most of us would like to become financially independent, to be emancipated from our jobs, yet millions of people got up this morning and drove to jobs that they can't stand. Were you one of them?

Would you like to get out of the rat race and travel a bit more, or play a little more golf, or spend more time with your family, or become more self-reliant and not dependent upon your employer? Would you like to have some extra cash in the bank?

The fact is: no one has to be stuck on a treadmill or in a job they hate. You can choose to make financial independence and investment success a reality in your life if you make plans and goals and most importantly commit to them! I think it was Steve Jobs that said: "It's not your fault if you're born poor, but it is your fault if you die poor."

But, first, let's look at some cold hard facts so you understand what's at stake if you don't.

Retirement reality

Across the world, people are living longer but unfortunately most won't have enough money to live comfortably in their retirement. In fact, many people will have to rely on the meagre provisions of the pension, or equivalent, in their home country. A report by Mercer found that 54 per cent of Australians expect to have less money than they need for the lifestyle they desire in retirement.

Retiring comfortably is increasingly looking like a distant dream for most Australians with nearly half of the country's population expected to outlive their savings. In fact, nearly 10 per cent of the population may be forced to rely only on the age pension for 15 years or more.

Key findings of the research included:

- One in four Australians will outlive their retirement savings by more than 10 years.

- 54 per cent of Australians expect to have less money than they need for the lifestyle they desire in retirement.

- On average, people expect to have half the amount they need to retire comfortably, falling short by almost $500,000.

With so many people staring down the barrel of a miserable retirement, what can you do to make sure you're not one of them?

Your wealth plan

The bottom line is that if you want to become a successful investor you must start on your journey today and that involves formulating a wealth plan.

Planning is bringing your future into the present so you can do something about it now, meaning your wealth plan will be the road map you can follow to turn your hard work and investing into your future financial freedom and security.

Throughout this book I'll discuss many of these steps in detail but as we're just at the beginning of your road to investment success, here's an overview of how to create your wealth plan.

Step 1. Your strategic financial assessment — determining exactly where you are at financially.

Step 2. Setting your financial goals — for the short-, medium- and long-term.

Step 3. Educating yourself and *overcoming your fears* — about investing money and strategically planning to invest.

Step 4. Choosing your investment vehicles — ones that suit each of your talents, knowledge, and risk profile and will eventually convert your assets into passive income.

Step 5. The right structures — setting up the correct finance, ownership and tax structures for your investments.

Step 6. Investing wisely — saving and investing your savings to slowly build your asset base.

Step 7. The importance of reviews — involves regularly reviewing the performance of your investment portfolio.

Step 8. Continuing education — continually educating yourself to gain insights into your wealth-building so you can leverage your efforts and ensure your investments outperform.

Now that you have a good understanding about the Wealth Pyramid, the reality of retirement and the importance of developing a wealth plan, let's take a look at how to start your investing journey towards success in the next chapter.

CHAPTER 4:
GETTING STARTED

Ready to get started on your investment journey?

What you do next will depend upon what investor level you are at, because at each level you will have different learning requirements and leverage points to accelerate your investment success, as well as to minimise risks.

Let's start with my advice for beginners …

Level 0, Level 1 and Level 2

Don't worry if you are at these investor levels — everyone has to start somewhere! My advice if you're just getting started is you should begin by investing in your financial education.

It's important that you learn the essential skills of investment as well as becoming financially fluent (understanding the language of money, finance and tax) by reading books, attending seminars and subscribing to investment blogs.

And you're already on the right track to increasing your financial education by investing in this book!

Now is the right time to establish sound financial habits — get rid of your bad money debt and continue to work more on yourself than you do on your job so you become more valuable to your employer (which will help you earn more money) and as an investor.

INVESTMENT SUCCESS FACT

This is the perfect time to find a mentor who will speed up your learning curve and it's a great time to join a mastermind group of like-minded people who are equally committed to achieving financial freedom through investment.

Don't be tempted to make substantial investments at this early stage, no matter how enticing they seem. You haven't yet developed the skills or the perspective to fully understand the risks involved and the landscape is littered with casualties of enthusiastic, but amateurish, investors who lost it all before they really even began.

Many of these people weren't actually investors at all, even though they thought they were. They were actually speculating with the hope that the value of what they bought would increase in the short-term, even though they often didn't understand the fundamentals.

This is also the time to build your professional network of contacts that you will later rely on to help you along your investment journey. Your mentor should be able to help you as you should also have access to their address book.

Level 3

As an active Level 3 investor your focus should be on building your asset base and continuing to improve your financial skills.

You'll have to choose which investment vehicles you will use to grow your wealth — don't worry too much about this at the moment because I'll cover this in detail in future chapters.

The key at Level 3 is not to invest for cash flow, but to invest for asset growth — to build an asset base. I'm not saying cash flow isn't important — it is essential to keep you in the investment game, but the only way you'll get out of the rat race is by building a big enough asset base that will then become your Cash Machine.

Next I'm going to suggest you only invest when you can generate wealth-producing rates of return — and this is often through forced appreciation. What I mean is when you buy an asset, whether it is a property, a business or any other asset, rather than letting the marketplace do the heavy lifting, you should be able to add significant value through the work you add to it after buying it.

A great example of this is a property to which you add value through renovations and thereby manufacture capital growth as well as increasing rental returns and depreciation allowances.

This is a great example of "forced appreciation" as the increase in value had little to do with the market and a lot more to do with how you forced the property to become more valuable by the skills you brought to the deal and improvements you made.

Much the same can happen if you buy a business and add value, however it's virtually impossible to force appreciation when you buy stocks in a publicly listed company.

INVESTMENT SUCCESS FACT

This concept of forced appreciation is important to Level 3 investors as it speeds up their wealth creation journey and is extremely tax-efficient because in general the gains in the value of the asset won't be taxed.

To use the power of forced appreciation early in your investment journey, you'll have to put in time and energy to educate yourself, or better still, to harness the power of a good team of experts who have already achieved the sort of results you're wanting to achieve.

While I suggested that beginning investors display caution, as you become a successful Level 3 investor and aggressively grow your asset base, it could be time to take some calculated risks and magnify your returns by using leverage.

At this stage it's critical to get sound tax advice and grow your asset base in a tax advantaged way. I'll explain what I mean in a future chapter, but at this point just note that this is a powerful strategy that can help you grow your asset base faster and safer.

This is also a good time to get legal advice regarding asset protection and estate planning, especially if you're looking towards setting up a lifetime legacy for your children and grandchildren.

As you progress up the rungs of the investment ladder as an advanced Level 3 investor you will start transitioning from the asset growth stage to the passive income stage of your investment journey.

The skills and strategies you used to become a Level 3 investor won't necessarily make you a professional Level 4 investor. This means you'll keep working on yourself as much as you do on your investment business. Can you see a theme here? Successful investors never stop learning!

The reality of investing

You'll find a lot written about investing in books, on the internet and in magazines — and the topic can be as broad, deep and complicated as you want it to be. You can dig deep and try and master the complexities of the alpha or beta variation of your portfolio or assessing the impact of the rising middle-class in China on the Australian tourism economy.

On the other hand, you can make it as simple as you want to be, by mastering a handful of principles that, if adhered to, will help grow your wealth and allow you to obtain financial freedom.

INVESTMENT SUCCESS FACT

The secret to investment success is to spend less than you earn, save, become financially educated, develop a strategy, and invest early and often.

There are really only two things you can do with money — spend it or save it. Since spending is obviously more fun that is what most people do, but those who learn the discipline of saving and investing will have a lot more to spend on even more fun things at a later date!

Those who learn to delay gratification always seem to get better things, don't they? It's much the same for those who learned to save and invest in their future financial security.

Why aren't more investors successful?

You're probably thinking; if investing is so easy, why do most investors fail to achieve this type of return?

In my experience, there are generally four reasons why so many investors fail to ever become successful:

1. Most people don't ever start investing because they're too busy leading their lives.

2. Many of those who do invest start too late for compounding to work its magic. I'll discuss this concept in more detail in a future chapter.

3. Some investors pay too much in fees or tax along the way, which erodes their returns and therefore their overall financial success.

4. Many investors make poor investment decisions. Most investors follow the herd, investing near the end of the boom because they've been carried away by the optimism in the media. To make matters worse they then sell up when market sentiment changes and pessimism prevails. They usually get into the property or the stock market just in time to capture a market downturn and then sell up just in time to miss the beginning of the next upturn in the market!

In my view, each of these factors can really be attributed to one thing — financial illiteracy. Since you weren't taught about investing at school and it's unlikely you've had wealthy mentors, in this book I want to begin teaching you how to manage your money because the cost of financial illiteracy is very expensive and will ultimately extract a significant learning fee from you.

Ready to start your investment journey?

As I frequently say: life is too important to simply work for your money! You should be enjoying life by having your money work for you. You need to transition from working for your money to having your money work for you.

No matter what level of investor you are today — whether you're a beginner or a seasoned professional — I believe you will benefit from the advice in this book.

Investing can be intimidating. There's lots of big numbers, concepts, money, emotions, salespeople and your future involved. And your journey to financial freedom will be a long one but you won't arrive at your final destination any sooner by rushing, looking for the next get rich quick scheme, or cutting corners.

The next step in your journey is understanding the different investment options available because if you want to live a comfortable life now and in retirement you need to learn how to turn your income into appreciating assets that will set you up for life.

CHAPTER 5:
YOUR INVESTMENT OPTIONS

OK, now that you understand *why* you should invest, in this chapter I'd like to look at the various options available and then we will examine some of these in more detail.

In reality, when it comes to investing, you really only have four options:

1. Cash — either deposits in the bank, bonds or term deposits.

2. Business — the wealth creation strategy of many multimillionaires.

3. Property — my favourite investment vehicle.

4. The stock market — you're probably already investing in this without even knowing through your superannuation or pension fund.

1. Cash

The only thing that many people seem to think they "know" about investing is just putting their money in the bank because they've been told that saving is a good habit, which it is, but in my mind it's not a way of getting rich. Here's three reasons why:

Firstly, the bank pays you a measly few per cent interest rate on your money and lends your money out to other people at a much higher interest rate — now that's a great investment ... for the bank!

Sure, there are ways of getting slightly higher interest rates, such as special savings accounts, term deposits or bonds, but to become wealthy your money is going to have to be invested at wealth-producing rates of return and that doesn't happen in a bank.

Secondly, the government taxes the interest you earn, which reduces your returns.

Thirdly, inflation eats away your savings. If, perchance, over the next 20 years you managed to somehow save and invest $200,000, after inflation in 20 years' time, your money will buy you far less than it will today.

I know some investors try and achieve a slightly increased interest rate by investing in bonds, which is effectively lending money to a government or company who pays you more interest than the bank. However not all bonds are the same — some are safe and others very risky.

To my mind you need to invest in assets that grow in value, have wealth-producing rates of return, outperform inflation, have the benefits of being able to leverage against them and work in a tax-effective environment. So don't try and save your way to wealth.

2. Business

Many of the wealthiest people are in the business of business.

Every year *Forbes* magazine lists the world's wealthiest people, while Credit Suisse and Cap Gemini annually report the number of high net worth individuals around the globe and you will always find a preponderance of businessmen and women in these rich lists.

But while a small group of businesspeople build their businesses into a truly profitable enterprise that can work without them, which clearly makes this a great form of investment, the majority of businesspeople never become rich.

It's often quoted (but never actually been statistically proven) that 80 per cent of new businesses fail in the first five years, and of those who do survive, 80 per cent don't make it through the next five years.

I've found many people start a business, sometimes a franchise (thinking this is more secure) because they're sick of working for a boss who is usually not as "smart" as they are. In truth, they just bought themselves a job and are as much, if not more, in the rat race than the average employee.

They've just swapped working five days a week for a guaranteed pay packet, to working six or seven days a week, often for no pay, and exchanged one boss for many bosses (now called customers or clients).

Worse still, many borrow money using the equity in their homes to commence their business, meaning that if the business fails they've not only lost their business but potentially their home.

Despite the fact that we all like lattes, to borrow a couple hundred thousand dollars to buy a Starbucks franchise, when there's another coffee shop around the corner and one across the road, means you're in for a lot of hard work and you've really just bought yourself a job, not an investment.

In my mind, businesses are a high-risk investment, and most people are not cut out to run a business because they don't have the right skills, mindset or enough money behind them.

Now let me give a quick disclaimer here — I run a very successful business based in three Australian states that employs over 80 people and has been in operation for well over two decades. So I know businesses can be a great investment, but I also know that's the rarity.

INVESTMENT SUCCESS FACT

If you're looking to make your investments in business, you need to set up an enterprise that will work for you without you having to be there.

This means that if you want to take a prolonged vacation, you could and your business would still be creating passive income while you're away. Your business will have systems in place and people to run them and this will make it saleable to other potential investors — now you will own a real asset.

There are many good books available about entrepreneurial skills and how to set up a business — this is not one of them. Instead I'm going to recommend you invest in real estate or possibly the stock market or perhaps both.

3. The stock market

When you invest in the stock market (the great companies of the world) you're investing in real companies, who sell real things to real people.

That's why many investors "have a go" at investing in the stock market.

Some invest directly in shares, others in indexed or mutual funds. Some trade in the short-term to create income and others trade complicated derivatives trying to beat the markets. While they may think they're investing, these people are really speculating with very few getting any reasonable type of return.

However, some who accept that they don't understand how the stock market works and consider it risky, tend to hand their money over to financial planners who invest in managed funds and earn a nice commission along the way. These are really Level 2 (passive) investors who see it as a safe option to allow somebody else to look after their money, while in reality this is not a way to get wealthy — at best you'll get average results.

I've found that one of the biggest risks in the stock market is not being in it.

4. Real estate

Real estate is a popular form of investment, probably because everyone lives in a property, either as an owner or a tenant, so many people think they know a little bit about it and perceive property to be less risky.

Having said that most property investors fail.

In Australia, the statistics show that 50 per cent of people who get involved in property investment sell up in the first five years. And of those who remain in the game, less than eight per cent ever own more than two properties and only one per cent of all property investors own six or more properties.

What's the ideal asset for you?

So what's going to be the best investment in the years ahead for you? Which vehicle is going to assist with your goal of investment success?

One thing is certain: there is no such thing as a perfect investment. If somebody tells you they have found "*the* perfect investment" be very sceptical and ask lots of questions, because chances are they're trying to sell you something you just shouldn't buy.

The things I look for are:

- Liquidity (the ability to take your money out by either selling or borrowing against your investment).

- Easy management.

- Strong, stable rates of capital appreciation.

- Steady cash flow.

- A hedge against inflation, and

- Good tax benefits.

When you look at the major categories of investments, you will recognise that not many fit the bill when it comes to all five of these criteria.

INVESTMENT SUCCESS FACT
To grow your wealth in the current uncertain world economic environment you're going to have to invest in assets that are both powerful and stable.

By *powerful*, I mean that they must have the ability to grow at high, wealth-producing rates of growth. In other words, you're going to have to be able to leverage or borrow against them.

By *stable*, I mean your investment should grow in value steadily and surely without major fluctuations in value.

Many investments are powerful, and many are stable, but only a few are both. Prime residential real estate is one of the investment vehicles that has both power and stability in spades.

Now that doesn't mean it's perfect, because as I've mentioned earlier, property is not as liquid as many other investments. It can take months to get cash out of your portfolio if you sell a property. Or you may be able to get cash out quicker by refinancing against the increased value of your properties, but even this can take a month or so to organise.

While some might see this as an issue, I would argue that a relative lack of liquidity is one of the virtues of property as an investment vehicle. Why?

Because the only way for an investment to achieve liquidity is to relinquish some of its stability. If it is liquid (easily sold like shares) it is more likely to have wide, more volatile fluctuations in value.

Liquid vs. illiquid

Let's examine this concept a little more closely by looking at the stock market.

The stock market is another potentially powerful investment vehicle because you can borrow against the shares you own, which is called buying on margin. But in order to achieve the liquidity the stock market provides you give up some stability. Share prices are volatile and fluctuate up and down and then down and up again! Sure, you can get your money out quickly, but you also run a bigger risk of making a loss.

But what about putting money into a savings account? This type of investment is both very liquid and pretty stable, but it won't ever give you a wealth-producing rate of return.

If I had the choice (and I do), I'll take stability (lack of big swings in price) over liquidity every single time.

Just look over the past two decades. In Australia we've been troubled by a pandemic, a number of world economic crises, experienced both high and low interest rates, had a mining boom and then a bust, and been governed by too many prime ministers to keep count of.

And during those past 20 years the properties in my real estate portfolio have doubled in value and doubled in value again but have been relatively illiquid — that is, it would have taken time to sell up. However, over the same period, the value of many shares that were very liquid *decreased* in value by 30, 40 and even up to 50 per cent and have only recently reached the same levels they were at a decade ago. I will stick with real estate any day!

Now I know that many financial planners recommend "when-to" investments, which means you have to know when to buy and when to sell. But timing is crucial with these investments — if you buy low and sell high, you do well. If you get your timing wrong, though, your money can be wiped out. Stocks, commodities and futures tend to be "when-to" investments. And it seems the same with the latest fad of crypto currencies which are very volatile.

I would rather put my money into a "how-to" investment such as real estate, which increases steadily in value and doesn't have the wild variations in price, yet is still powerful enough to generate wealth-producing rates of return through the benefits of leverage.

While timing is still important in "how-to" investments, it's nowhere near as important as how you buy them and how you add value.

"How-to" investments are rarely liquid, but they do produce real wealth. Most "when-to" investment vehicles (like the stock market and cryptocurrencies), on the other hand, produce only a handful of large winners but there tends to be millions of losers. You don't want to be one of them.

However, I believe that investing in well-located, capital city residential real estate produces millions of wealthy people (both homeowners and investors) and only a handful of losers. I much prefer those numbers.

Let's now move on to the next chapter, which is where I'll explain the concepts of leverage and the power of other people's money.

CHAPTER 6:
USE THE POWER OF COMPOUNDING TO GROW YOUR INVESTMENTS

Most people earning an average income believe their only shot at financial freedom is to win the lottery. But I've read the odds of anyone winning the lottery are less than the odds of being struck twice by lightning in your lifetime.

However using the power of compounding can slowly help you build a Cash Machine.

Compound interest is like planting an oak tree. One day's progress shows nothing, a few years' progress shows a little, 10 years shows something big, and 50 years creates something absolutely magnificent!

Just in case you may be new to the concept of how compounding works, here's a simple explanation:

Imagine you invest $100 and make 10 per cent return on your money, you'll earn $10 in interest and at the end of the year you'll have a total of $110. If you leave both your original investment and the earned interest in the account, the next year you will earn 10 per cent on the $110, which is $11. The third year you'll earn 10 per cent on $121 and so on, for as long as you leave it there. At this rate your money would actually double every seven years because you not only make money only on the money you started out with, but also on the accumulated interest.

Another way to look at is:

$100 Growing at 10%

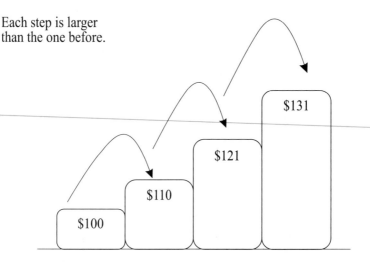

Each step is larger
than the one before.

$131

$121

$110

$100

Hold your nerve over the long-term

You'll hear some experts say *time in the market* (using the power of compounding) is much more important than timing the market. Let me explain …

Napoleon's definition of a military genius was "the man who can do the average thing when all those around him are going crazy" and it's the same with investing.

Building wealth over a lifetime doesn't require a lifetime of superior skill. In fact, it requires some pretty mundane skills — basic arithmetic and a grasp of investing fundamentals — practiced consistently throughout your entire lifetime, especially during times of widespread mania when everyone is bullish and at times of panic when everyone tells you to sell up.

It's important to remember that most financial advice is about today and what should you do now, what stocks look good now, etc. But over my years of investing, I've learned that the vast majority of the time that isn't that important. It really is all about just buying well (property, shares, etc.) and waiting, and then waiting some more.

INVESTMENT SUCCESS FACT

Most of what matters as a long-term investor is how you behave during the one per cent of the time everyone else is losing their cool.

To demonstrate this, let's take a look at Yale economist Robert Shiller's stock market data going back to 1900 to create three "investors". Each has saved $1 a month, every month, since 1900.

The first is Michelle. She doesn't know "anything" about investing so she invests $1 in the share market every month, no matter what is happening in the national or global economy. She diligently invests that $1 every single month and does nothing else.

Bob, on the other hand, thinks he knows a thing or two about investing so he also invests his $1 in the share market every month as well. But he also tries to "protect" his wealth by squirreling away cash during economic wobbles. Once the economy gets back on track he then funnels that additional cash back in the share market.

Karen, a mutual fund manager whose only incentive is to look right in the short run, invests $1 a month, but stops investing in stocks six months after a recession begins and only puts her money back into the market six months after a recession ends.

After more than 100 years of investing, if hypothetically they were still alive of course, who's won? Michelle takes it by a country mile.

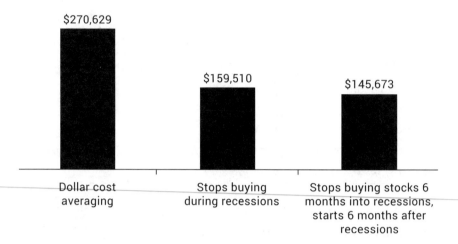

The lesson here is not to try and time the financial markets but to invest regularly whether the market is moving up or down. In fact disciplined investors in the stock market will be able to buy more shares when the market drops and they recognise that every one of the financial market's top days took place during periods of sheer terror.

Stock market volatility is always temporary, always expected and always feared by those who don't understand it. When the markets are down strategic investors often refer to this as "the big sale" — they buy stocks when they're cheap. The advance of the stock market is permanent, the declines are temporary.

In fact, some of the best market days of all time were during the Great Depression, one was a few days after the crash of 1987, two were during the depths of the 2008 Global Financial Crisis and there were great opportunities created by the Coronavirus Crash of 2020 when stock markets around the world crashed 30–40% as economies went into lockdown as the virus spread throughout communities.

Missing these days devastated investors' long-term returns. And most investors who missed them were those who sold out or stopped buying, after stocks crashed and everyone around them was busy panicking.

Successful investing in the share market is about "time in" the markets and certainly not about "timing" the markets.

Fact is, anyone who owned shares in the great companies of this world yet lost money in the stock market during these downturns did so because they sold out, because the share market rebounded and reached new highs following these downturns.

Those who try to avoid these short-term losses consistently end up missing even larger gains. That's why Michelle's strategy of regularly investing no matter what ends up above average overall.

A pilot once described his job as "hours and hours of boredom punctuated by moments of sheer terror". You can think of investing the same way (but hopefully without the terror bit).

INVESTMENT SUCCESS FACT

Your success as an investor will be determined by how you respond to punctuated moments of terror, not the years and years spent on cruise control.

Patience is the true wealth generator

Carl Richards, *New York Times* columnist and blogger on my *www.PropertyUpdate.com.au* website drew this little table napkin diagram:

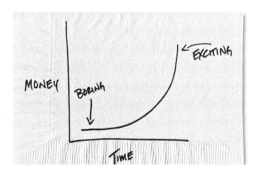

You've probably heard that starting early is one of the best investing decisions you can make. That's because investing done right is short-term boring but long-term exciting.

The reason? Once again, it's the power of compounding.

It should come as no surprise that Albert Einstein is credited with calling compounding the most powerful force in the universe, but whether he actually said that or not is somewhat debatable.

However, here's a point that we often miss in the discussion about compounding. Despite it possibly being one of the most powerful forces in the universe, it's clearly not one of the most exciting — at least in the short-term. Nothing really great happens until after years and years of discipline, and most importantly, of patience.

Take this silly (but true!) story that's often used to demonstrate how powerful compound interest is — if you start with one cent and double it every day for 30 days, you'll end up with $5,368,709.12.

Of course, if someone offers you an investment that promises to double every day then you should probably run for the hills as quickly as possible! But compounding — such as you achieve from capital growth investments such as property — has a powerful outcome. It just takes a really long time to become fun and exciting.

So, let's take a look at that example. One cent doubled is two cents. Two cents turns to $0.04, $0.04 to $0.08, $0.08 to $0.16, $0.16 to $0.32, $0.32 to $0.64, and $0.64 to $1.28. Nothing very exciting there apart from basic arithmetic.

But when you stick with it, it's those last few times when the figure doubles that it gets very, very exciting. In the last few days of that month

$1,342,177.28 becomes $2,684,354.56, and $2,684,354.56 doubles to $5,368,709.12.

And that's the case with your investments, too. It's not very exciting at the beginning, but compounding becomes a powerful force after years of patience and discipline.

Let me give you a real example: Say Sarah decides at 25 to save $1,000 a month. She does that for 10 years. And then she stops. Then there's Roger, who waits until he's 35, and he saves $1,000 a month for 30 years. They both earn seven per cent a year on their savings.

Now, 30 years after she stops contributing Sarah would have $1,262,089.05, but Roger, who would have put away three times as much as Sarah, would only have $1,133,529.44.

Now that doesn't seem fair, does it?

Here's how it works — the reason Sarah only saved a third as much as Roger but ended up with more money is because she simply started earlier. That's the secret.

But here's what you have to understand: Nothing too incredible happened during those first 10 years that Sarah was saving and Roger wasn't. The exciting part happens years down the road. So, you have to be patient and disciplined, counting on the well-known fact that compounding is going to do its work in its own time.

It's kind of like planting an oak tree. Warren Buffett famously once said that "Someone's sitting in the shade today because someone planted a tree long ago." The same thing applies to compounding of your assets.

INVESTMENT SUCCESS FACT
We have to live through the boring bits in order to reap the benefits a long way down the road.

And here's the key: Every day you wait, you're not cutting off the flat end of the curve like in the sketch at the start of this section. You're cutting off the steep end. You can't skip the boring part and get right to the excitement.

That's why we have to get started investing today!

The sad reality of life is that many people don't start investing when they're young because they don't think they can afford to.

The point I'm trying to make in this long-winded section is that they can't really afford not to get started investing because every year you invest is one closer to your success.

If you're like many other readers of this book, and haven't actually started investing yet, consider this: If you're 45 and haven't started, you don't want to be 55 and in the same (actually a much worse) position — do you? So start now.

Compounding building blocks

It should be fairly obvious by now that my strategy for helping you to build your Cash Machine is by growing a multimillion-dollar property portfolio, then to refinance and use your increasing equity in your investments to buy further properties.

So I'm commonly asked, "If we keep refinancing whenever we have equity and are in a position to do so, when do we ever pay off our mortgages and will we ever own these properties?"

Now I am not talking about your home mortgage here, because the interest on a home mortgage is not tax-deductible and it needs to be considered in a different light. But when it comes to residential investment properties my opinion is clear — why on earth would you want to pay them off?

I can probably best explain my reasoning as follows:

Imagine that you had an investment property worth $450,000 with a mortgage of $350,000 against it. Let's say you suddenly got hold of $100,000 lump sum cash. It could be a lottery win, an inheritance or a bonus.

Why would you apply that $100,000 to paying down your $350,000 mortgage when you could use it as a deposit on another $400,000 property that would give you greater exposure to the market and produce more gains?

Paying off your mortgage would reduce the leverage you have on your investment and therefore reduce the return you receive on the equity in your investment. In fact, it almost halves the return on your funds, as shown in the table below.

Further, by reducing your mortgage from $350,000 to $250,000, you are reducing your interest payments and therefore the amount of tax deductions that you can claim.

The yield on your property won't change; the rental income and purchase price remains the same, but the internal rate of return goes down. The situation is even more perplexing if you consider that after a number of years, you will probably refinance the property to release some equity so that you can buy even more properties, and you will pay the bank more fees to borrow again.

Let's have a look at the figures:

	Don't pay off mortgage	Pay $50,000 off the mortgage
Property value	$450,000	$450,000
Growth + Yield %	8% + 4%	8% + 4%
Growth + Yield $	$36,000 + $18,000	$36,000 + $18,000
Annual return	$54,000	$54,000
My money	$100,000	$200,000
Borrowed funds	$350,000	$250,000
Interest rate	6.5%	6.5%
Interest cost	-$22,750	-$16,250
Profit	$31,250	$37,750
Return on money	**31.25%**	**18.87%**

The response I usually get from this position at seminars is another question: "Okay, but I don't have a lump sum of cash; can I just use a principal and interest mortgage and pay off the loan slowly over time?"

Sure you can. There is nothing wrong with doing that, but it is really achieving the same thing. At the end of the day, you can either pay off your debt or use the surplus funds to save up a deposit to buy further properties.

If you have a home loan that is not tax-deductible it may be more sensible to use any surplus income to pay off that loan, but if not, it makes more sense mathematically to buy further properties.

I think the final decision comes down to how comfortable you are with debt and how much exposure you want to the property market. But you can probably use your money more wisely than paying off your home loan. I'll show you how in a minute.

"But Michael, reducing the principal increases equity ... "

Some see an advantage in reducing the principal as a form of increasing equity in the property. Sure it is a form of forced saving, but it does not actually create new value for you. You are simply transferring money from your pocket into the property. Only capital growth of the property can create new wealth for you without you having to contribute time or money to the deal. And the best way to access the most capital growth is to own a larger number of properties or add value to your properties through renovation or development.

"But then ... how do we ever own it?"

This is the final question that these discussions often lead to. My response is that a paradigm shift is required in investors' thinking if they feel they need to own all of their properties outright.

If we borrow only for investment purposes the aim is not to own our properties outright, but to maximise the use of our available income to own as much property as we reasonably can, and to receive the future benefit of capital growth and live off our increasing equity and future rents.

At the end of the day, if you have a lot of loans but lots of equity in multiple properties that bring you in surplus cashflow, what does it matter?

Should I pay off my home loan or shouldn't I?

I'm often asked whether it's better to pay off your non-tax-deductible home loan rather than investing. Many people see this as a form of forced savings, and even though it is, I've ready explained that you can never save yourself to wealth.

To explain my thoughts I usually ask people to do the following exercise: Write down on a piece of paper your mortgage interest rate — say three per cent. On the other side of the paper write down your best guess at how your investments will perform — say 10 per cent (combining the capital growth and rental return of your investment property) or maybe eight per cent (the dividends and growth of your share portfolio.)

So you have two potential investments — one is going to earn you three per cent (guaranteed) and the other is going to give you a chance at getting around eight to ten per cent per annum. Which one would you choose?

For most people it's clear that it makes little sense to pay off your mortgage (especially because you're using after-tax money to pay off your mortgage) when you could use the money to invest for a better return.

Of course the underlying assumption is that you can successfully invest your money without significant risk and achieve eight to ten per cent per annum. But what makes the sums look better still is that this return is on the value of your investment property or shares, not on your invested capital. If you take into account the benefit of leverage on your investments, it's clear that investing your funds gives a better return than paying off your mortgage (saving).

Let's look at these figures in a different way.

Imagine that you have received $20,000 as a bonus. You could use this windfall to pay off some of your home loan and save interest each year.

On the other hand, if you took that $20,000 and used it as a deposit to purchase a property, you could buy $100,000 worth of property using 80 per cent debt. Now of course you can't buy any decent sort of property for $100,000, but if you just follow my example — for every $20,000 that you have, you could buy $100,000 worth of property by borrowing 80 per cent of the value of that property.

If you bought a well-located property in any capital city, your property would increase in value by about eight per cent per annum (over the long term — not each and every year) and you would get about four per cent rental return. This means that you would realise a total investment return of 12 per cent. At the same time, you would have to pay about three per cent interest on your money and maybe one per cent of the value of the property would go in outgoings such as rates, taxes and insurance and managing agents' fees.

This means that you would have 12 per cent return coming in (some in cash and some in capital growth) and three or four per cent going out, leaving you a net return of eight per cent!

INVESTMENT SUCCESS FACT

The compounding effect really kicks in once you have multiple properties that benefit from a market upswing. It's during these times that your wealth starts to grow right before your eyes — just make sure you don't then rush out and overspend on non-wealth producing assets, of course!

Don't forget inflation

Most people fail to take inflation into account when they create their financial plan. Of course the trouble is by the time they retire, inflation will have taken a huge chunk out of their savings ... unless they have a wealth accumulation strategy that will allow their assets to grow at wealth producing rates.

It's kind of ironic that the same principles of compounding and inflation that defeat the average person actually benefit property investors.

Well-located properties have, in the long-term, increased in value by considerably more than inflation, while the value of the mortgage that investors hold against those properties has relatively decreased in value due to inflation.

What this means is that if you were to buy a property today for $800,000 with a $600,000 mortgage — 10 years down the track your property could be worth $1,600,000, while the mortgage would remain at $600,000 (assuming an interest-only loan). Of course in the future, that $600,000 won't buy as much as it would today — so although your property is worth much more your mortgage against it is worth relatively less. Pretty nifty — hey?

Compounding investments

Now here's an interesting fact and one of the reasons the rich keep getting rich …

Around 80 to 90 per cent of their ultimate asset base will consist of money they never saved or invested. When I explain this to people they're usually shocked. But it's true.

INVESTMENT SUCCESS FACT

The fact is that no matter how much of an investment you start with, if you invest in high growth assets your money will grow exponentially due to the power of compounding.

Compounding means you not only earn money on your investment, but you also earn money on the entire previous balance.

Let's use the property example from the last section to illustrate this more clearly. Imagine you put $100,000 down as a deposit on that property worth $500,000. The value of your property doubles in value in 10 years to $1,000,000. This means that your original $100,000 deposit would have compounded into $600,000 ($1,000,000 less your original mortgage of $400,000). As you can see, most of your profit will come from capital growth and leverage.

Most of the greatest fortunes have been made through the power of compounding.

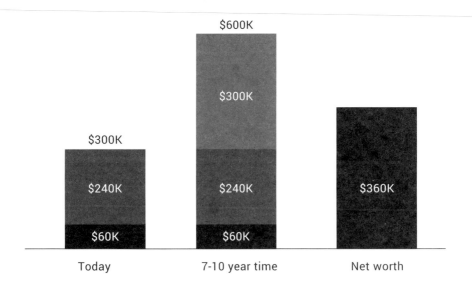

Time is your friend

Let me share a little story that clearly illustrates the power of compounding.

This story is about the humble water lily and its ability to replicate itself. I'm sure you've seen ponds covered by water lilies, right? All you need to start off with is one water lily in a pond and that single lily will multiply until it eventually swathes the entire pond. For argument's sake, let's say that the number of water lilies doubles every month. So, by the end of the first month, there are two water lilies floating in the pond, which then doubles to four in the second month, and then to eight, and then those eight water lilies turn into 16 and so on.

Fast forward two years (24 months) down the track and 12.5 per cent of the pond is covered with water lilies. By now, it will only take one more month for the lilies to envelop 25 per cent of the pond and after that, only another two months for the lilies to cover the surface of the water entirely. This means that it has taken one lily 27 months to cover the entire pond with plants!

The most amazing aspect of this is that in the very last month, the increase of lilies that occurred was the equivalent to the total overall increase for the previous 26 months — in other words it took 26 months for the lilies to cover half the pond and only one more month to cover the remaining 50 per cent of the water and engulf it completely.

It's much the same with investors; compounding has a similar effect on their asset base as the water lilies covering the pond, as demonstrated by the following graph which shows how the value of a property purchased today could increase over the next 15 years to $1.4 million if it grew by an average of seven per cent per annum.

Here's another way of looking at it — when you look at the power of compounding in the graph below you'll see it grew steadily in the first five years then even more in the next five years, but almost half of the growth in value occurred in the last five years.

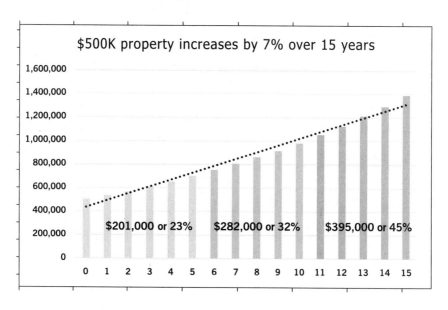

The point I'm making is the sooner you start saving, and the sooner you buy your first investment property, the longer you have compound interest working its powerful magic for you.

In other words, despite what most people want to believe, money does make money. It breeds quietly and quickly like rabbits. It prefers to hang around in big groups and that's why the rich get richer. They understand and use the concept of compounding which means it's easier for the rich to get richer than for the poor to keep up with them.

The truth is that it's easier for the rich to keep getting richer than it is for the average Australian to keep up.

Remember the key is to enter the market as soon as possible and then duplicate as soon as you have usable equity, but while you invest your equity into your investments, ensure that you invest your time into education. Investment knowledge will help you to avoid costly mistakes.

Let's now move on to the next section, where I'll take you through how you can use leverage, or gearing, as well as other people's money to fast-track your path to investment success.

CHAPTER 7:
THE POWER OF LEVERAGE AND OTHER PEOPLE'S MONEY

By now you're probably getting the hint that I prefer real estate as my investment vehicle.

But I'd like to let you in on a little secret … the returns you get from real estate, if you pay for your purchase using cash only (without getting a loan), isn't much higher than what you can achieve with other types of investment.

Of course, with real estate, you usually don't pay using raw cash; instead you use someone else's money to buy your properties. That is, you put down a small deposit, generally 20 per cent, and the bank finances the balance. This is called *leverage*. Because of its history as a secure asset that provides stable income and proven capital growth, residential real estate is regarded as a prime security for loans, meaning that banks may lend you as high as 90 per cent of the value of your property.

This gives residential real estate investment a distinct advantage, as no financial institution would ever dream of lending this sizeable proportion of funds on any other type of investment. Even if you buy shares in the banks themselves, they may only lend you 50 or 60 per cent of their value and they will not lend beyond 70 per cent or so for commercial properties.

So in essence … financial is the leveraging tool to get the property and property is the vehicle I recommend you consider to become wealthy, because the ability to leverage borrowings makes residential property a very appealing vehicle for building wealth because, effectively, you're able to buy property using *other people's money* to make yourself wealthy.

In fact, as a property investors you use other people's money in three ways.

1. The bank's money for leverage,

2. Your tenant's rent money for income and …

3. The government's money as they provide you with tax incentives to become a property investor.

This allows you to achieve the wealth generating rates of return that a Level 3 investor needs to help you grow a substantial asset base and become a Level 4 professional investor.

In the technical sense, leveraging, or gearing as it is also known, means using a small effort to move a large object, like the gears on your bicycle that allow you to pedal a small rotation in order to turn the large back wheel.

In the financial sense, leveraging is the act of using a small amount of money to control a large asset.

INVESTMENT SUCCESS FACT

The ability to use leverage with real estate allows you to purchase a considerably larger investment than you would normally be able to and, therefore, has the potential to significantly increase the profit you can realise.

The power of other people's money (OPM)

To demonstrate what a significant difference borrowing OPM can make, let's look at an example in which there are five investors, each with $100,000 of their own money. Let's assume that they all buy an investment that returns 10 per cent growth per annum and has a yield (or rental return) of four per cent.

Investor 5 is very conservative, chooses not to borrow any money and only puts down his initial $100,000. However, all the other investors take on some amount of debt in varying degrees. At the other end of the scale, Investor 1 borrows 90 per cent of the value of his or her investment ($900,000) and buys an asset worth $1 million, while the other investors borrow lesser amounts as illustrated in the following table.

	Investor 1	Investor 2	Investor 3	Investor 4	Investor 5
Equity (your money)	$100,000	$100,000	$100,000	$100,000	$100,000
Growth + yield	10%+4%	10%+4%	10%+4%	10%+4%	10%+4%
Interest rate	7%	7%	7%	7%	7%
Leverage (Loan to Value ratio or LVR)	90%	80%	50%	30%	0%
Debt (other people's money)	$900,000	$400,000	$100,000	$42,857	Nil
Value of investment	$1,000,000	$500,000	$200,000	$142,857	$100,000

At the end of each year, all the investors have received their returns and paid their interest as shown in the table below.

	Investor 1	Investor 2	Investor 3	Investor 4	Investor 5
Interest repayment	-$63,000	-$28,000	-$7,000	-$3,000	$0
Yield	$40,000	$20,000	$8,000	$5,714	$4,000
Capital growth	$100,000	$50,000	$20,000	$14,286	$10,000
Net profit	$77,000	$42,000	$21,000	$17,000	$14,000

As you can see, Investor 1, who borrowed the most (used the highest leverage), received the highest return. The cash return on the amount invested ($100,000 for each investor) is shown in the following table.

	Investor 1	Investor 2	Investor 3	Investor 4	Investor 5
Cash return	77%	42%	21%	17%	14%

Clearly, Investor 1 is out in front by considerably more, with an impressive 77 per cent return on his or her initial outlay of $100,000 — that's the power of leveraging or gearing a property portfolio using OPM! That's the stuff that makes property millionaires out of ordinary people!

But that's not the only advantage of using OPM to buy residential property investments. To make things even better, the people who lend you the money do not take a share of the increase in value of your asset. That's all yours to enjoy!

So, essentially, we're talking about taking on good debt to grow your asset base and your long-term wealth but you must understand the difference between good and bad debt so I'll explain further.

The more highly you're geared, the more money you have borrowed and the lower your invested capital in relation to your borrowings, the more your ROI (return on investment) will be.

But be warned, gearing not only magnifies your profits, if the value of your investment falls, your losses are magnified as well.

Debt recycling: How to earn money from your debt

You were probably taught by your parents to get a good education, a good job, buy a home, work really hard, and pay off your debt.

But, in my mind, that's not a productive use of the equity in your home or your investment properties.

Instead, you should recycle the equity in your home and convert it into productive debt to buy income-producing assets.

But before we start delving into all things debt recycling, let's start out by clarifying the difference between good and bad debt, and how having debt can actually benefit you, and set you on the path to financial freedom.

There are three types of debt:

1. **Bad debt:** This is a debt against assets that depreciate in value. Bad debt generally refers to things like credit cards or other consumer debt that does little to improve your financial outcome.

2. **Necessary debt:** This is the non-tax-deductible debt against your home, but it's something essential that can't really be avoided.

3. **Good debt:** This is a tax-deductible debt against income-producing and appreciating assets. Think loans against residential investment properties business loans. This is the type of debt that can help build wealth and bring you cash flow over time.

INVESTMENT SUCCESS FACT
Good debt is the money you borrow to make more money.

Somewhere along the line, you were probably taught that debt is a problem. But, I don't agree with that. Not all debt is bad debt.

Having debt is not a problem. Not being able to repay your debt (or interest on your debt) is the problem and that's why it's so important to understand the difference between good and bad debt.

Having said that, in today's economic environment I believe good debt is an asset.

Now I know that may sound counterintuitive but let me explain …

In the old days, when you owned an investment property your mortgage repayments would have likely been more than the rental income you received meaning most "investment grade" properties were negatively geared — and this resulted in a cash flow shortfall.

The tenant would have contributed to some of your mortgages by paying you rent, the taxman would have assisted with depreciation allowances and negative gearing benefits, but each month you would have had to contribute to your mortgage repayments.

However, today, taking on good debt and borrowing at historically low-interest rates and using leverage to grow your assets while at the same time receiving rent that is likely to cover your interest payments is a sound investment strategy.

Your cheap debt is an asset because you are using it to create more equity (as the value of your investment property improves) plus cash flow.

And you can accelerate this by using debt recycling.

Simply put, debt recycling is a strategy that turns your current home equity into a tax-deductible investment loan.

If like many Australians you bought your home a while ago and have been slowly re-paying your mortgage debt, and all the while your property has increased in value, you would now have significant equity in your home.

So my suggestion is to borrow against this unused equity and buy an investment property.

Previously that debt against your home was "necessary debt" but re-borrowing or recycling those funds means you now have "good debt" because, as I just explained, you can use this to buy an appreciating asset that will bring in cash flow every month.

But here's the catch — to recycle your equity into good debt, the debt can't just be used for anything. If you borrow against the equity in your home to buy a car or as other debt used for personal purposes, the interest payments are not tax-deductible.

Just to make things clear, it's not the security against with you borrow the money (your home) which determines if the interest payments are tax-deductible. It's the purpose of the loan such as borrowing to invest, which makes interest tax-deductible.

The concept of debt recycling may be a little confusing, so let's explain it with a seven-step guide.

1. Over time you will have paid down a portion of your home mortgage with a principal and interest loan and during that time your home would have increased in value. The difference between the current value of your home and the outstanding amount on your mortgage is your equity.

2. The bank will often lend you up to 80% of the value of your home as long as you can show serviceability.

3. You would take out a new investment loan using your available home equity as security and the purpose of this loan would be to use the funds as a deposit on an investment property.
Imagine your home is worth $600,000 and your available equity is $300,000 because you'd paid your mortgage down to $300,000. You could recycle $150,000 of this equity as a loan — in other words, take out a new investment loan for $150,000 which would be then used as a deposit for an investment property, using the equity in your home as security.

This would leave you with a loan to value ratio of 75% ($450,000 loan on a $600,000 property) well within bank's lending parameters.

4. You could use this $150,000 to invest in assets that produce both income and capital growth such as a managed fund, shares or as a deposit against an investment property.

5. You could even use the income generated from your investments, plus any tax advantages of a geared investment, to pay off the non-deductible debt in your home loan.

6. Over time you will build your wealth as your investment property or share portfolio should increase in value over time and the cash flow you receive in the form of rental or dividends should also increase.

7. At the same time you will slowly be paying down the mortgage on your home, so that when you reach your retirement years and start enjoying the longest holiday you will have in your life, you will own your own home with no debt and have an investment portfolio of properties or shares (preferably both) with a manageable level of debt.

In order for a debt recycling strategy to work you need the following:

• A regular, independent income you can rely on to deliver a surplus cash flow to cover the interest payments on your investment loan.

• A long-term investment focus.

• A willingness to increase your debt and hold an investment loan.

• Tolerance for risk and short-term fluctuations in investment value.

• Income protection insurance — which would provide replacement income in case you're sick or injured and unable to work.

- And a financial rainy day, cash flow buffer to see you through the ups and downs of your property investment journey — this could be in the form of money in an offset account

So now that you understand a little more about debt recycling, you can see that good debt isn't really a problem — in fact, you can be an asset.

INVESTMENT SUCCESS FACT

Becoming comfortable with the concept of good debt and understanding that in order to make money in property you need to borrow money is a crucial aspect to building your own real estate empire. Smart investors purchase debt.

One of the ways the rich get richer

Because wealthy people can access other people's money (through lenders) to make more money for themselves, most real estate fortunes have been built on borrowed money. Remember, debt against investment property is good debt and rich people borrow this way during the wealth accumulation phase of their investment journey to become even richer.

To come to terms with this idea, which is foreign to the vast majority of people who are at the bottom of the Wealth Pyramid and still working for a living and who would prefer to avoid debt at all cost (regardless of whether it's good or bad), it's important to remember that the point of what I'm trying to teach you in this book is to build yourself an investment business and grow an asset base that will one day replace your personal exertion income.

This step of borrowing large amounts of money to invest in real estate worries many beginning investors because they were taught by their parents not to buy things they can't afford, not to borrow large amounts of money from the banks and to pay down their loans as quickly as possible.

While that's the money strategy of the average person, (the non-wealthy who relied on welfare for their golden years) you need to do things differently so that you can get different results — don't you?

CHAPTER 8:
THE SECRET TO
FINANCIAL FREEDOM

When I speak with investors, I soon discover they all want similar things and it's not actually the properties or shares they're after. Some want the financial security or financial freedom or the lifestyle that comes with wealth. Others want the toys such as imported European cars or holiday homes by the beach.

Now there's nothing wrong with that. The desire to obtain security and material things is basic to most humans. It's nothing we should feel bad about; it's a reality. These things make us happy.

Think back — as a child it was toys, dolls or bikes that we wanted. As teenagers it was computers, mobile phones or the latest fashion clothes. Now as adults we're after new cars, bigger houses, longer vacations and security for our families, or maybe it's all of the above.

If the last few economically challenging years taught us anything, it's that we need to start taking a different approach to money and how we value it, procure it and use it. In the past many people felt their job was secure and their superannuation or pension would see them through retirement.

But now many feel uncertain about their job security, realise they're going to have to work longer than they hoped and when they eventually retire they'll find their superannuation or pension will give them a (very) modest living at best.

In reality your pension or superannuation was never enough — and it's a fact that only about one per cent of people (even in our wealthy Western countries) become truly financially free. Most try to stretch their savings, superannuation or pension so it won't run out before they die. Some end up taking a part-time job to supplement their pension, which is not what any of us want after we've already been working most of our lives.

I've said it before, but it's such an important concept so let me remind you that the steps to financial freedom are to simply:

1. Spend less than you earn;

2. Save to invest;

3. Build your asset base by reinvesting, using leverage and forced appreciation.

What does wealth mean to you?

Most people say wealth means a big salary with a lifestyle to match. They equate it to money, but that's not how wealth works.

You need a lot more than money to be truly wealthy. You need your health, your friends and family to share it with, you need personal growth, spirituality (this means different things to different people) and contribution to society.

As you can see, to me wealth is a product of the mind and no amount of money will make you wealthy.

INVESTMENT SUCCESS FACT

To be truly wealthy you have to be grateful for what you have in life, and you have to be living a life where you know you are contributing or giving back to society.

Financial freedom is different to wealth, of course. It means you never have to work again to live your desired lifestyle. Now that's what you're really investing for, isn't it?

My suggestion is that you should be committed to being *wealthy* as well as *financially free.*

Just to make things clear ... income by itself does not make you financially free. In fact income is one of the worst predictors of financial freedom. You spend some, maybe you save some, and taxation takes away a portion of it. Most people never become wealthy and they never develop real financial independence.

For most people the bills keep mounting up and despite working more and more hours they can't make ends meet. So it's not income you are after. To secure your financial future you need to acquire assets that grow in value and bring in income.

As I see it there are a number of levels of financial evolution and ultimately financial freedom.

1. Pay cheque existence

Most people live what I call a "pay cheque existence"— OK, nobody gets paid by cheque anymore, but you know what I mean — their main source of income is their regular pay cheque and they hope the month doesn't run out before their money does. The problem is they've usually spent their pay before they've received it and they need each pay packet to pay off their credit cards.

2. Passive income

Those who've moved to the next level of financial independence achieve an element of their income as passive income. This is money that they receive whether they get up and go to work or not — like interest from investments and rental income. Believe me, it's a nice feeling to know that when you wake up each morning you're richer than when you went to bed.

3. Financial security

At this stage your investment covers your basic needs — your housing, cars, food and basic entertainment. Interestingly, the investment income you need to achieve this is usually less than what most people think and it's much less than required for financial freedom.

4. Financial independence

At this level of financial freedom your passive investment income is sufficient so that you don't have to work and "all your expenses" are covered.

5. Financial freedom

At this level you don't have to work and your passive investment income is sufficient that everything you can think of is covered. Obviously the income you would need for this is substantial. In fact, it's so big that some people are scared off by the concept and never get started on the journey to financial freedom.

Let's face it, few people reach this level. I know people who are rich because they have good incomes, but they're not what I call "financially free" because they still need to go to work.

The wisdom of multiple streams of income

One of the important concepts that you need to understand to achieve financial freedom is that you need more than one source of income to be wealthy today. If you think back to the 1950s when, in most families, only the husband worked, how many streams of income did a family need to survive?

Only one.

Yet today, very few families can survive on less than two streams of income, with both the husband and wife working. And the way things are going, that won't be enough in the future. It would be wise to have multiple streams of income flowing through your adult life.

Wealthy people have always known this. They generate income through wages or their businesses and also from their various investments such as property, shares and managed funds. If one stream dries up, they have many more to support them. If one of their businesses goes broke, they have other sources of income available.

But ordinary workers are much more vulnerable. If they lose their income stream, for example their job, it can wipe them out and it often takes them years to recover.

Imagine you have a portfolio of income streams — not just one or two, but many streams from completely different and diversified sources, perhaps from a portfolio of investment properties. If one stream of income disappears (for example a property becomes vacant), you'll barely feel the bump. You will be stable. You will have time to adjust. You will be safe.

Do you have multiple streams of income flowing into your life at this time?

Maybe it's time to add another one!

Be in control of your financial destiny

I hope you realise that by many measures you're already wealthy because true wealth is much more than how much money you've got in the bank or how many properties you own, but it's interesting to realise that Credit Suisse's annual global wealth report shows that Australians have the highest median wealth in the world, and we have a very low percentage of poor people.

COVID-19 has made the rich even richer

Despite the many challenges the Coronavirus put in our way, over the last few years Australian households just kept getting wealthier.

A combination of surging property prices and solid share market gains saw total Aussie household wealth grow by 20.2% in 2021 — the strongest annual gain in eleven-and-a-half years.

Australia's total household will hit an all-time high of $13.9 trillion, with wealth per person of $540,179 also sitting at record levels. And a large part of this growth in wealth is related to owning a home.

Just look at these figures … the total value of all the residential property in Australia was $7.2 trillion at the end of November 2020, this grew to $8 trillion by April 2021, and by the end of 2021 finished breaking a record with the value of all residential properties now being worth more than $9.4 trillion.

In fact, Australia has become a millionaire factory. The total number of millionaires in Australia rose 31% from 485,000 to 635,000 during 2021 — the biggest rise in recent history.

Again a large part of this is related to their ownership of real estate and their superannuation and share portfolio.

A recent report by Credit Suisse estimates that as many as 1.8 million Aussies are considered to be millionaires today, based on estimates of net household wealth.

And the number of Australian millionaires is expected to grow to 3,100,000 by 2025.

But while the rich keep getting richer many Australian household budgets are beginning to feel a financial squeeze. In particular those who don't own their own homes and are finding their rent is increasing significantly more than their incomes are.

Moving forward other Australian families will find themselves in financial difficulty as inflation creeps in, as the cost of living increases, and interest rates rise more than their wages meaning their mortgage or their rent will eat up a bigger proportion of their pay packet.

INVESTMENT SUCCESS FACT

Property is the investment vehicle that more average Australians use to develop their wealth than any other asset class.

So in spite of all the economic challenges that have been thrown our way, simply owning their own home over a period of 10 years or more has made money for an incredible number of people. Over this period many homes doubled in value, which meant that many homeowners saw their household wealth increase substantially. And it's much the same in many of the world's big capital cities.

But another group discovered how to profit in ways other than just owing their own home. They became real estate investors and bought additional properties. They took their future into their own hands and set themselves on a path to financial freedom.

How the rich are different

If you study how the wealthy have achieved financial freedom you will realise it has very little to do with how they earn a living, and much more to do with their mindset — how they think about wealth.

Although this may be true, when it comes to how people make their money we can all be placed in one of four categories: employees, self-employed, investors and business owners.

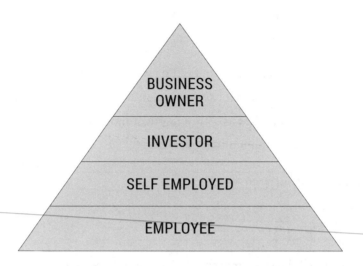

In his *Rich Dad, Poor Dad* series of books, Robert Kiyosaki suggests that we all fit into one of four categories when it comes to how we earn our income.

1. Employees — have a job and receive an income from their employer, trading their hours for dollars; however before they even see their money the government takes its share in taxes.

You're probably thinking, "Of course they do, isn't that what happens to everyone?" Interestingly that's not always the case — some investors and business owners only pay tax on what's left over after their bills are paid.

2. The Self-Employed — own a job and are typically small business owners or professionals who work hard and expect to get paid for their efforts.

In reality, though, they have swapped one boss for hundreds — called customers or clients and are still swapping time for money. If they take time off or fall sick, they simply don't get paid.

3. Investor — money works for them. Unlike employees and self-employed people who trade time for money, investors make money with their money. Some build a sufficiently large investment portfolio so they don't have to work, because their money works for them.

Regardless of how you make your money today, if you hope to become rich, successful or financially free in the future you'll have to ultimately become an investor.

Obviously you won't become a full-time successful investor overnight, but you can start moving in that direction by establishing your own property investment business. Done correctly, income-earning residential real estate can be your vehicle for getting out of the rat race!

There are also many tax advantages available to property investors. One of the reasons the rich get richer is because in some cases, they can make millions and legally pay very little tax because they build their asset base, not their income.

For example, if you own a $1 million investment property portfolio that increases in value by seven per cent in a year, your asset base will have increased by $70,000, yet in Australia no tax is payable on this capital gain. You could then borrow against the increased value of your assets and use this money to reinvest or live off.

4. The Business Owner — owns a system and people work for them. The true business owner not only doesn't have to do the work, he doesn't even have to be at work every day. Why?

Because he has a system and has hired people to do it all for him, along with qualified supervisors to manage his team. The true business owner asks, "Why do it yourself when you can employ someone to do it for you?"

One of the best ways to earn more and work less is by owning a business, because "the tax system" favours business owners who understand finance, tax and the law.

As a businessperson you could own a McDonald's franchise and have a group of teenagers serving Big Macs or you could have a portfolio of investment properties working hard for you.

Can you see the difference?

As an employee you would have to pay for many of life's pleasures (such as a new car) with after-tax dollars, whereas a business owner can pay for his new car with before-tax dollars, as long as it's used for business and meets certain requirements. They can even pay for things like movie tickets and holidays with before-tax dollars if they qualify as legitimate business expenses.

Does that mean you're going to have to set up a business?

I'm not advocating that you open up a conventional business; I believe it's just too hard to make money that way as most small business go broke in the first five years.

However, I've seen some investors become very rich by growing a multimillion-dollar property portfolio and treating it like a business. They get the right type of finance, set up the correct ownership and asset protection structures and know how to use the taxation system to their advantage.

INVESTMENT SUCCESS FACT:

Owning income-producing residential real estate is just like owning a business because your tenants go to work or run their businesses to earn a living and then pay you.

Your tenants will pay you for the use of your property to live in. This puts you in a position whereby you can profit from the efforts of other people — think about that!

These people get up every day, get dressed and go to work. You don't have to supervise them, pay their tax or worry about paying for vacations or sick leave. Yet every month you get a portion of their income in the form of the rent they pay for the use of your property. The more of these people you "employ", the more income you get.

Now before you get all moralistic, understand that this is not a "bad thing" if it's done fairly and with a genuine concern for others. You should not feel guilty if you position yourself to profit from the earnings and efforts of others, as long as you are providing fair value to the relationship.

Best of all, you can set up your property investment business while you're still an employee; that's what I did and what every wealthy property investor I know has done. They built their portfolio one property at a time, while living off the income from their day job.

They started with one property, then leveraged off its capital growth to invest in another and another until one day they found themselves with a true property investment business that gave them financial freedom.

Now that we've talked about a few strategies to set you on the path to investment success, it's time to take a look at another key concept because many people still don't understand it.

It's the strategy of always paying yourself first.

CHAPTER 9:
PAY YOURSELF FIRST

"Don't save what is left after spending; spend what is left after saving."
Warren Buffett

The decision to spend less than you earn and invest the difference is by far the most important decision you need to make on your path to investment success. You see, without surplus income, your wealth accumulation opportunities are extremely limited.

But what does it mean? The phrase "pay yourself first" refers to prioritising the allocation of your income. That is, make it the number one priority to allocate a certain amount of income towards securing your future — your personal future fund.

So the first step in building your own Cash Machine is to decide what portion of your pay you are going to keep and then put it aside before you spend a dollar of it. What portion of your pay will you leave untouched, no matter what else is going on in your life, and pay yourself first with it?

I'm not really being melodramatic when I say that the rest of your life will be determined by this decision to keep a percentage of your income aside because this money is not really savings, it's money you're *investing* in your financial future.

INVESTMENT SUCCESS FACT

By initially saving money, and then investing it intelligently, over time you'll have your money working for you.

Now, of course, when I say pay yourself first I don't mean hopping online and buying the latest gadget or rushing down to the shop and buying a new pair of jeans. That's not paying yourself — it's paying somebody else with your hard-earned money.

The concept of paying yourself first means setting aside a percentage of your income for investments that will grow for you.

Do you find it difficult to save?

Most people do. Good reasons to pull out your credit card always crop up, don't they? But there is an answer.

Consider this: The government has it all worked out! Every time you get paid the government automatically takes a share in the form of income and other taxes. I guess they do this because they know that if they had to rely on everybody coming up with this money at the end of the year, most of us would have trouble doing so because we would've spent it! But by making it happen automatically, the government ensures it always gets its share.

So, why don't you do the same? Every time you get paid, automatically deduct a portion and pay yourself first — into your bank account or, better yet, into wealth-producing investments.

Some would call this an automated investment plan. This is an incredibly powerful concept if you do it right: the money is deducted automatically and regularly (in other words you have no choice) and this money is then invested.

Four critical steps of saving for success

Before you start paying yourself first, there's some equally important ideas to consider and they have quite a bit to do with having the right mindset. You have to want, and believe in, your desire to have a better life.

To help you get there, no matter what your current circumstances might be, here are four critical steps that will get you moving in the right direction.

Step 1: Decide it's OK to become rich and be successful

Many people are held back by their thoughts about money. They think it's an unworthy goal to become wealthy; it's wrong or maybe even immoral to be a success. So before you begin your journey to wealth creation, search your attitudes and make sure you're willing to create wealth in a way that will support your inner beliefs and values.

INVESTMENT SUCCESS FACT

It's important to understand that your thoughts lead to your feelings, your feelings lead to your actions and your actions lead to your results.

You have to start by thinking about money in the right way. You see, everything begins with a thought. The verb for turning your thoughts into tangible things or physical experiences is to "manifest". So when you manifest something, you metaphorically reach inside your thoughts and pull your desired object into existence; first you think it, and then you manifest it — you materialise it and cause it to appear.

I bet you're thinking, "What are you on about, Michael? This all sounds a bit 'rah, rah' to me."

But look around you – everything you see began as a thought in someone's mind: the chair you're sitting on, the car you drive, the clothes you wear, even you as a person were born from a thought ... and everyone manifests their thoughts.

Of course depending on their attitude, some people manifest abundance while others manifest scarcity. If you don't have what you want in life or are not where you really want to be at the moment, it's time to examine your thoughts. Ask yourself, "How did I manifest this reality? What thoughts led me to my current situation?"

Then you have to decide that it's okay to be wealthy and manifest the right thoughts to get you there. I'll discuss more about the traits of successful investors later in the book.

Step 2: Spend less than you earn

It may sound too simplistic, but it's a fact that most people's financial problems are caused by living beyond their means.

Think about it: If you need to borrow on your credit card just to get by, you are spending more than your take-home pay. It sets up a vicious cycle because when you borrow, the repayments on those loans reduce all future pay packets. Then it's even harder to cope, and the situation will get worse and worse.

"But I can't spend less," you may be thinking, "I don't earn enough now as it is." The simple solution is that you are going to need to budget so you understand where your money is going. More on this in a minute.

You can't become rich by spending all that you earn (or more).

Step 3: Pay yourself first

Way back in 1926 George Glasson wrote one of the classic success books called *The Richest Men in Babylon*. In this fable Akrad, a simple scribe, convinced his client, a money lender, to teach him the secrets of money.

The first principle he was taught was *"A part of all you earn must be yours to keep."* He was shown that if he first set aside at least 10 per cent of his earnings and made that money inaccessible for expenses, Akrad would see this amount build over time, and in turn, start earning its own money. And in time, it would grow into a fortune because of the power of compound interest (as mentioned in chapter five).

This principle is as effective today as it was in 1926 — many people have built their fortunes by paying themselves first. The problem is that many can't grasp the power of this principle and instead look for a "get rich quick scheme".

Starting right now, unless you are in some dire financial situation that you must clear up first, you must start deducting at least 10 per cent (and preferably closer to 20 or 30 per cent) of your income to deposit into an investment account. That's not a "savings account" or an "emergency fund" — it's an account where you will accumulate money to invest in a high growth vehicle. You also have to eliminate your bad debt, including your credit card debt, and live on whatever's left over.

Step 4: Invest

Invest the money you've saved in the step above into assets that will generate wealth-producing rates of return. Remember $1 a day invested at 10 per cent becomes $1 million in 65 years. Put in more or invest in a high return investment vehicle like property, and you can get there much, much quicker.

So why don't people do it?

All financial planners speak of this same concept — an automated investment plan to pay yourself first — so why don't more people do it?

I guess it's for the same reason that most of us understand we should eat more healthily and we know we should do more exercise but we never get around to it. We've also all heard that we need to put some money aside for the future, but we never get around to it. Likewise, most people know they should budget, but they never do that either. I know many people reading this are possibly thinking, "I can't afford to save", but frankly you can't afford not to save. They probably think budgeting is keeping track of where their money went, when in fact budgeting is deciding where to put their money in the future.

The next step is to reinvest your investment returns to get the benefit of compounding as mentioned in an earlier chapter. So, to achieve this, you must:

1. Spend less than you earn.

2. Pay yourself first.

3. Invest and then reinvest your investment returns.

4. Don't be tempted to steal your money to consume — leave it alone and watch your investments grow through the power of compounding.

5. Invest in assets that grow wealth-producing rates of return.

6. Don't try and get rich quickly — get rich patiently.

You can organise an automatic plan by asking your employer to put a certain percentage of your wages into a different bank account or you can organise this automatically online yourself.

The first step in moving from a consumer to an investor, which is really the first step up my Wealth Pyramid, is simply deciding what percentage of your income you will set aside for you and your family's future.

Now that you've agreed to set up an automated savings plan — remember it's actually an *investment plan* — the question you're probably asking yourself is where do I put the money? And maybe you're wondering how much do I really need to set aside to achieve financial freedom? Well, hold tight because I'll answer both of these questions in future chapters.

How to do it

The lesson from all of this is that you should resolve, from today, that you are going to save and invest at least 10 per cent of your income throughout your working life. Take 10 per cent of your income off the top of each pay, each time you receive one, and put it into a special account for financial accumulation.

Remember, developing the lifelong habit of saving and investing your money is not easy. It requires tremendous determination and willpower. You have to set it as a goal, write it down, make a savings plan, and work on it all the time. But once this practice is locked in and becomes automatic, your financial success is virtually guaranteed.

For some it will mean that you'll initially have to practice frugality. You'll need to question every expenditure and often delay or defer important buying decisions for at least a week, if not a month. The longer you put off making a buying decision, the better your decision will be.

You see … the major reason that people retire poor is because of impulse buying. They see something they like and they buy it with very little thought at all. They become victims of what's called "Parkinson's Law", which says that "expenses rise to meet income". This means that no matter how much you earn, you tend to spend that much and a little bit more besides. You never get ahead and you never get out of debt.

I know what you're probably thinking, "I can't afford to save 10 per cent of my income" and that's okay. But start today by saving one per cent of your income in a special savings or investment account. Put it away at the beginning of each month, even before you begin paying down your debts and live on the other 99 per cent of your income.

As you become comfortable living on 99 per cent, which will be much more quickly than you think, then increase your savings level to two per cent of your income, then three per cent and so on. Create a savings plan that you are comfortable with and then commit to it. I'll talk about that more in an upcoming chapter.

Within one year, you will be saving 10 per cent — and maybe even 15 per cent or 20 per cent of your income — and living comfortably on the balance. At the same time, your savings and investment account will be growing.

A great side effect of this is that you will also become more careful about your expenditures and your debts will begin to be paid off. In fact, you will become a *money saving expert*. Within a year or two, your entire financial life will be under your control and you will be on your way to becoming a self-made millionaire. This process has worked for everyone who has ever tried this savings plan. Try it and see for yourself.

Finding money to save

We've all heard the traditional savings advice of not buying those lattes, packing your lunch and avoiding impulse buying.

That's where putting a budget together will help.

In his book *The One-Page Financial Plan*, Carl Richards suggests you implement the 72 hour test. Apparently he struggled with impulse buying on Amazon. Now instead of buying immediately, he keeps items in his shopping cart for 72 hours before hitting the checkout button. He finds when he returns to the site he rarely feels strongly about buying what's in his cart.

This is a good test you can use in many areas of your life because very few things need to be bought *right now.*

The B-word

No one likes the B-word — budgeting — do they?

If currently you're not spending less than you earn, don't worry. Most of us need a little help getting control of our money.

And this usually starts with the basics of creating a budget.

The good news is budgeting is neither as scary nor as onerous as it sounds. But since budgeting is such big subject I've created a special report for you together with some spreadsheets. Just go to _www.InvestingSuccessfully.today_, register your copy of this book and you'll find these resources waiting for you.

Unfortunately getting control and keeping control of your financial situation are two different things, and there's no guarantee you won't fall off the straight and narrow at some time. But when this happens, just take stock of why you fell so you can learn from your tumble and calmly and proudly climb back on the horse.

The conclusion is that you must get into the habit of paying yourself first before you can ever achieve anything like investment success. I've found that the discipline of saving money to invest works every time, so what are you waiting for?

CHAPTER 10: UNDERSTANDING YOUR TRUE FINANCIAL SITUATION

Income and assets; liabilities and expenses.

Wait a minute, you say. Isn't income an asset? Aren't expenses liabilities?

Why do accountants use all this confusing terminology?

There's a very practical reason for separating income from assets and expenses from liabilities. This will become clear in this chapter as I explain how, by having a picture of your assets and liabilities on the one hand and your income and expenses on the other, ultimately you'll be able to manage your cash flow and increase your assets.

But most people don't have a handle on this. Month after month, they look at their bank and credit card statements and are surprised by what their balance is and how much they spent.

Think about it this way …

If you asked someone "What's your salary?" or "How much money do you make?", 99 per cent of the population could tell you an exact dollar amount. However, if you asked those same people how much profit they had at end of the year, less than 10 per cent could give you an answer.

And it's amazing what else those 10 per cent could tell you. They'll know exactly how much money they have left on their car loan or their mortgage and when they plan to pay it off.

Can you describe your current financial situation?

For most people the answer is probably not.

The problem is before you can move forward you have to know where you are now because your current situation is the result of the choices you've made so far and those you've chosen not to make.

If you want to work your way up the Wealth Pyramid, the best tool for assessing and then managing your situation is to regularly create personal financial statements, similar to those that businesses use to evaluate their finances.

Now don't be intimidated — you don't need all your numbers to be spot-on to get started — the actual numbers are nowhere near as important as the "picture" the spreadsheets tell you.

Even if you're not into numbers, don't be tempted to skip this exercise. You really must sit down with your financial account information. And if you financial situation is not that rosy it's important to face up to reality and then take positive steps to move forward.

You can do it on paper but it's usually easier if you create a series of Excel spreadsheets with two sets of numbers:

- Your personal cash flow statement, and

- Your personal balance sheet.

Let's explore these in more detail.

Your personal cash flow statement

Your personal cash flow statement measures your cash inflows (money you make) and outflows (money you spend) in order to show you your net cash flow for a specific period of time. For example, you could assess your typical cash flow on a monthly or annual basis.

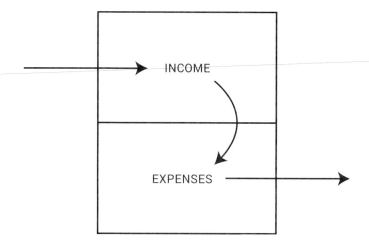

Cash inflows (your income) generally includes anything that brings in money such as:

- Salaries, bonuses, commissions earned

- Investment income — rental, dividends and interest

- Capital gains.

As you can see there are three basic types of income:

1. Earned — your salary or self employed wages

2. Passive recurring — from your investments (your money is working for you)

3. Capital growth of the value of your property or shares — in Australia this is not taxed unless you sell.

To become rich you have to convert more of your income into passive recurring income as I've been mentioning in previous chapters.

Cash outflow (your expenses) is the money leaving your pocket and could include:

1. Rent or mortgage payments

2. Interest including credit and store cards (hopefully you're taking my advice about getting rid of these!)

3. Tax payments

4. Utilities, rates, phone and internet bills

5. Living expenses: food, groceries, household expenses

6. Childcare and medical expenses

7. Clothing and personal care

8. Transportation: fares as well as car expenses including petrol and insurance

9. Entertainment, gifts and recreation: vacations, hobbies, sport, movie tickets, restaurant meals, cigarettes, alcohol, etc.

10. Miscellaneous: you'll always forget some expenses.

The purpose of determining your cash inflows and outflows is to find your net cash flow, which is simply the result of subtracting your outflow from your inflow.

Your income pays your expenses and if you don't have enough income you may have to incur additional debt to pay your expenses.

So, if you currently have a negative cash flow or you want to increase your positive net cash flow, the only way to do it is to assess your spending habits and adjust them as necessary.

INVESTMENT SUCCESS FACT

Regularly updating your personal financial statement helps you become more aware of your spending habits and net worth, and helps you move up the Wealth Pyramid.

Your personal balance sheet

Your balance sheet is the second part of your personal financial statement; it balances the value of your assets (what you own) against the value of your liabilities (what you owe) and provides an overall snapshot of your wealth at a specific period in time (your net worth = assets minus liabilities).

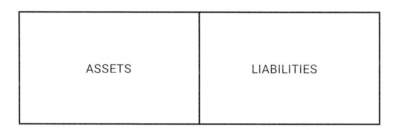

Assets are things you own and could include:

- Cash on hand

- Bank account balances

- Property — your home or investment properties

- The value of stocks or mutual funds owned

- Any other investments

- Your superannuation or retirement funds

- The net value of the business you own

- Other personal property like jewellery, cars, boats, artwork and furniture.

Liabilities are things that you owe or have a binding agreement to repay at some point in the future. They decrease your net worth and include:

- The mortgage on your home or investment properties

- Personal loans

- Current bills: medical, utilities, repairs, etc.

- Payments still owed on some of your assets like cars

- Credit card balances and other loans including personal and school loans

- Tax owing.

It helps to consider this balance sheet as just a snapshot of what you have and what you owe. You are not creating a ledger for the week, month, or year. You are simply trying to take a picture of your net worth at one moment in time.

Your net worth is the difference between what you own and what you owe. This figure is your measure of wealth because it represents what you own after everything you owe has been paid off. If you have a negative net worth, this means that you owe more than you own.

Bringing them together

Personal financial statements give you the tools to monitor your spending and increase your net worth. The thing about these two spreadsheets is that they are not just two separate pieces of information, they actually work together.

You'll be using your net cash flow from the cash flow statement to help increase your net worth. If you have a positive net cash flow in a given month, you can apply that money to acquiring assets or paying off liabilities. Applying your net cash flow toward your net worth is a great way to increase assets without increasing liabilities or decrease liabilities without increasing assets.

INVESTMENT SUCCESS FACT

Remember the true measure of how successful you are as an investor is your net worth — the size of your asset base — not your working income.

While it may take a little time to set up all this up the first time around, it will just be a matter of updating the numbers to create a new personal financial statement every month. Doing this can help you determine your current financial status and control your spending. Comparing this year's position to last year's will help you track your progress towards your financial goals.

Where is all your money going?

The aim of all this is, of course, to understand where your money is going so you can get better control of your personal finances.

Depending where you are on the Wealth Pyramid, your cash flow pattern will look different.

Level 0 Wealth

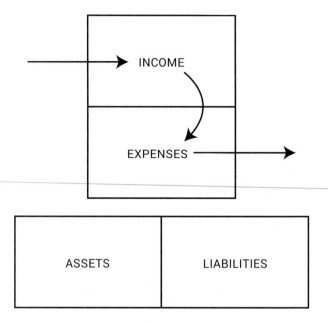

If you're at Level 0 on the Wealth Pyramid all your earned income is immediately spent on "things". This cash flow pattern corresponds to immediate gratification.

You'll have few assets and if you do their liabilities are equal to or more than the value of your assets.

Let's compare this to someone further up the Wealth Pyramid at …

Level 2 Wealth

At this level you'd be focussing on buying assets that generate income, so you're not as reliant on your personal exertion income.

You'll still have expenses and liabilities and still rely on your earned income to some extent. But at Level 2 you'll use any surplus money that does not go to expenses to buy income-producing assets — like real estate or shares.

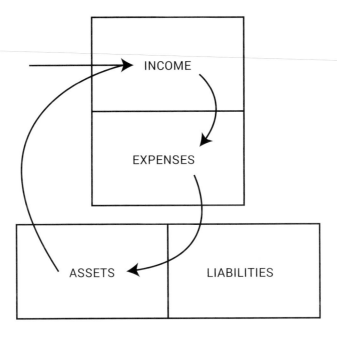

Level 3 Wealth

You'll notice in the diagram below that when you're financially independent the earned income arrow is gone.

At Level 3 or 4 all your expenses are paid from the passive recurring income from your Cash Machine and you no longer need a job.

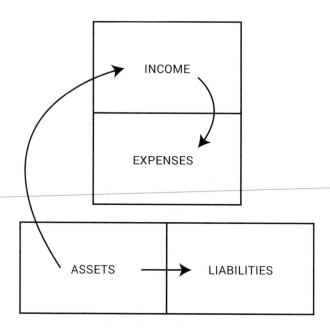

Analysing your personal financial statement

Now that you've prepared your own financial statement and seen the examples, it's time to do an analysis of your own financial health. The numbers will indicate where you are and suggest ways to move you forward financially. Consider things like:

- How much do you keep each month after you subtract your expenses from your income? Then plan to increase this amount over time.

- Does your money work for you or do you work for your money? Plan to increase your passive recurring income. If you have no passive income start by buying assets that generate income.

- How much are you spending on thingies? Sure you're allowed to reward yourself for a job well done, but don't do so at the expense of building assets.

- How much tax are you paying? Make sure you're claiming all legitimate deductions.

- How wealthy are you?

Far too many people have their financial lives run by their whims and spending. Their financial accounts look a bit like this:

Now take a look at how the wealthy people spend their money. They take the money they earn and invest a large portion of it into income-producing assets like real estate, shares or businesses. If you want to become a successful investor follow their lead.

I first remember learning these concepts I've just outlined in Robert Kiyosaki's book *The Cash Flow Quadrant*. I've since watched many clients and those I have mentored exhibit the exact same cash flow patterns outlined above.

People at level 0 and 1 on the Wealth Pyramid work for their money, but as they move up the pyramid they get their money working for them.

INVESTMENT SUCCESS FACT

Put simply — the rich buy assets, the poor only have expenses and the middle-class buy liabilities that they think are assets!

So while the poor try to increase their cash flow, the rich are busy building their asset base. That's why the rich get richer — their assets generate more than enough income to cover their expenses and they reinvest the balance to buy more income-producing assets.

Your strategic financial assessment

Let me be clear: to really make the most of your strategic financial assessment you should compare the results from last year with your current status. This way you will not only see where you are financially, you'll also see the trend — which way your finances are heading and how fast.

In the future, I suggest you look at your financial results every three months or so as this will give you more regular feedback to fine-tune your investing.

A simple formula you could use to give you the percentage increase or decrease that you're looking for could be:

(Net worth this period – Net worth last period)/Net worth last period

This way you can see how your net worth is trending. Is it rising, staying the same or falling?

By now, I hope you've realised that as well as understanding your true financial situation you also need to set goals to work towards on your journey to investment success.

The concept of setting your financial goals in writing may sound so simple that you would be tempted to skip this stage — but please don't!

INVESTMENT SUCCESS FACT

I've found that one of the biggest differences between investment success and failure is the critical initial step of goal-setting — not just in your head or just thinking about it, but putting goals down in writing.

Whether you're single or have a partner, it's important to have clear goals that you can work towards. If you don't, it's just too easy to keep going round in circles and never move up the Wealth Pyramid, as you don't actually have any goals to aim for.

So let's start by asking yourself these questions:

1. What are my/our *dreams*? What are our goals? What do we want to accomplish in life? What toys do we want?

2. What type of *lifestyle* do we want now during our working years and in the future?

3. *When do we want to retire?* Or don't we want to stop working?

4. When we retire *how much income* do we want?

5. What is the *goal of our wealth building* — spend our nest egg or grow a Cash Machine and continue growing wealth?

6. Are we investing for our *lifetime* or to leave a *legacy* for our children and grandchildren? If you plan to build a multigenerational wealth machine you're going to need more time, a larger asset base, more aggressive investment strategies and sound risk minimisation strategies as well as the correct ownership structures.

7. What is our *risk tolerance*? Low, medium or high tolerance for risk?

8. *What am I / are we good at?* Your unique talents are what will help you consistently outperform the market in a specific niche. Maybe it's real estate, possibly shares or maybe you're a good business person. Maybe you're a good negotiator or maybe you're analytical and good with numbers. Your unique advantages should be harnessed and taken advantage of to magnify your investment returns.

9. Do I want to be *actively involved in the management* of my wealth creation or do I want to have others do this for me?

10. What *charitable legacy* do I want to leave?

What all this means is that you'll need to decide how much money you'll need to enjoy the lifestyle you desire and to do the things you want, in today's dollar value. You also need to understand how much your asset base will need to grow to achieve the financial freedom, and the future, that you desire. Chances are you'll discover you'll need a much, much bigger asset base than you thought.

Now that you have a better idea of where you're heading I suggest you set yourself two financial goals: a realistic goal — one that you should be able to achieve — and a stretched goal — one that will push but also inspire you.

Put these in writing and include:

1. Your financial freedom date

2. The passive annual income you want your Cash Machine to produce

3. The size of your asset base at your financial freedom date.

With these financial goals written down you know exactly what you're working towards and how your journey towards achieving these goals is going during your regular reviews.

Hopefully now you have a good understanding of what your true financial position is, which is a great start because now it's time to consider why most people just don't make it financially.

CHAPTER 11:
WHY MOST PEOPLE DON'T MAKE IT FINANCIALLY

Why don't most investors succeed? Even in wealthy countries like Australia, the UK and USA most people never make it financially.

They live a life that's dictated by their boss or one that's constrained by the size of their income and then, sad but true, they live out their final years hoping they die before their savings run out. How depressing is that?

But, it doesn't have to be that way.

Often it's because they're making some simple but common investing mistakes that are sabotaging their chances of reaching their financial goals.

Whether you're investing in real estate, stocks, bonds or any other investment vehicle, it's possible you're also unintentionally hurting your own financial results.

I received an email from a listener of my podcast the other day and I was shocked when he told me of the "dud" investment property a property promoter had "sold" to him on the pretext of giving "advice". This poor choice literally cost him over $150,000 of potentially better investment returns over the past few years, increased his portfolio risk and almost sent him broke as he had difficulty servicing his loans and had negative equity in his property!

And this is not an isolated occurrence. I see this happen all the time where well-intentioned people keep making very similar investing mistakes that keep them trapped financially.

Before I discuss some of the common mistakes I see and how you can avoid making them let's first unwind some thinking that most of us learned about money from our parents.

The wrong type of education

You see … we learn our financial programming from our parents and often, in turn, pass on this financial *illiteracy* to our own children.

So consider this: If you have children, will they be rich or poor?

You have a big say in it, so if you've got children or are planning to have children at some stage in your life, this chapter is a must-read for you!

What messages are you giving *your* children and what lessons are you teaching them about money, wealth, success and rich people?

Unfortunately, most of us are setting up our children to fail financially in life.

In his book *Rich Kids*, my friend, author Thomas Corley, explains that his study found the poor are poor because they have too many Poverty Habits and too few Rich Habits. And poor parents teach their children the Poverty Habits and wealthy parents teach their children the Rich Habits.

Here are some of the statistics from his five-year study of the daily habits that separate the rich from the poor:

- 80% of the wealthy are focused on at least one goal vs. 12% of the poor

- 79% of the wealthy believe they are responsible for their financial condition vs. 18% of the poor

- 79% of the wealthy network five hours or more per month vs.16% of the poor

- 73% of the wealthy were taught the 80/20 rule (live off 80% save 20%) vs. 5% of the poor

- 72% of the wealthy know their credit score vs. 5% of the poor

- 67% of the wealthy watch one hour or less of TV per day vs. 23% of the poor

- 63% of the wealthy spend less than one hour per day on recreational Internet use vs. 26% of the poor

- 63% of wealthy listen to audio books or podcasts during their commute vs. 5% of the poor

- 62% of the wealthy floss their teeth every day vs. 16% of the poor

- 21% of the wealthy are overweight by 30 pounds or more vs. 66% of the poor

- 9% of the wealthy watch reality TV shows vs. 78% of the poor

- 8% of the wealthy believe wealth comes from random good luck vs. 79% of the poor

- 6% of the wealthy play the lottery vs. 77% of the poor

INVESTMENT SUCCESS FACT

The rich have good daily success habits that they learned from their parents.

My children are grown up now and have children of their own. But if I had my time over again here are 11 lessons I would have taught them when they were young.

1. The sooner you save, the faster your money can grow through compounding

It takes money to make money so teach your kids the importance of spending less than they earn, saving the difference until they have sufficient money to buy appreciating assets.

Part of this is learning how to budget. You can start by teaching your children the art of saving for "big ticket" items once they're old enough to earn a few bucks for washing the car or bathing the dog.

2. You may have to wait to buy something you want

This is a hard concept for people of all ages to learn, however the ability to delay gratification can also predict how successful one will be as a grown-up. Children need to learn that if they really want something, they should wait and save to buy it.

The problem is we all want the best for our children, which is why a common trap for parents is giving their kids everything they feel they missed out on growing up. Trampoline in the backyard? Check. Brand new clothes each season? Check. Entitled, impatient attitude geared towards instant gratification? Check!

It may make you feel good to give your child all the toys and gadgets they desire, but in doing so you're not doing them any favours. The lesson you want to demonstrate is not one of instant gratification, but one that shows how much reward comes from putting in incremental amounts of effort.

If your child patiently saves $2 per week for a few months to buy a $20 toy, how much do you think they're going to love their new prize? And more importantly, when lessons like this are learnt young, it will encourage them to manage their money more smartly as they get older.

3. You need to make choices about how to spend money

It's important to explain to your child that money is finite and it's important to make wise choices, because once you've spent it, you don't have more to spend!

4. Today's debt equals tomorrow's slavery

When we're younger we tend to think in very narrow time increments, seek immediate gratification and don't like delaying the purchase of something that we really want.

Unfortunately, this leads many to fall into the credit card trap we've spoken about. But today's debt will rob them of tomorrow's earnings because they're sacrificing money they don't yet have.

INVESTMENT SUCCESS FACT

Limiting debt obligations when you're younger will mean having more control over your personal finances later in life.

---

5. He who dies with the most toys is not the victor

We all like our toys. Well … at least I know I do. But expectation is a dreadful enemy of money management.

We see so much of how "the other half live" in glossy magazines and on television these days; glorified as something to aspire to, making many of us think life is all about working just so you can be one of the "have mores" of the world.

Consumerism is the "new black".

The truth is possessions don't make for a rich life; it's the experiences and people — the things that money can't buy — that make you truly wealthy and successful. In my mind "true wealth" is what you're left with if you lose all your money and possessions.

6. Taking responsibility makes you the master of your own destiny

Fact is: there are no rich victims.

Yet unfortunately people are too quick to blame others for their own failings in life. We have become a society of litigious finger pointers and as a result, many people feel they've been unjustly dealt a "bad hand".

The truth is, if you're courageous enough to cast a critical eye over your life, recognise you are where you are as a direct result of your own choices and take ownership of your decisions; you build confidence, self esteem and self respect.

In turn, you'll feel an inner strength in knowing you are master of your own destiny, rather than handing your power and control over to someone else who, let's face it, won't have your best interests at heart the way you do.

And just to make things clear ... hope is not an investment strategy — you need to plan your destiny.

7. Patience and waiting is ...

When you fly the family coop, no doubt you'll want everything yesterday — the flashy car, new furniture and the biggest TV money can buy. But in all likelihood you'll have to work your way up the food chain, learning to prioritise how to make the best use of your fortnightly pay cheque as you go.

Understand the difference between wants and needs, and recognise that all the money you spend on those material items you just "had to have" today is less that you'll have to fund your retirement with tomorrow.

It's that delayed gratification thing again isn't it, knowing that if you work hard and invest even harder your purchasing power will increase over time!

8. Luck is made through hard work

Many of us like to attribute the success of others all to "good fortune". Perhaps they were in "the right place at the right time", or knew "the right person". While a handful of people have lucked out by winning the lottery, truly successful people do the hard yards to reach the pinnacle of their chosen field or endeavour.

INVESTMENT SUCCESS FACT

If you can find something that you're passionate about and make a living doing it, you'll be far more likely to achieve great things because you'll work harder to reach your goals ... and every day won't be a struggle.

---

9. You don't need millions to achieve financial freedom

Plenty of millionaires are up to their eyeballs in debt and that's the truth of it. Many of society's rich power players are asset-rich, but cash-poor whereas other people, who earn $50,000 a year, are without debt and have more financial freedom.

Financial freedom is not dependent on money itself, as I've outlined in a previous chapter, but it is dependent on your relationship to it and the level of personal responsibility and fiscal discipline you're prepared to exercise throughout life.

10. Only use a credit card if you can pay the balance off in full each month

Buy now — interest free! No repayments for 24 months! It's all too easy to slide into credit card debt, which gives your child the burden of paying off credit card debt at exorbitant interest rates. Plus a default could affect their credit history, which could make it difficult to, say, buy a car or a home.

11. *Your youth won't last forever, so use it wisely*

Compounding to grow your wealth relies on more than money — it relies on time.

In fact given enough time compound interest — that is the interest earned on the interest earned on your high growth assets — is so effective that Albert Einstein called it the most powerful force in the universe.

Start saving and investing early in life and you're likely to secure your financial future.

Now let's look at some of the common mistakes and how you can avoid making them yourself so that you can increase your returns and reach your financial goals —faster and safer!

Common mistakes that trap the unwary

1. *Following the wrong financial plan*

As I've already explained, the first big problem is that most people have never set themselves clear financial goals.

Despite the fact that they've never really planned for their future, they are in fact following a wealth plan, even though they don't realise it.

Now this is an important point because it's your wealth plan that will either lead you to financial freedom or to financial mediocrity, but if you're like more than 90 per cent of the country, your plan is designed to give you financial mediocrity at best and financial failure at worst.

And most people unknowingly follow a plan they've been handed down by their parents and the result is a huge percentage of those who reach retirement age wind up dependent on the government, their family or a job as the main source to fund what should be their "golden years".

That's because their financial plan is to:

1. Get a good education so they can land a "secure" job.

2. Work for 40 years or so, saving as they go.

3. Buy themselves a house and pay it off.

4. Invest their leftover money in conventional investments such as stocks, superannuation (or your 401(k) in the USA) or managed funds, so they can retire at 65 or 70.

5. Then hope that their money doesn't run out while they're still alive.

Not a very inspiring plan, is it? But sadly the average person doesn't know any better.

2. Blindly turning your investments over to a "professional" to do your investing for you

Since most people don't understand about investing and are overwhelmed with the myriad of options, they're tempted to hand over their future to a financial planner and invest in a "diversified portfolio of professionally managed securities" and hope for the best.

As for me, I am not comfortable passively allowing other people, most of whom are still financially struggling employees themselves, to be in control of my financial destiny.

To be frank, seeing the results this has achieved for others, that scenario scares me!

Instead you should invest the time and energy to cultivate your investing skills so that you will be the one in control. You will be the one who can make sure you reach your financial dreams.

Does this take more effort? Of course it does. But remember that the stakes are incredibly high and the price of not making the investment in yourself could be financially fatal for you and your family.

3. Focusing on the "investment" and forgetting about you the investor

The media tells us that the way to protect yourself and be "safe" is to focus on the specific, individual investments that you are making.

But in my experience mentoring over 3,000 investors over the past two decades I've found that risk cannot be isolated from the investor.

In fact, in my mind, investment risk has more to do with the investor than it does with the investment.

What's risky for one investor may be a bread and butter investment for another investor.

For example, I'm an experienced property developer. When I find a great development site I can produce returns two to three times that of passively investing in real estate.

But I'm not an expert in investing in shares. Virtually any investment I make in shares will be quite risky for me.

As Warren Buffet aptly says: "Risk comes from not knowing what you are doing."

By the way — I've got a whole chapter on this later in the book.

4. Focusing on "saving" versus investing

There's a big, big difference when it comes to saving versus investing.

You just can't save your way to wealth, but that's what a lot of people try to do. In fact most don't save to invest — they may think they do, but they usually save to consume.

Let's look at it this way …

Level 0 and 1 investors don't build wealth. Their focus is on getting through today. Unless they do something radically different they will end up financially dependent and struggling their entire lives.

Level 2 investors build wealth from their income. To them investing is a process of scrimping and saving a small amount of their after tax "left over" money to build their "nest egg" bit by bit over 40 years. Many hand their money over to a "professional" manager to invest for them. Never mind that this professional manager is probably no better off financially than they are and is most likely a salesperson working on commission.

On the other hand …

Level 3 investors are not trying to build a "nest egg" to live off. They're building an asset base so they can become Level 4 investors and live off their Cash Machine — their future income comes from their wealth.

It's important to understand the difference — *Level 4 investors* use their wealth to build more wealth they don't spend down their wealth like Level 1 or 2 investors. Rather than drawing down on their nest egg and hoping it will last the distance, they let it keep growing because they have a perpetual motion Cash Machine.

5. Falling victim to the prevailing investment myths

It disappoints me to see hardworking people underperform financially simply because they follow flawed financial advice and investment myths.

I've written whole chapters about these in my other books.

One of the common ones is when financial "experts" recommend, "Diversify, diversify, diversify." They suggest that you shouldn't put all your eggs in one basket, but instead buy a number of shares or units in different managed funds.

You may agree and think, "If I put all my money into a bad investment, I could lose everything."

Yet, the best investors in the world don't diversify. Warren Buffet, the world's richest investor, says, "Diversification is protection against ignorance. It makes little sense for those who know what they are doing."

And Robert Kiyosaki asked, "Whose ignorance are you being protected from? Yours … or your financial advisor's?"

He then goes on to say: "One of the keys to being successful at anything is to know what you are doing. When you know what you are doing, you make more money because you buy only great investments … not a basket of wishful thinking."

In other words, risk is really a measure of your investment knowledge.

Almost a century ago when Napoleon Hill wrote *Think and Grow Rich* he recognised one of the characteristics of successful people was that they specialised.

When you study the way the wealthy have become rich, rather than diversifying which leads to mediocrity and an average outcome (because you make money in one investment and lose it in another) successful investors specialise.

They become an expert in their niche and take active control of their investments. This is particularly relevant when you're just beginning to create wealth.

You need to pick a strong, sound investment (and in general I would advocate income-producing residential real estate) and throw your whole energy into studying it, learning about it and gaining a thorough understanding of how it works.

Don't dissipate your energy trying to comprehend a number of different asset classes.

When starting out, you need to keep it simple, as there's a steep learning curve ahead. As you become a Level 3 and 4 investor you can start to diversify into other areas.

To achieve wealth-producing rates of return you'll need to become an expert in your niche and I'm sure you won't be surprised that I suggest it should be residential investment property.

But as you build up your property portfolio, then you should diversify. Considering the cost of investment properties, you can't diversify when you first start off, but over time you should do so by owning a number of properties, a number of different types of properties, properties in different areas and properties in different states or territories.

For example, I own residential, commercial, industrial and showroom properties, as well as apartments, houses and townhouses and I own properties in a number of different geographic locations.

So while I specialise in property, I'm diversified within that asset class.

INVESTMENT SUCCESS FACT

My point is that diversification isn't the best way to lower risk, cultivating the skills and advantages you need to make better smarter investing moves is.

6. Not treating your investments like a business

Most investors have a "set and forget" philosophy. While I agree you should invest for the long-term, you should also regularly review your investment portfolio and evaluate its performance.

This means you need to understand what constitutes a great investment for you and you need to know how to evaluate its performance.

Having these guidelines let's you sort through various investment opportunities fast to choose the ones that you want to pursue further. It also sharpens your focus when you are looking for deals and dramatically increases your odds of finding winning opportunities.

I know that I've made more money by saying "no" to perceived opportunities than I've made by saying "yes" to opportunities.

Let's now move on to learning about financial advisors and whether they are really useful or not.

CHAPTER 12:
HOW USEFUL ARE
FINANCIAL ADVISORS?

Why is investing so complicated?

A comfortable retirement is supposed to be the reward for a lifetime of work, and yet it seems we must pass an entrance exam to reach it and that's probably why many people think they need to see a financial planner for advice on how to invest.

And that's why most investors remain Level 2 passive investors. Rather than becoming financially fluent, they let a "professional" handle their investments. It could be a financial planner, a stockbroker or a real estate agent, because the average investor hopes these "professionals" know more about investment then they do.

But do they really?

You see … most financial advisors, but certainly not all, are really salespeople working for banks, insurance companies and other financial institutions selling their products for a commission.

Most property "advisors" are selling products from a stock list (you know … project marketers, real estate agents or brokers who are representing their clients) and most stockbrokers earn commissions every time you buy or sell shares.

Sure they may have had some training, but giving financial advice does not make them a financial expert. In fact, it doesn't mean the advice they give is even correct. It is often the same advice regurgitated by the financial planning industry for decades and is usually plain wrong.

If you peek behind the curtain you'll find that many financial advisors are in much the same financial situation as their clients, struggling to make ends meet and worrying about the bills. They are not making money from their investments, but rather making money from selling investment products to their clients.

If I was to go to a marriage counsellor, I wouldn't want to go to one who has written the books or knows what to say. I'd to go to the counsellor who has the happiest marriage and the best relationships. Similarly, you shouldn't choose your financial advisor based on what they say, but on what they have achieved personally and retained over the long-term.

While many financial advisors may be looking after your best interests, usually the advice they give you will, at best, be average. You need to develop financial fluency yourself so you have the knowledge and perspective to properly evaluate the advice given to you.

Now I'm not a believer in doing it yourself — if you want to get a good job done employ a professional. While I have no issue with you outsourcing the implementation of your investment strategy to a buyers' agent to purchase your property, to a financial planner to buy managed funds or to a stockbroker to purchase your shares, I'm very much against you outsourcing your financial education.

Get a good team around you, but remember the performance of your investment portfolio will only be as good as the weakest link in your team — so get a good team and make sure you're not the weakest link.

You need to become financially fluent so you can assess the quality of the "advice" you're being given.

Legal considerations

The provision of true financial advice is regulated in most countries, yet many people defer to unqualified people for "advice", which can have disastrous consequences.

Unfortunately many would-be investors decide that the fast-talking salesperson they saw on stage one day has the answers to their financial dreams and blindly follow them without completing their own due diligence.

In Australia, providing advice regarding shares, life insurance and managed funds is regulated by ASIC, yet the history of Australia's financial planning industry is littered with stories of banks, insurance companies and financial planners who've at best put their own interests before their clients and at worst committed outright fraud.

On the other hand, in Australia, the provision of property investment "advice" is largely unregulated, and all manner of "advisors" are out there to assist inexperienced investors. That's probably one of the reasons most property investors fail.

Some unfortunate stories

The internet is littered with stories of how financial advisors took advantage of average mums and dads. This all spectacularly came to a head during the Global Financial Crisis when bad advice caused the downfall of many Level 2 investors.

In the early days of the GFC in Australia, the collapse of Storm Financial Ltd was the result of reckless advice, which cost 3,000 to 4,000 investors in Queensland, New South Wales and Victoria around $3 billion.

In early 2022 the collapse of Dixon Advisory, one of the nation's largest wealth managers, exposed the heavy personal and financial cost of the 36-year-old firm's highly conflicted business model that steered the retirement savings of thousands of middle-class Australians into its own poorly performing high-fee property fund. Thousands of the firm's clients who followed its allegedly conflicted advice were left with their retirement plans in tatters as a result of the losses that have occurred in an otherwise buoyant period for financial investments.

Financial advice is too expensive

A number of years ago, renowned financial columnist Alan Kohler wrote in *The Australian* newspaper that the problem with financial advice is that it's too expensive. He explained:

> *A financial plan costs at least $2,000, usually more* (It's more like $3,000 today). *The truth is, it's not worth it.*

> *It has become so expensive not because of the years of study by the practitioner or the expensive equipment being used. In fact, health check-ups usually cost less than wealth check-ups, even though they're carried out by someone who has studied for at least seven years and who is probably using very expensive equipment indeed.*

> *Why has financial advice become so expensive? Because of regulation. Clients are paying for attempts to protect them as much as they are paying for the advice itself.*

> *Over the years, regulation has focused on disclosure, so that any financial advice now comes with huge volumes of expensive paperwork that no one reads. That's why clients know the advice is not worth the real cost. Most of the price pays for disclosure that they're not going to read.*

And the reason that sort of misguided regulation was introduced was that financial advice arose from a sales culture — that is, from life insurance.

The early financial planners were insurance salespeople who switched to selling investment products. Calling themselves financial planners, or advisors, was a brilliant idea. It set up a very profitable knowledge gap in which they knew they were selling but the clients thought they were advising.

The definitions in the laws that control what advisors do, and the training now required to be a financial planner, are all about products and disclosure rather than simply financial advice.

The result is that regulation has had the perverse effect of driving people towards disguised ways of paying for it: that is, commissions and percentages. Would you go to someone who sends you a bill for $5,000 or someone who says: "Don't worry about the cost — someone else will pick that up."?

In other words, the regulation of financial advice has created a kind of whirlpool effect, where the regulation increases the cost and the high cost produces the need for more regulation.

Who to trust?

Just to make things clear … I'm not suggesting you don't engage advisors to assist you. All the wealthy people I know have a number of advisors and mentors while the poor rarely have advisors.

However, the financial advisors that the wealthy engage tend to be different to the ones the poor people go to. The rich and successful are prepared to pay for good advice, understanding that it's an investment not an expense, however the average person naively thinks the free advice they're getting from a salesperson is in their best interest.

So perhaps this leads to the question: Who do you get your financial advice from? One source is to find a financial mentor, which is what we'll learn about in the next chapter.

And this is clearly a good time to once again declare my financial interest in two separate financial planning firms as well as Metropole, which gets paid by our clients to give strategic property advice.

CHAPTER 13:
HOW TO FIND A
FINANCIAL MENTOR

A mentor is somebody whose hindsight can become your foresight.

A mentor is a trusted friend, counsellor or teacher who is more experienced than you to help advance your career, your education and your network.

When I learned that I didn't have to do things on my own or to reinvent the wheel — that I could instead stand on the shoulders of my mentors — I got to the next level of investment success very quickly and so can you.

In his study on the habits of the rich and poor, Tom Corley (*www.RichHabits.net*) learned three things about mentors:

Mentors are hard to come by — only 24 per cent of the wealthy had a mentor in life.

Finding a mentor is the fast track to accumulating wealth — those 24 per cent who found mentors also happened to accumulate their wealth at a younger age than the rest of the millionaires.

Having a mentor produces the greatest accumulation of wealth — almost all of the millionaires in his study who had a mentor, also happened to have accumulated the most wealth.

So it seems the goal for anyone who wants to invest successfully is to find a mentor to help you on your journey.

Why mentors matter

People at Level 3 and 4 on the Wealth Pyramid recognise the need for mentors who they can look up to and from whom they can seek guidance and inspiration. These mentors have been successful and achieved many of the things that the investor is still aiming to accomplish in life.

Mentors have been critical in my success — they have helped me see things that I couldn't see. They identified my blind spots, encouraged me to think differently and made me accountable for my decisions.

Successful people employ mentors who have already done what they want to do and are successful at doing it. On the other hand, the poor take counsel from advisers who tell them how to do it, but have not personally done it.

INVESTMENT SUCCESS FACT

One of the things that changed my life and helped me grow my financial independence was when I realised that I had to go out and seek teachers and role models who would help me to end up where I truly wanted to be.

Let's be clear — your mentors should not be the teachers that impart those traditional lessons learned at school, but coaches who've had real life experience in wealth creation. I don't mean to be critical of the education system, but you'll find that most teachers — even those teaching economics, business and investment — base their lessons on theory rather than actual experience.

As I built my business and investment skills, I sought mentors who had already produced real life results. I realised that this wouldn't come for free, but I sought their counsel and went to their seminars, bought their books, listened to their tape sets (there weren't CDs, DVDs, podcasts or webinars around when I started off!) and absorbed as much of their life-gained knowledge as I could.

By the way ... we all have mentors.

You will already have people you model. Sometimes you pick them consciously, sometimes you pick them unconsciously. Some people (unconsciously) pick the people from *Keeping Up With The Kardashians*, *Desperate Housewives* or *The Bold and the Beautiful* as their models — interesting, isn't it?

How mentors can help you

Mentors can help you to become a successful investor by contributing to your wealth creation in the following ways:

1. Imparting knowledge: A mentor can bring a wider range of experience to the table and offer you the opportunity to gain years of knowledge in a short space of time. This could be a personal mentor or you could learn from someone who has done it before through a book, a DVD or seminar.

2. Sharing experience: We're often taught to learn by trial and error, but I'd rather learn from somebody else's mistakes, rather than make costly errors myself. A good mentor will have a thorough understanding of the dos and don'ts to help prevent you making your own mistakes.

3. Mentors make you present your ideas and then make you *think long and hard* about your ideas and what you're planning to do and make you *justify* what you are planning to do.

4. Providing contacts: A good mentor will have contacts that can help you to seek out and identify opportunities you wouldn't have found yourself. In this world, it's not who you know, but who you know knows. No, I'm not stuttering. Having a wide range of contacts will help you enormously.

5. Mentors can *motivate* you and help you achieve in different areas that you may not have thought you could find success in.

6. Mentors can *save you time*: Having done it before, they can show you the shortcuts and teach you the potholes to avoid, helping you to navigate and take the right turns on your road to riches.

7. Mentors are *independent* and won't have a vested interest in what you do, so they can offer you support. They'll understand when you're feeling high and why you're feeling low at times and they can relate to the challenges you will go through on your climb up the investment ladder.

Finding a real estate mentor

All the successful property investors I've dealt with over the years have hung out with like-minded investors and followed in the footsteps of the others who have already done what they wanted to achieve. This helped them see the landmines before stepping on them and helped them achieve success more quickly.

The problem is there are lots of people out there calling themselves "real estate experts" and many do a great job. However, the recent property boom made even some below average investors look like geniuses.

What to look for in a property mentor

When looking for a mentor you should identify people who have got at least the following credentials:

1. They must be *currently actively investing* in real estate using the strategies they are teaching. There's no room for theorists here.

2. An absolute bare *minimum of 40 property transactions* to their name so they have experience dealing with different buying and selling situations.

Currently there are books and educational courses written by people who have bought five or six properties. I would be wary of these.

3. Somebody who has been hands-on investing for *no less than 15 years*, so they have had experience in different market conditions. They must have successfully used their strategies through a full property cycle.

If somebody has managed to survive through the early 90s (the recession we had to have), the middle 90s (during low inflation), the late 90s when we had a real estate boom and the early 2000s when we had a real estate bust and through the ups and downs of the last decade and are still able to prove that their system works … then I want you to listen to these people.

However, the recent property boom where almost every property in Australia increased in value by more than 20% made a new generation of young "advisers" look good. The problem is they don't have the perspective to understand that it is the market that did the heavy lifting not their input.

4. Somebody who *doesn't have a property to sell you*. Now this isn't necessary in all cases, but just something of which to be aware. Ensure there isn't a potential conflict of interest.

5. Somebody who is *not selling to your emotions*, such as act now or you will miss out and somebody who doesn't put others down to make themselves look good. Look for somebody with integrity and a commitment to disclosure.

6. Don't be scared to pay the right people to mentor you. Of course your mentor is going to make money, if they are good they deserve to do so.

If everything is disclosed upfront there should be no conflict of interest.

7. Avoid somebody who is offering you something exciting, speculative, new or the latest thing. Don't look for excitement in your investments. Your property investments are your way of securing your financial future.

INVESTMENT SUCCESS FACT

Don't be distracted from your long-term plans or strategies by promises of quick riches. Find the system that focuses on long-term wealth creation.

Who could you ask for property investment advice?

Here are the people you could turn to:

1. **No One** — many beginning investors think they understand real estate because they've lived in or rented a home or an apartment. That's a big mistake and probably one of the reasons around fifty per cent of first-time investors sell up within five years. While they may know their local neighbourhood, that's very different from understanding the property market.

2. **Friends or family** — I understand people may do this, but the question to ask is: are they financial experts? How many millionaires do you have in your family? If not, don't ask them because often their advice will be to avoid property investment because of the "risk".

3. **A real estate agent** — remember agents work for the vendor to help them achieve the best price, and they're unlikely to tell you about the other great properties for sale in the area by other agents.

4. **A mortgage broker** — while it's important to have an investment savvy mortgage broker on your side helping you through the finance maze, most don't understand the property market well enough to advise on what is an "investment grade" property.

5. **An accountant** — your accountant should advise you on tax matters and structuring, but most don't have the intimate knowledge of the property market required to give investment advice.

6. **Financial planners** — while financial planners are licensed to sell financial products, most are not able to advise on real estate. Not only because they lack a sound understanding of property, but the company they work for doesn't allow them to. Those who do recommend property usually have a biased view as they make commissions based on the investments they sell from their "stock list".

7. **A property marketer** — while these salespeople may seem to be on your side, they're really selling "product" for a property developer who is most likely going to make the biggest profit out of the deal.

8. **Investment webinars, seminars and workshops** — ask yourself: Is the person conducting the event an investment expert in their field? How long have they been financially secure, or do they make their money teaching others?

9. **A property mentor** — there seems to be an abundance of property mentors around — some who give great guidance, while others are really property sellers or marketers in disguise. Let's make it clear: It's important to have mentors. They see your blind spots, give you guidance and support and expand the way you think. Just be careful who you choose and ensure they have achieved the results you want to achieve.

10. **A buyer's agent** — these can be a great help in selecting the right property, but most are just "order takers" — they don't devise a plan that takes into account your family's future needs and your risk profile.

However, when you look at this list you can now see why you need an independent, unbiased property adviser or strategist. In my mind, it is critical to have a trusted advisor when making property investment decisions. It's just too hard to do it on your own or by trial and error. There's a huge learning fee involved — of time, money, effort, and heartache.

So what do Property Strategists actually do?

I see my role as a property advisor as helping our clients grow, protect and pass on their wealth using property as a vehicle.

While people come to the team at Metropole for property advice, in fact, they're really coming for something else. Some are looking for financial freedom; others for more choices in life like working because they want to, not because they have to; and yet others want to leave a legacy for their family or the community.

So, as I've already explained, property is really just the vehicle they're keen on using to achieving their end goals.

While most property advisors come from a real estate background, the property strategists at Metropole come from a wealth, financial planning or banking background, but have a good understanding of property and are successful investors themselves.

You see ... at Metropole our property strategists' job is not to sell clients properties, but to help them safely increase their wealth over the long term.

Many years ago, when I first saw a gap in the market for sound strategic advice, I set about providing my services as a property strategist.

I was the first one I knew of — today many people call themselves property "advisors" or "strategists", yet quite a few are thinly disguised salespeople, or are not really qualified to give in depth advice.

So, let's look at what a good strategist can and can't do …

Here are some of the things a good property advisor can (should) do:

1. A good advisor will first start by getting to know their clients' hopes and fears and then be future-focused to help them achieve their long-term financial goals.

2. With so many mixed messages about property investing out there (many coming from parties with vested interests), a good property advisor will help remove his client's anxiety by simplifying the complex. They will provide clarity around the complicated world of wealth creation which involves much more than just property — but includes finance, tax, economics and the law. They will advise their clients about the risks as well as the rewards of property investment.

3. While most buyers' agents or property salespeople are transactional and think of the current "sale" or purchase, a professional property advisor will aim to develop a long-term relationship and help their clients understand the next two or three steps even before taking the first step. A good property advisor will "sell" advice, not a product or a property.

4. Many clients come to a real estate advisor looking for the next big thing — some are looking for a shortcut, or the next hotspot, or a way to get rich quickly. Instead, a qualified property strategist will stop their clients from speculating by recommending proven strategies that have always worked.

5. A good independent advisor will not have any properties for sale but will have a list of potential options and refer their clients to a buyers' agent who is part of their team to find the best opportunity in the market to suit their client's budget, plans and risk profile.

6. A strategic advisor will never put any pressure on their client to make an investment decision, but their knowledge, research and experience will help their clients select an investment property that is the highest and best use of their funds, and one that will work hard for them over the long term.

7. A wise property strategist will help their clients avoid the big mistakes made by the average investor and will earn their fees simply by helping their clients avoid the devastating errors made by many investors such as those who lost significant amounts of money by investing in mining towns, regional locations, house and land packages or off-the-plan properties.

8. Of course, a great advisor will do a lot more than that for their fee. By being a student of history, a good strategist will be able to provide perspective, insights, and often optimism at a time when the media is being pessimistic, and vice versa. Remember the information in the media is general and therefore doesn't necessarily relate to your specific circumstances.

9. They will also advise their clients to invest their money the way they do themselves — they must be experienced investors — not enthusiastic amateurs.

10. A good strategist will regularly meet with their clients to objectively assess the performance of their property portfolio and ensure they are heading in the right financial direction.

As you can see — it takes years of learning, experience, and the perspective that only comes from investing through a number of property cycles to become a great property strategist.

Some things a property advisor can't do

As you read on you'll find that some property "advisors" will claim to be able to do some of the things on the following list — things they really can't do. I guess they tend to do this because they're not able to deliver on many aspects on the list above — the things skilled, professionals advisers can deliver.

1. Even a good advisor cannot predict the future. They won't be able to tell you how the market will perform, what will happen to interest rates, or what capital growth rate a particular property will achieve.

2. They won't be able to find the next hot spot for you, yet many so-called advisors suggest they can. In essence, they give their clients what they are requesting, rather than what they need — sound, solid advice.

3. Even the most qualified advisor won't be able to pick the best time to purchase an investment property other than to remind you that the best time to invest was 20 years ago, and the second-best time is today.

4. A good advisor won't be able to help you get rich quickly or achieve extraordinarily high returns without taking on extra risks. The problem is many investors take a short-term approach to real estate which is really a long-term investment. They try and make a quick profit such as buying cheaply, or looking for the next hotspot, which is a short-term approach and then wonder what to do next; rather than taking the long-term approach of owning the best asset they can which will give them long-term compounding growth and in time produce substantial wealth.

The bottom line …

Like me, you were probably told that "experience is the best teacher". This is wrong — it's very slow hard and demoralising. Instead, with a qualified mentor on your side, your path to investment success gets much easier. You have too much to lose not to do it this way. In the end, your financial success will have nothing to do with the advisory fees you pay or don't pay, however it will have a lot to do with the quality of the advice you get or don't get.

But, even at this stage, many people retain some fears about investing and success. Let's now take a look at a few of those perceived "risks" and make you aware of one you probably hadn't thought of.

Don't forget to register your book at <u>www.InvestingSuccessfully.today</u> to access extra resources to help you on your path to investment success.

CHAPTER 14:
IS INVESTING REALLY RISKY?

In this chapter I'd like to share with you some of my thoughts on risk and how it relates to your investment success because I believe that what most of us have been taught about risk is wrong.

In fact, it's probably holding you back from obtaining real wealth and success!

Most people are overly concerned with security and when faced with what they perceive as risk, they opt for so-called "safe investments" — you know, the type of investments that don't actually produce riches.

Similarly, I've found that many financial advisors place too much emphasis on avoiding "risk", trying to preserve your money rather than grow your assets — they see it as a form of "insurance". This means that the average investor becomes defensive and more concerned with saving their money than making it grow.

If you are like most investors somewhere along the line you've probably heard that there is a continuum of risk associated with different investment vehicles, with low-risk investments at one end and highly speculative ventures at the other.

Most believe that any investment can be placed somewhere along this continuum and that in general the higher the risk the greater the reward.

The innate problem with this approach is that while we are taught to evaluate the level of risk in the investment itself, as well as general market risk, there is a critical factor missing — you the investor.

Imagine you are considering undertaking a small residential property development. Is this risky?

In isolation, this question is impossible to answer because I don't know enough about you. Have you ever invested in property? Have you completed a development? If you have no knowledge about residential developments, or you've never owned an investment property, no matter how good the deal seems a development is a risky proposition.

Essentially, it's impossible to distinguish discussions about risk from an assessment of the investor.

So as we start to talk about the different forms of investment in later chapters, and how risky or not they are, we're also going to have to consider you — the investor — and your expertise.

Of course, you could always turn to a trusted advisor to help make up for your lack of knowledge, but the only way to unfailingly lower your own investment risk is to become an expert in a particular area.

Don't get me wrong — I'm not saying don't have advisors, because all the wealthy and successful people I know do, and I'm not saying don't outsource the execution of your investment plan, because you can have stockbrokers and property buyers help you. But to become a successful investor, you must have the fundamental knowledge and you must become an expert in your field.

There are many obvious reasons why you should become an expert but one most people don't consider is because you'll then be able to evaluate the value of the advice you get from others.

How do you know when you're an expert?

You have to consistently outperform the market in the given investment niche over time — preferably a couple of investment cycles.

An element of risk is inherent in any investment, but the truth is that you, the investor, are the biggest risk variable of all.

The difference is generally in the individual's skills, contacts and expertise.

INVESTMENT SUCCESS FACT

Sophisticated investors manage to obtain higher returns without taking a higher degree of risk, which is the exact opposite to what conventional wisdom tells us.

Over the years, I've seen people make a lot of money out of real estate, but I've seen just as many people lose money. Similarly I've seen some investors become very rich investing in the stock market, but I've seen many more lose money investing in shares.

Let's consider the primary factors that determine the degree of risk associated with an investment:

1. Expertise

Your experience and network of contacts can be your biggest competitive advantage or your most potent risk factor. Investing in your specialty area allows you to achieve a higher return because, as an expert, you will be able to find opportunities the average person can't.

What contacts do you have who can help you make an informed decision or let you know about an opportunity before others? What do you know about an investment opportunity that others don't, about timing in the property cycle, or a change in government legislation?

For instance, a visit to the local council might uncover plans to re-zone a particular area, allowing multiple units on a site where before you could only build one dwelling. This in turn can make the property more valuable and the investment less risky.

That's why I love investing in real estate — it's what I call an imperfect market.

If real estate was a perfect, liquid marketplace, you wouldn't be able to buy property considerably below value. Information, contacts and expertise help you in an imperfect market — they make the investment less risky.

2. Control

The more control you have over your investment, the lower your risk.

When you buy shares you have no real control over their destiny. That's one of the reasons I prefer real estate — I have control over my property. I can add value through renovations or redevelopment, change property managers if I am unhappy with their service or furnish the apartment if it's appropriate.

3. Transparency

Is all the information about your investment disclosed? The more you know, the lower the risk.

When you invest in shares or managed funds, you have partial disclosure. There are also guidelines on how publicly traded companies should report to their investors, but if these worked well there wouldn't be as many stock collapses as have occurred over the years.

4. Liquidity

Liquidity means the ease with which you can recover your money by selling the investment and converting it (or part of it) to cash. The greater the degree of liquidity, the lower your risk.

Real estate is not as liquid as shares or managed funds, because even though you can sell your property it takes more effort and time. However, this makes property prices less volatile than share prices.

Your own liquidity is another major risk factor. That's why you need a financial buffer in the way of a line of credit, an offset account or even a savings account to weather the inevitable storms you'll encounter as an investor.

Without a sufficient buffer, especially in more turbulent times, you're at risk from things such as interest rate hikes, extended vacancy periods, stock market dips, illness or the loss of your job.

5. *Returns*

Investors gain returns from their investments via:

- Cash flow — the rent you receive from your properties or dividends from shares.

- Capital growth — the increase in the value of your property or stocks.

- Forced appreciation — the value increase you "manufacture" by undertaking renovations or redevelopment of your properties (you can't really do this with shares can you?).

- Tax benefits.

The more secure the returns, the less risky the investment will be.

6. *Is your principal at risk?*

Is your financial outlay secure if the investment fails?

An initial cash investment (your principal) in a bank term deposit is considered very secure, whereas if you buy shares it's possible for the company to fail and the shares to be worthless.

With property you generally have to put down a 20 per cent deposit, so if it drops in value by more than 20 per cent your equity (or deposit) would be wiped out.

The overall median house price in the capital cities of Australia has never fallen more than five per cent in one year, even through wars and depressions.

But I have come across many investors who have had their equity wiped out.

Some were highly geared who bought at the top of the market then values fell, while others paid too much buying off-the-plan and on completion, the value of the property was less than what they paid.

Occasionally, the value of individual homes has fallen more than 20 per cent, especially in mining towns, holiday locations or regional areas.

The more secure your principal, the less risky the investment.

7. Are you personally liable?

When you make an investment, do you have to provide a personal guarantee? This gives others (usually the banks) the right to pursue you if things go wrong.

If your liability extends beyond the asset itself, such as when you are personally guaranteeing the loan for a property bought in a company or trust, your personal assets could be at risk.

In this instance, if things go belly up and the bank sells your property and can't recover all its debts, they'll chase you for the difference.

Obviously, the more you are personally liable, the higher the risk to the investment.

8. Market risk

When weighing up risk, consider what impact general economic changes to the marketplace could have on your investment.

For example, if you invest in tourism you are subject to your investment market collapsing if there is a natural disaster, war or disease. Just look how the economies of many popular tourist destinations crumbled over the past few years after they were struck by natural disasters or even worse — terrorists.

And I don't have to tell you what happened to those who invested in mining towns, do I?

When assessing risk, most investors only look at the last two factors — the market and specific investment risk. They rarely focus on these other factors, which in many ways are more significant.

Is the fear of risk holding you back?

In my experience, the most common reason that people never start investing is because of fear. They see investing as risky.

Fear takes many forms but the four most common are:

1. Fear of failure

When I first contemplated investing in real estate, everyone told me I was crazy. My friends warned me about the dangers of property investing. The funny thing is that none of them had done it themselves, yet all of them were willing to share their horror stories of a "friend" who tried to invest in property and failed. They filled my head with "what ifs".

What if you can't find a tenant? What if interest rates go up? What if you lose your job and can't make the mortgage repayments? What if … What if … What if? I tell you, I was getting pretty nervous.

If the fear of failure is holding you back, you can reduce your risks by educating yourself or by surrounding yourself with a good team and leveraging off their knowledge.

2. Fear of debt

This is another common fear that holds many people back. Most of us have been taught that debt is bad and not to take on more debt. Over the years I have come to realise that debt in itself is not necessarily bad, rather it's not being able to repay your debts that's a problem.

3. Fear of success

Interestingly, some people put off their investment decisions because they're haunted by a fear of success. While this may initially seem strange, this fear generally stems from a feeling of unworthiness, where people convince themselves that they are undeserving of wealth or it's the mistaken concept that wanting to accumulate wealth makes them a bad person.

Because they feel undeserving, they always somehow manage to find ways to sabotage themselves. They do so subconsciously because in their minds, they are not deserving of the prize.

You need to substitute these fears with empowering beliefs about money and wealth. Beliefs that you are deserving of wealth and success and that many wealthy people add value to their communities in lots of different ways. Essentially, you need to redefine your perception of money and your own self worth.

4. Fear of the unknown

Fear of the unknown is the last of the big four. Who wants to go into a dark room? Who wants to go to a party where you don't know anyone? Who is not nervous about buying their first investment property? Whenever the outcome is uncertain, fear rears its ugly head.

With investing in general, and with real estate investing which is my preferred plan of attack, the way to conquer a fear of the unknown is through knowledge. You gain knowledge by reading books, attending seminars and networking with people who are already doing what you want to do. But the quickest shortcut to investing success is finding a mentor who's already achieved what you want to achieve.

INVESTMENT SUCCESS FACT

You can also opt to fast-track your investment knowledge by surrounding yourself with a good team of advisors and leveraging off their experience and know how.

While fear is the most common reason many people don't start investing, do you realise that there can be no courage without fear?

Why worry about tomorrow?

While many people lay in bed at night worrying about tomorrow and what it might bring (and which bills might crop up), most people fail to pay enough attention to their long-term future in a productive way. Tolstoy once said: "The most unexpected thing that happens to people is old age."

We all think we are going to remain young forever. It's not until we look in the mirror and see an elderly face staring back at us that we realise this just isn't the case. And by then, it's already happened and we can't turn back the clock.

As a member of the Baby Boomer generation, I hear many peers say, "I don't have to worry. I'll just keep working." They don't want to acknowledge, or they can't even imagine, that the day will come when their body simply won't allow them to work the way they want to anymore.

INVESTMENT SUCCESS FACT

It's critical that people start to realise that tomorrow will catch up with us all one day. There's no escaping the hands of time.

Denying that one day you will have to support yourself financially, without the security of a regular pay cheque, is simply irresponsible. So if you think, "I don't need to invest yet. I have plenty of years ahead of me to think about that", just remember that your parents probably felt the same way when they were your age. And are they rich today?

The fear of debt

This is a big one — the fear of taking on debt holds many potential investors back. After all, as kids we were all taught that debt is bad and risky.

But if you take a look at the *AFR* Rich List in Australia, *The Forbes* list in the US or in fact any Rich List, you will find that the rich use debt — other people's money, such as banks or shareholder's funds to grow their businesses, which we talked about in chapter six.

INVESTMENT SUCCESS FACT
Sophisticated investors use other people's money before their own. They understand that debt itself is not risky. They know that debt is only risky if you are not able to get more debt.

While sophisticated investors use debt as a tool to build their wealth, the average person gets into trouble with debt. They buy depreciating assets with their credit cards, pay massive interest on this debt and once the cards are maxed out they are in big trouble.

However, if you were still able to keep borrowing more money, without a limit on your loan size, you could afford to make your repayments couldn't you? Now you're likely to be thinking, "That would be great, but I'd end up with a massive debt," and that is true. But the wealthy and successful have worked out that the way around this is to have their assets growing quicker than their debt so that their net asset position is improving.

As I've already explained, in today's low interest-rate environment, debt borrowed against appreciating assets is really an asset rather than a liability because of the income it can generate — in other words smart investors "purchase" as much debt as they can safely.

What's your relationship with debt?

How you handle debt will vary depending on what level of investor you are.

If you are a Level 0 investor, it's likely that your relationship with debt will be built around spending — it will involve consumer debt. You probably use debt to pay for your lifestyle and in the process will be mortgaging your future. You just want to get stuff and will spend money on things that decrease in value, such as consumables, cars and the latest TV.

Level 1, and to a lesser extent Level 2 investors, are scared of debt. Sometimes it has taken them so long to get out of consumer debt that they are scared of falling back into that hole. Their goal is to have no debt.

On the other hand, Level 3 investors want to use debt. They want to harness it and use leverage to create more wealth. They recognise that debt is a source of power as long as they control it, as opposed to having the debt control them. They are not worried about debt that pays for itself because they invest in assets that increase in value like residential real estate.

Level 4 investors have got the whole debt thing figured out. They balance their levels of debt to enable their assets to spin off sufficient cash flow to provide the lifestyle they desire while still growing in value, and at the same time they take advantage of the tax benefits that leverage provides.

So, what I'm saying is that you need to increase your financial fluency so you can create your own luck and take whatever happens and make it better. Yes, that's right! Luck is created and so is money and wealth.

In my experience, financial fluency falls into four broad areas, which you need to master on your journey to investment success:

1. Money management — this is vital if you want to become financially independent and includes budgeting as well as personal asset and liability statement.

2. Investing — this involves strategies and formulas for successfully making your money work harder.

3. Accounting — the tax system favours business people and investors (more about this in an upcoming chapter), so it's important to understand how to use these legally to your advantage.

4. The law — you don't have to be a legal expert but you need to understand how the law relates to ownership structures and asset protection.

Finally, to become a successful investor you must understand that investing, and debt, are not inherently risky. Of course, both are necessary if your dream of becoming wealthy is to ever become a reality — but you must have the skills, knowledge and expert support to make it so.

Let's now move on to my favourite wealth creation vehicle — property investment. So, in the next section, I'll take you through the basic rules of investing in real estate.

CHAPTER 15:
THE BASIC RULES OF PROPERTY INVESTMENT

So by now you might be considering getting involved in residential real estate investment, which is my preferred investment strategy — but how do you start?

In this chapter I'll take you through some of the basics of property investment including how you can use the equity in your current home to start you on your path to investment success.

Equity must be used for the greater good

Before I show you how to gain access to your home equity, I want to make sure you respect it and use it wisely.

When used correctly it can help you get into the investment game, but I've seen too many people borrow against their homes to eliminate credit card debt and just slide back into debt at the same level as before (or, more often than not, into even more debt) within two or three years.

This is because after wiping the slate clean, they haven't altered their relationship with money or their spending habits. They max out their credit cards all over again and find themselves in an even deeper hole, because now they not only have the same amount of credit card debt as they started with, but they also have a bigger home equity loan that they need to repay.

Equity equals assets

I've already touched on the concept of recycling equity in a previous chapter so you probably already understand the concept of equity, but for the novice investor I'll briefly outline it so we're all on the same page.

If the value of your home is worth more than what you owe on it, then you have what's called *equity*. Accessing this equity involves refinancing your home, but the good news is that banks are generally happy to lend against your home because this represents one of the safest forms of security for them.

While some people then use this money to do an extension to their home, or to go on a holiday, I'm proposing you use this money to get into the world of real estate investing.

But before you run off to the bank or a mortgage broker, it's best to understand the concept of "borrowable equity".

By and large, banks will lend you up to 80 per cent of the value of a property, and if you want to borrow more than 80 per cent of its value, you'll need to take out Lenders Mortgage Insurance (LMI), which protects the bank (not you) if you default on your loans.

Now your borrowable equity is the amount the bank will lend you minus whatever amount is still outstanding on your mortgage. In other words, if your home is worth $800,000 you could theoretically borrow $640,000, which is 80 per cent of its value. But if you still owed $400,000 on your home loan then your *borrowable equity* would be $240,000, which is $640,000 minus your existing $400,000 loan.

OK, now that you've got some seed capital for investment, the question you may be asking is:

Why invest in residential real estate?

Well, property is just one of several investment vehicles that you could choose to try to get you from where you are today to where you'd like to be financially in the future.

And if you want to move up the investment ladder and become a Level 4 investor, you need to choose an investment vehicle that will generate wealth-producing rates of return. I know of no better option than property based on its reliability and performance advantages compared to the alternatives.

This is the reason that I advocate the purchase of well-located *capital city* residential property that will grow in value. Simple, safe and reliable over the long-term if you know what you're doing.

But why property?

In my opinion, two important elements of a good investment are:

1. High *capital growth*, which allows you to grow your net worth, and;

2. *Secure income*, which increases over time.

So what this means is that residential property must be a significant part of your wealth-building program.

So, let's look at the reasons to invest in property in more detail.

1. More millionaires

If you look at the results others have achieved, you would have to say that property makes pretty good investment sense. According to the annual *AFR* Rich 200 List, property has consistently been the major source of wealth for Australia's multi-millionaires. And it's the same all over the world.

Those that haven't made their money out of property generally invest their money in real estate.

Remember, there's nothing wrong with seeing what successful people do and applying those principles to your own life. If the majority of extraordinarily wealthy people have used real estate profitably, it stands to reason that there's money to be made in this sector.

2. Anyone can do it

Property investment is not just for the wealthy. It doesn't really take large sums of money to get involved in real estate. This is because banks will lend you 80 per cent or more of the property's value to help you purchase it, which means that most people with a steady job and a little capital behind them can afford to buy investment properties.

INVESTMENT SUCCESS FACT

It has been shown over and over again that careful and intelligent use of real estate can enable ordinary people, like you and me, to become property millionaires in about 10 years.

If you truly intend to become one of the wealthy people in the future, you should probably take a serious look at using property to your advantage.

3. Income that grows

The rental income you receive from your investment property allows you to borrow and get the benefit of leverage by helping you pay the interest on your mortgage.

INVESTMENT SUCCESS FACT

Over the years the rental income received from property investments in Australian has increased at a rate that has outpaced inflation.

But will this continue in the future? Well, statistics show that the level of home ownership is slowly decreasing. There are a number of reasons for this but, in particular, as property prices keep rising fewer people are able to afford their dream home. And despite falling interest rates, rising tertiary education debts, high rents and mounting consumer debt mean that for many first homebuyers the great dream of owning a house remains just that — a dream.

4. Consistent capital growth

Perhaps the most compelling benefit of real estate is its proven performance over time — its capacity to provide those wealth-generating rates of return that you need to grow your asset base as a Level 3 investor. Well-located capital city residential property has an unrivalled track record of producing high and consistent capital growth. Over the past 50 years the value of the average property in all Australian capital cities has doubled every 10 years or so. However, in the short-term the picture is much more uncertain and confusing, and at times capital growth stops and even reverses for a time, as we saw in the early '80s, the early '90s, in the slump of 2008-09 and more recently in some capital cities.

Yet the resilience of our residential property markets really shone through in the challenging economic time the Coronavirus recently inflicted on us.

By the way, there's another great thing about property. You can outperform the average by researching areas of strong capital growth, by buying your properties below market value and then adding value, which increases your capital growth and rental return.

You may have read that some commentators suggest that the strong rate of capital growth over the past few decades have been an aberration and property values can't keep increasing at these levels forever. And that's true — in 2021 we experienced a once in a generation property boom the likes of which won't be seen again for a number of decades, however our growing population and increasing wealth will underpin long-term capital growth in property.

What does this mean to you?

I'll explain it with an example: If a property increases in value by seven per cent per annum (averaged out over a number of years) then the value of that property doubles every 10 years or so. Imagine you owned a property worth $500,000. In 10 years' time the same property would be worth $1 million and in 20 years it would be worth $2 million.

When you bought your property, usually you have some equity and you borrow the rest. Imagine you had a 20 per cent deposit and borrowed the balance ($400,000) from the bank.

How capital growth works

After 10 years you would still owe the bank $400,000 (assuming you had an interest-only loan) and your net worth would have increased from $100,000 to $600,000. That's an increase in your net worth of six-fold even though the value of the property only doubled.

HOW CAPITAL GROWTH WORKS

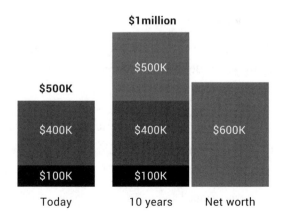

What would happen over the next 10 years?

Your property would once again double in value to $2 million and your net worth would increase to $1.6 million dollars. Your initial $100,000 investment would have increased in value 16-fold while your property only increased in value four-fold.

HOW CAPITAL GROWTH WORKS

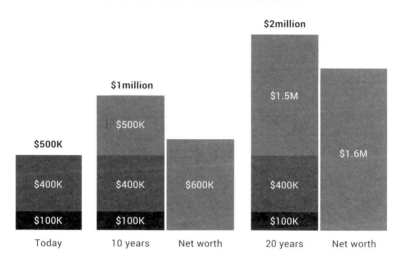

This amazing increase in your net worth is due to the combined effects of compounding and leverage, which we talked about in an earlier chapter.

5. You use other people's money in 3 ways

(i) The tenant's money — when you own an investment property the tenants go to work to earn a living and then pay you for the use of your property to live in.

Think about that. They get up every day, get dressed and go to work. You don't have to supervise them, pay for their sick leave, holiday pay or superannuation. Yet every month you get a portion of their income in the form of rent. The more of these tenants you employ, the more income you get!

(ii) The bank's money — your mortgage gives you leverage.

(iii) The Government's money — in the form of tax deductions such as negative gearing and depreciation allowances.

6. You are in control

Property is a great investment because you make all the decisions and have direct control over the returns from your property. If your property isn't producing good returns, then you can add value through refurbishment or renovations or adding furniture to make it more desirable to tenants. In other words, you can directly influence your returns by taking an interest in your property and by understanding and then meeting the needs of prospective tenants.

7. You can add value

There are hundreds of ways you can add value to your property, which will increase your income and your property's worth. These include little things like giving it a coat of paint or removing the old carpet and polishing the floorboards underneath. Or you could do major renovations or development works.

8. You don't need to sell it

Unlike other investments, when real estate goes up in value you don't need to sell in order to capitalise on that increased value. You simply go back to your bank or mortgage broker and get your lender to increase your loan.

9. Property is an imperfect market

When I look to invest, I want to invest in an imperfect market. This means that I'm more likely to be able to buy an investment below its true value or I can sell above its true value. Let me explain this in more detail ...

The world of shares is not a completely perfect market, but it's about as perfect as it gets. That's because it is a liquid market where investors are well informed. I can buy stocks at the same price as anybody else can. In general, the overall marketplace has the same information as I have, because for the most part the information is equal. This shared knowledge creates a more "perfect" market.

On the other hand, real estate is what I would call an *imperfect* market. I know many people who have bought properties at five, 10, or even 15 per cent below the real market value. If property was a perfect liquid marketplace, you would not be able to buy a property considerably below its intrinsic value.

10. You can insure against risks

Another factor that adds to the security of residential property as an investment is that you can insure it against most risks. You can insure the building against fire or damage and you can insure yourself against the tenant leaving and breaking a lease.

11. Most forgiving

Even if you bought the worst house at the worst possible time, the chances are good that it would still go up in value over the next few years. History has proven that real estate is possibly the most forgiving investment asset over time. If you are prepared to hold property over a number of years, it's bound to rise in value.

Mind you, I'm not advocating wasting time, money and effort buying not-so-good properties at the wrong time in the cycle. As your mentor I would prefer you learned how to choose wisely in the first place. If you do this, then even if you are a new investor, you can buy property and be comfortable so you won't see the value of your asset decline over the medium-term. There's really no other asset class quite like property!

Which property is best?

Now that you better understand the benefits of residential real estate as an investment vehicle, it's time to learn about which types of properties are the best.

While at any time there are hundreds of thousands of properties for sale, not all will make good investments. In fact most won't.

My top down approach

The property investment system that has helped me build a very substantial property portfolio uses what I call a top down approach.

1. It starts with buying at the **right stage of the property cycle**. I look at the big picture — how the economy is performing and where we are in the property cycle.

2. Then I look for the **right state** in which to invest — one that is in the right stage of its own property cycle. Each state in Australia has its own property cycle — select one that is heading towards the upturn stage of its cycle, not one near its peak.

3. Then within that state, I look for the **right suburb** — one that has a long history of outperforming the averages. I've found some suburbs have 50 to 100 per cent more capital growth than others over a 10-year period. Obviously those are the suburbs I target.

This is different to the speculative approach some investors adopt — they say things like, "Oh, this suburb hasn't had much capital growth, maybe its time has come," or, "That's a brand-new suburb. They're getting a train-line down there so it must grow in value."

4. Once my research shows me the suburb to explore, I then look for the **right location** within that suburb. Think about the suburb where you live — there would be areas you'd happily live in and areas you would avoid, like on main roads or too close to shops, schools or commercial areas.

5. Then within that location I look for the **right property**, using my 7 Stranded Strategic Approach, and finally I look for …

6. The **right price**. I'm not looking for a "cheap" property (there will always be cheap properties around in secondary locations). I'm looking for the right property at a good price.

I choose my properties in that order — a top down approach — which leads many people to ask why price is at the bottom of the list. I guess this is because they've heard you make your money when you buy your property. While that is correct, it's not because you pay a cheap price or because you get a bargain. You make your money when you buy because you buy *the right property* — one that will be in continuing strong demand by both owner-occupiers (who push up property values) and tenants (who will help you pay off your mortgage).

To ensure I buy a property that will outperform the market averages I also use this **7 Stranded Strategic Approach**.

1. I buy a property below its intrinsic value — that's why I avoid new and off-the-plan properties that come at a premium price.

2. In an area that has a long history of strong capital growth and that will continue to outperform the averages because of the demographics in the area. This will be an area where more owner-occupiers will want to live because of lifestyle choices and one where the locals will be

prepared to, and can afford to, pay a premium price to live because they have high disposable incomes.

3. I buy the type of property that would appeal to owner-occupiers because they're the ones that drive up property values.

4. I look for properties with an element of scarcity — not look alike Lego Land apartments or houses in estates where there is no shortage of land. Abundance of supply is the enemy of capital growth.

5. I look for properties with a high Land to Asset Ratio — that doesn't mean necessarily mean a large amount of land, it means more valuable land because of its location, including the land below underneath family-friendly apartments in low density blocks.

6. I look for a property with a twist — something unique, special, different or scarce about it and finally…

7. I buy a property where I can "manufacture" capital growth through refurbishment, renovations or redevelopment.

While most investors read a book or two, do a little research and then buy one of the first properties they come across, strategic investors are smarter than that. They follow a system that is rooted in the real world and has stood the test of time in changing markets.

By following my *7 Stranded Strategic Approach,* I minimise my risks and maximise my upside. Each strand represents a way of making money from property and combining all four is a powerful way of putting the odds in my favour. If one strand lets me down, I have two or three others supporting my property's performance.

Three cardinal rules of property

I'm not suggesting property investment is easy, but it is simple and that's not a play on words. Successfully investing in real estate is a learned skill and can be simple if you know the rules.

So, before we move on to the next chapter, let me leave you with my three cardinal rules of property.

1. If you want to become financially independent through property investment you're going to have to do things differently to most other property investors.

2. You will need to find others who have invested successfully over a number of property cycles, achieved what you want to achieve and maintained their wealth, and then use them as your mentors. The road you want to travel on is one many people have travelled before you — find role models and learn how they think and what they do. Follow their footsteps and obey the rules they play by, because there is no need to reinvent the wheel.

3. Property investment is not a "get rich quick scheme". To be successful you must treat it like a business and use systems that are proven, because your property portfolio can make more money than you can earn.

CHAPTER 16:
PROPERTY INVESTING FOR CAPITAL GROWTH OR CASH FLOW

When it comes to property investment you'll often hear two somewhat conflicting philosophies advocated.

Some suggest you should invest in property to achieve positive cash flow (rental returns that are higher than your mortgage repayments and expenses leaving money in your pocket each month).

Others suggest you should invest for capital growth (an increase in the value of your property).

But there is a third element to investment that many commentators forget to mention and that is risk. Considering cash flow, capital growth and risk, when investing in residential property you can only typically have two out of the three.

If you want a property investment that is low-risk and has a high cash flow you will have to forgo high capital growth. If you are looking for a low-risk investment that has strong capital growth, you will usually have to forgo high rental returns (cash flow).

Of course, in an ideal world we'd all like to buy properties that have all three elements and while this combination is possible, it's far from the norm. I manage to achieve all of these by purchasing properties in high growth areas and then adding value by renovating them or redeveloping them into townhouses. The extra rent and the taxation benefits I achieve give me high-growth properties with high yields.

INVESTMENT SUCCESS FACT

There's no doubt in my mind that if I had to choose between cash flow and capital growth, I would invest for capital growth every single time.

So let me explain why investing for capital growth is the best wealth creation strategy in my experience and how you can harness it to achieve investment success.

The power of capital growth

The fact is that in Australia (but not necessarily other parts of the world) residential real estate is a high growth, relatively low yield (cash flow or rental return) investment.

Now I know that's not how some people see it. Podcasts will flaunt the next positive cash flow "hotspot" and courses will lure you with the promise of instant "cash flow" from property — but that's not how successful property investment works.

Sure in secondary locations or regional centres you could achieve a higher rental return on your investment property but, in general, you wouldn't get strong long-term capital growth.

If you have any doubt about the importance of capital growth, the calculations in the table I'm about to discuss may change your mind.

Over the long-term, "average" property investments in Australia's four big capital cities tend to return around seven per cent capital growth (averaged over a number of years) and four per cent rental yield. The table would be turned the other way in many regional areas that may only achieve five per cent capital growth, but a higher rental yield of, say, seven per cent.

The argument then continues: If you're going to achieve 11 or 12 per cent per annum from your property why not go for the high rental returns? I guess that's why many new investors make the mistake of viewing their property investments as income-driven rather than striving for capital growth.

The problem with this argument is that while the first part is generally correct — properties with high growth will give a low return and vice versa — the second part is clearly wrong. The two types of investments do NOT give similar results over time.

This is easy to explain with the following example.

Imagine you bought a property worth $500,000 in a poor growth area delivering five per cent capital growth and seven per cent rental return. The calculations in the table below illustrate that in 20 years your property would be worth around **$1.3 million**.

If you bought a different property for $500,000 in a higher capital growth area, showing seven per cent per annum capital growth and four per cent rental return, this property would be worth over $1.9 million at the end of the same period. That is a big difference in the final value of your investment property — **more than $600,000 more**.

In the meantime, the rent on this property would also grow substantially, in line with its capital growth, and they'd slowly catch up to the rent you'd achieve on the first (high return) property.

Capital growth vs. rental income on a $500,000 purchase				
	7% capital growth	4% rental return on property value	5% capital growth	7% rental return on property value
Year 1	$535,000	$21,600	$525,000	$36,750
Year 5	$701,276	$29,387	$638,141	$44,670
Year 10	$983,576	$43,178	$814,447	$57,011
Year 15	$1,379,516	$63,443	$1,039,464	$72,762

| Year 20 | $1,934,842 | $93,219 | $1,326,649 | $92,865 |

Let's look at the same information graphically — using the concept of compounding you can see how different levels of capital growth affect the value of your asset base over time.

I'm trying to show you that if you could outperform the averages — which you will after learning the lessons in this book — and find a property that goes up by, say, 10 per cent per annum (averaged out over a property cycle) over the next 20 years you would make a further $1.5 million in equity.

THE IMPORTANCE OF CAPITAL GROWTH

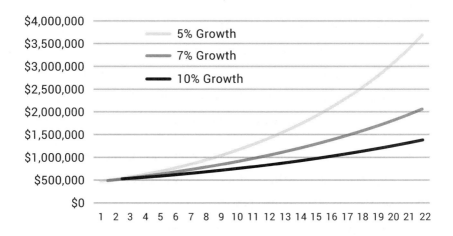

The real bonus for the investor who bought the high growth property is that they would be able to access the extra equity and borrow against it to invest in more assets. It's very hard to do this with properties that have high rental returns but poorer capital growth.

The few dollars a week you get in positive cash flow isn't really going to make much difference to your lifestyle or your ability to service other more desirable properties. Wealth from real estate is not derived from income, because residential properties are not high-yielding investments.

INVESTMENT SUCCESS FACT

Real wealth is achieved through long-term capital appreciation and the ability to refinance to buy further properties.

Capital growth beats cash flow

I know I've gone on and on about capital growth, but not understanding the significance of this has led to so many would-be property investors missing out that I feel I should go into a little more detail.

Of course I understand why new investors would be keen to buy a property with positive cash flow. They tend to be cheaper and it's easy to purchase and support this type of property. While these properties will give you short-term income, which may be attractive, the problem is they will never allow you to accumulate the equity necessary to become truly wealthy.

And while the rent may seem relatively high initially, it's the ongoing capital growth of your property that will underpin its long-term rental income, which means that if you buy in low capital growth areas, your rents won't increase that much over the years.

Sure, cash flow is important, but it won't make you rich or to ever be classified as a successful investor. Remember your focus should be on building your asset base (safely) so you can eventually develop the passive income from your assets that will allow you to enjoy the freedom of a Level 4 investor.

One of the main reasons properties increase in value is the scarcity value of the land they sit on, meaning you should buy properties with a **high land to asset ratio** (the land component should make up a substantial portion of the value of the property).

If you think about it, when you buy a cash flow-type property in a regional area where prices are lower, the land value per square metre tends to be much lower because there's plenty of land available. This means the building accounts for most of the asset's value. In these areas the building may lose value faster than the land can gain value, thus hampering long-term capital growth.

Let's compare this with buying high growth property. When the property price is high, the land value probably is as well. You're likely to have purchased in an area with a limited supply of land relative to buyer demand and your land-to-asset ratio is likely to be high, meaning the land component makes up a higher proportion of the property's overall value, giving the asset strong capital growth potential. In general, this makes this type of property lower risk than positively geared property over the long-term.

On the other hand, properties with positive cash flow could be seen as more of a liability as the years go by and capital growth fails to occur. They are dependent on achieving high rents and you may need to undertake regular and significant renovations to attract suitable tenants and to maintain an acceptable income.

Now don't misunderstand me, cash flow is the ultimate aim — but that's only once you've built your Cash Machine. Before then your investment journey will comprise three stages:

1. The Accumulation Stage — is when you build your asset base (net worth) through capital growth of well-located properties. You can speed up your wealth accumulation through leverage, compounding time and "manufacturing" capital growth through renovations or development

2. Transition Stage — once you have a sufficiently large asset base, you slowly lower your Loan to Value ratios so you can move on to the …

3. Cash Flow Stage — now you can live off your property portfolio.

What makes a good investment property?

There are around 10.4 million dwellings in Australia and at any time there are around 300,000 properties for sale.

But not all properties make good investments! In fact, in my mind, less than four per cent of the properties on the market currently are what I call "investment grade".

Of course, any property can become an investment property — just move the owner out and put in a tenant and it's an investment, but that doesn't make it "investment grade".

To help you better understand what I consider an *investment grade* property, let's first look at the characteristics of a great investment, and then let's see what type of properties fit these criteria.

The things I look for in any investment (including property) are:

- Strong, stable rates of capital appreciation.

- Steady cash flow.

- Liquidity (the ability to take my money out by either selling or borrowing against my investment).

- Easy management.

- A hedge against inflation.

- Good tax benefits.

So, as you can see, residential real estate fits the bill pretty nicely.

How do you make money from an investment?

Well … property investors make their money in four ways:

1. Capital growth — as the property appreciates in value over time.

2. Rental returns — the cash flow you get from your tenant.

3. Accelerated or forced growth — this is capital growth you manufacture by adding value through renovations or development, and

4. Tax benefits — like negative gearing or depreciation allowances.

And although not everyone agrees with me, in my mind, capital growth is the most important factor of all.

But let me be blunt. Most property investors fail to achieve the financial freedom they aspire to and this is, in part, due to the fact that they follow the wrong strategy — many chase cash flow.

Like I said, your aim is to build a substantial asset base so you can work your way up the Wealth Pyramid. To build your asset base, and in turn your net worth, you need your investment properties to grow at wealth-producing rates of return. This is because capital growth builds your equity much faster than loan repayments and rental income will.

Not all properties are "investment grade"

OK back to my comment that less than four per cent of properties on the market are investment grade.

While there are a lot of properties built specifically for the investor market — think the many new high-rise developments that are littering our cities — most of these are not investment grade.

Some would call these properties "investment stock" — they are what the property marketers and developers sell to naïve investors, but they are not investment grade because they don't fit the criteria for my 7 Stranded Strategic Approach that I taught you in the last chapter.

- They have little owner-occupier appeal — due to their size and location.

- They lack scarcity.

- They are not purchased below intrinsic value.

- There is little or no opportunity to add value.

- They are not situated in suburbs — those that outperform the averages with regards to capital growth because of the wealthy and aspirational demographic that live there.

On the other hand, investment grade properties:

- Have **owner-occupier appeal** — meaning there will always be in demand.

- **Are in the right location** — and by this I don't just mean the right suburb — it's one with multiple drivers of capital growth, but also close to public transport (this will become more important in the future as our population grows and people want to reduce commuting time) and are a short walking distance to lifestyle amenities such as cafes, shops, restaurants and parks.

- Have **street appeal** as well as a **favourable aspect** or **good views**.

- **Offer security** — by being located in the right suburbs as well as having security features such as gates, intercoms and alarms.

- Offer secure **car parking**.

- Potential for **add value** renovations.

- A **high land-to-asset ratio** — this is different to a large amount of land — I'd rather own a block of land under my apartment block in a good inner suburb than a huge block of land in regional Australia.

Here's a few more things I look for in an investment grade property:

1. The type of property that will return above average **long-term capital growth**. I ensure this by choosing the right type of property to suit the demographics in the area — one that will have enduring value. Rather than thinking about who the tenant will be (like most investors do), I buy the type of property that will be in continuous strong demand by a wide range of affluent owner-occupiers because they're the ones that will buy similar properties and push up the value of my property.

Of course it must also appeal to a wide range of tenants, but that's a secondary consideration.

Years ago when I first started investing I used to buy houses, but now I generally prefer medium-density dwellings — apartments and townhouses, as these are now the favoured type of dwelling by an increasing percentage of the population.

With our changing demographics, more and more people want to live near the city and, if possible, near the water in medium-density dwellings — in other words in townhouses, units or apartments.

2. I avoid **new or off-the-plan properties** because the price of these properties generally carries a substantial mark-up to account for the developer's margin, marketing costs, agent's commission, GST and so forth. Instead …

3. I buy **established properties** that give me the opportunity to add value through renovations or redevelopment. This means I don't just count on the capital growth in the area or the growth of the property cycle, but I create forced capital appreciation.

4. The property must generate **cash flow**. While rent returns are not my main criteria for investing in property, of course it is important

to have steady cash flow from your tenants to help subsidise your mortgage costs.

5. I look for the type of property that **lenders are prepared to lend against**. To maximise the return on my money I want to maximise my leverage. Lenders are keen to lend 80 per cent, 90 per cent or in some cases even 95 per cent of the value of what they consider "well-located" residential properties.

However, they will not lend as much against serviced apartments, commercial property and properties in regional areas, or very small properties like studio apartments. Therefore I avoid these types of properties to maximise my leverage.

6. I like my investment to be **tax effective** so I look for properties that allow me to have high depreciation allowances. These are non-cash (money does not come out of my pocket) deductions that I can make at the end of the year to reduce my income tax payable.

While new properties tend to have high depreciation allowances, as I've explained they come at a premium price so I maximise my deductible allowances by adding value, refurbishing or redeveloping my investment properties and "manufacturing" depreciation allowances.

7. Once I have found the right property I then need to buy it at the **right price**. While I understand that you make the bulk of your profit when you buy your property, I also recognise that this doesn't mean you have to buy a bargain. It means you buy the "right" property by following the system I have just outlined.

While I don't want to overpay, and I undertake thorough research so I understand local property values, I am not prepared to lose that special property by looking for a bargain.

But it doesn't end there …

Regularly review your property portfolio

While most investors just buy a property and hold it for the long-term, strategic investors regularly review their investment portfolio's performance.

When I ask investors how their properties are performing they usually have no idea. They've just closed their eyes, crossed their fingers and hoped for the best. It makes no sense to invest in a property and then not review its performance every year or so.

I like to look at my property portfolio's performance at least once a year. Are my properties performing to my expectations? Are they outperforming the market? If that property was for sale today would I buy it again? Does this property still fit in with my overall plan?

This is the time to assess how our shifting markets will affect your property portfolio. What would happen to your position if interest rates were to rise 0.5 or one percentage point?

It's also the time to assess your Loan to Value ratio and your cash flow to see if you can afford to buy another property or two.

Over time you grow, your skills improve and your circumstances change. Treat your property like a business and evaluate your assets dispassionately.

CHAPTER 17:
HOW TO LIVE THE LIFE OF A
PROPERTY MULTI-MILLIONAIRE

Now it's time to understand the end game — how you convert the high-growth assets you have accumulated as a Level 3 investor into your *Cash Machine* as a Level 4 investor.

If, like many readers of this book, your retirement is 10–15 years away let's get a few things clear …

The rules have changed considerably since I first started educating property investors and recommended my *Living Off Equity Strategy*. More restrictive lending criteria since the Global Financial Crisis means that while this still works for a few high-net-worth property investors, it's likely to be difficult for many investors to use this strategy moving forward.

And it's likely there will be many more changes moving forward.

When you finally plan to live off your property portfolio I don't know if the government of the day will allow negative gearing or not. I really have no idea what interest rates are going to be then. Will you still be able to negatively gear properties or borrow in yourself and superfund? Will there be capital gains tax exemptions if you plan to sell some properties to release funds?

No one knows what the banks' lending policies will be or whether they'll allow you to have interest only loans or whether you'll have to pay down principal. And we don't know how they'll assess your serviceability which will affect your ongoing borrowing capacity.

But what I do know is that if between now and then (whenever *then* will be) you grow a substantial asset base, be it property or shares or both plus your superannuation, you'll have choices. And along the way you'll need to formulate a debt reduction strategy, because holding a significant amount of debt in retirement is not advisable.

While there's no exact formula, the end game I'd like to see is that you own your own home with no debt against it as well as a portfolio of investment grade properties with a Loan to Value Ratio of less than 40 per cent, as well as some income producing assets such as shares or managed funds which might be held in your superannuation fund.

The further away your retirement, the easier this will be to achieve because the capital growth of your properties over time will lower the overall Loan to Value Ratio of your portfolio.

If however you're planning to retire in the next 5–10 years, unless you already have a significant property portfolio or significant funds in your superannuation, it's almost impossible that you'll be able to live off your property portfolio. Which leads to the question …

How much money income do you want?

When I ask clients how much income they think they will need to fund retirement almost everyone seems to say "$100,000 per year after tax". Yet when asked how they arrived at that figure, there is rarely any real thought put to it.

To work out how much money you will need you should start with how much you spend today on living expenses and make some adjustments from there. It's likely that you will have fewer mouths to feed once your kids leave home — but don't count on that. Adult children still seem to get themselves into trouble and need help.

Also it's probable that you'll want to holiday more often or pursue certain hobbies or pastimes that you don't currently do. And unfortunately, there will be medical and other expenses you're not having to pay today.

While it's difficult to accurately assess your life expectancy, as it will probably be impacted by medical technologies and treatments that haven't even been discovered yet, meaning many Australia's will live well into their 80s or 90s, you're likely to have to fund 25 years or more of living expenses in your retirement phase.

Won't my superannuation be enough to fund retirement?

All working Australians contribute a portion of their income to superannuation and many hope this will see them through their golden years however, for most people, super will not be enough to fund the kind of comfortable lifestyle they're aiming for. This will of course depend on your superannuation balance and the type of lifestyle you hope to enjoy.

The problem with relying on superannuation is that the government can (and do) change the laws and move the goal posts. They decide when and how you can access the funds in your super. I don't know about you, but I'm not comfortable with putting my retirement plans in the hands of the government.

So how many properties do you need to retire?

If you're planning your financial future you're probably wondering how many properties you would need to quit your day job and live comfortably?

The simple answer … *It depends.*

OK that's not what you wanted to hear, but in fact it's the wrong question to ask. It doesn't really matter how many properties you own. What is more important is the value of your asset base and how hard your money works for you.

Why do I say this? Because I'd rather own one Westfield Shopping Centre than 50 secondary properties in regional Australia.

How will you live off your property portfolio?

While investors know they want their properties to replace their income, I've found most don't think about how they'll actually achieve financial freedom. Many just think that they'll live off their rental income, yet I rarely see this happen. It's just too hard to grow a portfolio of cash flow positive properties to a sufficient size to replace your income.

On the other hand, the wealthy investors I deal with have built a Cash Machine by growing a substantial asset base of high growth properties, and other income producing assets and then lowering their loan to value ratios so they can transition into the next phase of their lives.

Why can't I just live off the rent?

Here's why ...

Let's say you want an annual after-tax income of $100,000. How are you going to achieve that? How many properties do you need?

If you plan is to eventually pay down your debt and live off the rent, you'll probably need to own your home outright (without a mortgage) and at least $6 million worth of properties *with no mortgage* to get that $100,000 after-tax income.

Don't believe me?

The average gross yield for well-located properties in Australia is around 3.5% per cent.

This means if you eventually own $1 million worth of properties with *no* debt (you've paid off all the mortgages), you'll receive $35,000 rent each year. But you'll still have to pay rates, land tax, agents' commissions and repairs, leaving you with less than $30,000 a year. And then you'll have to pay tax on this income.

When you do the sums you'll see that you need an unencumbered portfolio worth $5–6 million to earn that $100,000 a year after outgoings and tax.

Remember that's $5–6 million worth of property and no mortgage debt, otherwise your cashflow will be lower. And as I said, you'll also need to own your own home with no debt against it. And those values are in today's dollar value.

Let me ask you a question … Will you ever be able to save $6 million? Will you ever build a portfolio of that size on a few dollars a week positive cash flow from your rentals?

In my mind the only way to become financially independent through property is to first grow a substantial asset base (by owning high-growth properties) and then transition to the next stage — the cash flow stage — by lowering your loan to value ratios. In other words, reducing your debt, but not paying it off completely.

Now you can see why most property investors fail to build a sufficiently large property portfolio to be able to live off its fruits.

Many start too late in life, they don't take advantage of their peak income earning years to trap spare cash and invest it. Others don't stay in the market long enough. It takes 20 and more likely 30 years to allow capital growth to build a large enough asset base.

Yet others don't buy the right assets to get sufficient capital growth. Fact is … you can't expect to invest in average properties (non-investment grade assets) and expect above average returns. Therefore, if you are going to invest you better make sure that you invest in the highest quality properties you can find. And this means properties that grow at above average rates of return. Capital growth must be your main focus. Everything else is a distant second.

All successful investors move through three stages of their wealth creation:

1. The asset growth — this requires leverage

2. Transitioning to lower LVR — where you slowly pay down your debt

3. Living off the Cash Machine of your property portfolio

Can't I just buy high yielding residential investments?

Yes you can! But a year ago the best-yielding area in Australia was the Queensland mining town of Blackwater, where there was an average rental return of 11.8 per cent for a median price house worth $120,000.

But I wouldn't invest in a mining town — would you?

I'd rather put my money into a well-located property in a gentrifying inner or middle ring suburb of our three big capital cities where there are multiple growth drivers including economic growth, jobs growth, population growth and infrastructure spending. And I would look for a suburb which has a large percentage of owner occupiers who are earning higher wages so that they can afford to and are prepared to buy houses in this location.

Sure these locations will provide lower rental yields, but they will have low vacancy rates, more stability of property values and stronger long-term capital growth potential.

Don't try and fight the trends. As I've explained — residential real estate is a high growth relatively low-yield investment. After all expenses, your net yield may be less than 3%. But when you consider the capital growth you'll achieve from a well located "investment grade" property, the overall returns are very good, especially in today's low interest rate environment.

And as this capital growth is not taxed unless you sell your property (and why would you do that?) this enables you to reinvest your capital to generate higher compounding returns. On the other hand, rental income is taxed, leaving less to be reinvested.

This means for investors in the asset accumulation stage of their journey, the more capital growth you achieve (even at the cost of lower rental income) the more wealth you will accumulate in the long term. When investors eventually transition to the cash flow stage of their journey, adding higher yielding commercial properties to their portfolio makes sense.

How are you going to repay all your loans before you retire?

Once you've built a substantial asset base you'll need to start thinking about lowering your debt levels, but it all begins long before that — you have to have a plan.

By now I've shown you that part of successful investment is having a strategy — a strategy for property purchases, a strategy for asset protection, a finance strategy — and now I'm explaining you need an exit strategy knowing how you're going to repay your debt before you retire.

Just to be clear, you don't need to fully pay off all your debt before you retire but, considering current lending practices, you must assume that the banks won't be comfortable extending you further debt in retirement unless you can prove serviceability.

They won't just keep lending you more money because you have equity like they did in the past. You'll need to prove serviceability which could come from your rental income (meaning you'll need a very low loan to value ratio) or from dividends from your share portfolio.

Since your ability to service debt will be very dependent upon interest rates at the time, it will therefore be important to go into your retirement years with a level of debt that is easily manageable, and which would not choke you financially if interest rates rise.

With that in mind, an ideal situation to be in would be to own a mixture of growth and income producing assets and would look a little like this:

- You would own your own home with no debt against it

- You'd have a substantial superannuation fund which should be delivering you regular income

- You would own a multi-million-dollar property portfolio which is no longer negatively geared and, if it does have debt against it, the LVR would be such that the portfolio generates income. This would not need to be a lot of income but needs to be sufficient so that your property portfolio is not draining your cash flow.

INVESTMENT SUCCESS FACT

With lower levels of borrowings, your properties will start generating positive cash flow and passive income that you could then use to enjoy your lifestyle.

I know many financial planners suggest you should go into retirement with no debt at all, but in my mind entering retirement with a conservative amount of leverage works well for those investors who have set themselves up correctly.

These investors often live off their superannuation assets and income for the first 10–15 years of their retirement allowing their property portfolio to once again double in value which allows their already low loan to value ratio to fall even further enabling their property portfolio to spin off even more cash flow.

Others achieve their cash flow in retirement through the dividends from shares or from the positive cash flow of commercial property investments.

So how do I transition to the cash flow phase of my investing?

1. Grow your portfolio at a slower pace

Once you've grown a substantial asset base, one option is to slow down the pace at which you grow your property portfolio.

In other words, rather than refinancing and buying more properties as the value of your properties increase, just sit tight and allow your Loan to Value ratio to progressively fall as the value of your loans becomes a smaller proportion of the total value of your property holdings. With lower levels of borrowings, your properties would start generating positive cash flow and passive income that you could then use to enjoy your lifestyle.

2. Convert to a principal and interest loan

In the asset accumulation stage of your investment journey your borrowings should be interest only loans if economically possible, thus lowering your monthly payments, allowing you to borrow more and accumulate surplus funds in an offset account.

As you transition to the cash flow phase of your investing, you could convert some of your loans to principal and interest, allowing your tenants to slowly pay off your mortgages, thereby putting you in a stronger cash flow position. Remember that while paying interest on investment loans is tax-deductible, paying off the principal portion of the loan is not. However, this is a common strategy investors use to reduce their debt and increase their cash flow.

3. Investing in commercial properties.

Different to residential real estate, commercial properties tend to have strong cash flow but less capital growth (this is linked to the rent increases which tend to be linked to the CPI). So adding commercial properties to your portfolio once you already have a strong asset base may be appropriate for you.

4. Use part of your Super or savings to pay off debt

When you reach the official age you may, if your advisor believes it's appropriate for your circumstances, choose to sell some assets in your Self Managed Super Fund, which under current legislation would not attract capital gains tax and then distributing the proceeds tax-free to help pay off debt outside the SMSF.

5. Redevelop a property or two to repay debt

It's possible that one of your investment properties has unrealised redevelopment potential. You can develop this property, make a profit selling the new dwellings and repay some of your debts, or even better — you could keep the new units and enjoy the rental income from two or three properties on the allotment where previously there was only one.

6. Sell a property or two and repay debt

You know I prefer to hold properties for the long term, but the purpose of owning these properties is to give you the lifestyle you want. This means sometimes the right thing to do is sell off one or two investments and use the proceeds to reduce your portfolio debt and increase your cash flow.

It will be important to consider the impact of capital gains tax (CGT) from the proceeds of your sale, but this could be avoided if you own the property in an SMSF and it is sold while you are in pension phase.

However, my favourite strategy is living off the increasing equity of my property portfolio. This allows me to retain my high-growth assets, avoid having to pay CGT and essentially, have my cake and eat it too. Let me explain this concept in more detail …

Here's how it works:

Fast forward 15 years and imagine you own your own home plus $5 million of well-located investment properties.

If you had a typical 80% Loan to Value Ratio (LVR), you would be highly negatively geared. On the other hand, if you had no debt against your property portfolio you would have significant positive cashflow but would forego the benefits of leverage.

Somewhere in the middle, maybe at 40% LVR, your property portfolio would be self-funding. And if you lower your LVR further you'll have sufficient cash flow to prove serviceability to the banks.

If you think about it, it will be much easier to amass a $5 million property portfolio with $2 million of debt than the same size portfolio with no debt.

You could then go to the bank and explain that you've got a self-funding portfolio that isn't reliant on your income and in fact, provides surplus cash for serviceability. You would also have your other income producing assets (shares etc) to bolster your serviceability.

You would then ask for an extra $100,000 loan, so you increase your LVR slightly.

The good news is that because it's a loan you don't have to pay tax on this money because it's not income. But you would have to pay interest, which would not be tax deductible if you use the money for your living expenses.

This means after the interest payments you're left with around $95,000 to live on.

Crunch the numbers ...

At the end of the year, you've "eaten up" your $100,000; but in a good year, your $5 million property portfolio would increase in value by say $400,000. In an average year it will have increased in value by $300,000 and in a bad year it may have only gone up by $150,000 or $200,000.

Of course, your rents will also have increased because your properties have grown in value.

Sure you've used up the $100,000 you borrowed, but because your portfolio has risen in value, along with rents, your LVR is less at the end of the year than the beginning, so you finish off the year richer than you began it. You truly have a Cash Machine, and then you can do this over and over again.

Does this really work?

In the old days living off equity was easy. You just had to go to the bank and get a low doc loan and as long as your properties increased in value it was smooth sailing.

Yes it's harder today, much harder. But it's definitely do-able if you own the right type of property and lower your LVR to show substantial serviceability to the banks.

Needless to say, you can't achieve this overnight. It takes time to build a substantial asset base and a comfortable loan-to-value ratio. But if you take advantage of the magic of leverage, compounding and time, it happens.

Of course this strategy depends on the growth in your property portfolio and your ability to ride the property cycle by having financial buffers in place.

My living off equity strategy

To ensure that you fully understand the concept, let's examine the numbers in more detail. To make things easy, let's just use today's dollar values when we make our projections otherwise things become a bit too complicated.

INSIDER TIP

The RICH think ASSETS — the POOR think CASH FLOW.
The RICH spend ASSETS — the POOR spend CASH FLOW

Again let's imagine you own your own home and have paid off the mortgage as well as now owning a substantial property portfolio. You've built your asset base and now transitioned into the cash flow phase of your investment life by slowly lowering your Loan to Value ratio to 50 per cent and you're ready to live off your Cash Machine. Your investment property portfolio could look a bit like this:

Total value of investment properties	$5 million
Loans	$2 million
Equity	$3 million
Net rental return before interest	$175,000

(This rent return is low, but keep in mind it's net after rates, agent commissions, repairs, etc.)

In the following table, we are going to see how these figures change over a 10-year period — which should encompass a complete property cycle. During this time I have allowed for periods of poor capital growth and strong property growth as well as periods of low interest rates and higher interest rates.

I have also assumed that because you're living your life to the fullest your cost of living increases by three per cent each year and your rental returns increase around the same as the growth in your property values.

These are the assumptions I've used:

	Inflation	Capital Growth	Interest Rates	Lifestyle Costs
Year 1	2.00%	8.00%	5.00%	$100,000
Year 2	2.00%	9.00%	5.25%	$103,000
Year 3	2.00%	10.00%	5.50%	$106,090
Year 4	2.00%	5.00%	5.00%	$109,273
Year 5	2.00%	4.00%	4.50%	$112,551
Year 6	2.25%	6.00%	4.50%	$115,927
Year 7	2.50%	6.00%	4.75%	$119,405
Year 8	2.75%	7.25%	5.00%	$122,987
Year 9	3.00%	7.50%	5.00%	$126,677
Year 10	3.00%	7.50%	5.00%	$130,477
Average:	**2.35%**	**7.03%**	**4.95%**	

Let's see what these assumptions do to the value of your properties and your loans over this 10-year period:

| Year | Equity | Value of Properties | | Loans & Expenses | | | | | |
		Start of the year value	End of the year value	Loans	Rent	Interest	Living costs	New loan balance	Loan to value ratio
1	3.375M	5.0M	**5.4M**	2.0M	175K	100K	100K	**2.025M**	38%
2	3.830M	5.4M	**5.886M**	2.025M	178.5K	106K	103K	**2.055M**	35%
3	4.381M	5.886M	**6.474M**	2.055M	182K	113K	106K	**2.092M**	32%
4	4.677M	6.474M	**6.798M**	2.092M	185K	104K	109K	**2.121M**	31%
5	4.930M	6.798M	**7.070M**	2.121M	189K	95K	112K	**2.139M**	30%
6	5.335M	7.070M	**7.494M**	2.139M	193K	96K	115K	**2.158M**	29%
7	5.761M	7.494M	**7.944M**	2.158M	197K	102K	119K	**2.183M**	27%
8	6.307M	7.944M	**8.520M**	2.183M	202K	109K	122K	**2.212M**	26%
9	6.917M	8.520M	**9.159M**	2.212M	208K	110K	126K	**2.241M**	24%
10	7.575M	9.159M	**9.846M**	2.241M	214K	112K	130K	**2.270M**	23%

As you can see from these calculations, even despite my prediction of average property value growth over the 10-year period (7%) and the fact that each year you borrow money to live off the increasing equity in your properties, each year you still end up with more equity than you began the year with.

Let's look at these same sums graphically. You can see that even though your loans are increasing each year, your net equity — how much you are worth after you subtract all of your loans from the value of your properties — is increasing faster than you can spend your money.

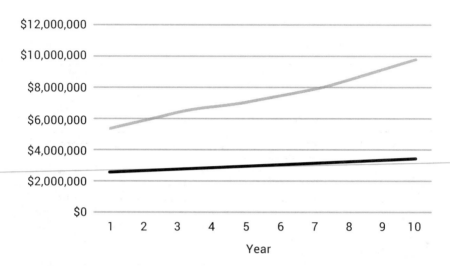

LIVING OFF EQUITY

To help you understand this concept better, I have included the spreadsheets for these calculations on the special resources web page you can access when your register your copy of this book at *www.InvestingSuccessfully.today*.

You can use this to run the numbers for your own personal circumstances.

Will the banks keep lending me money?

Before I answer this, remember that you are earning income — in fact, you're getting it from a number of sources:

1. The *Passive Income* you receive from the growth in value of your property portfolio. Of course, banks don't always recognise this capital growth as income. They would much rather see wages or rents cover the mortgage payments. The good news is you don't pay tax on this income.

2. Your *Rental Income*. Remember I suggested you lower your Loan to Value ratio so that your rental income at least covers your property

expenses and your mortgages? Depending upon your returns, this means your LVR will have to be around 40 per cent or less.

3. *Share, or dividend or superannuation income.*

At the time of writing, banks are cautious and reluctant to refinance property portfolios based purely on the prospect of capital growth. What this means today is that as you become a Level 4 investor, you are going to have to lower your Loan to Value ratios (decrease your debt as a proportion of your portfolio) using one of the strategies I mentioned at the beginning of this chapter.

And as you do, your property portfolio Cash Machine will start producing more cash flow. And if you substitute a commercial property or two for some of your residential properties this will increase your cash flow even more. Of course a by-product of not being as highly leveraged will be that your asset base will not grow in value as fast, but that's OK because as a Level 4 investor you are now in the cash flow stage of your investment life, not the asset accumulation stage.

Do you have an asset protection plan?

Remember this strategy depends on the growth in your property portfolio and your ability to ride the property cycle. This means that as you build your asset base, buying high-growth properties and adding value, you will need an asset protection plan to see you through the highs and lows that you'll experience.

After all, over the next ten years we'll have good times and bad. We'll have periods of strong economic growth, but there will also be downturns. And while interest rates are low at present, they may rise again — not that I'm expecting this any time soon.

Savvy investors count on the good times but plan for the downturns by having an asset protection plan, as well as a finance and tax strategy to make sure they set up their structures in the most efficient way.

Don't get me wrong

While I've just made gaining financial freedom from property investing sound simple, it's not easy.

If you want financial freedom from property investment to fund your dreams, you're going to have to do something different to what most property investors are doing. You're going to have to listen to different people to whom most Australian property investors listen. You're going to need to set yourself some goals and follow a strategy that's known, proven and trusted.

Then you grow your property investment businesses one property at a time and of course you need to buy the right type of properties.

CHAPTER 18:
HOW I LEARNED ABOUT
THE STOCK MARKET

We are not born knowing how to "do money" and we're not born knowing how to invest. This is a skill we need to learn and as a child much of what we learn about money comes from our parents — the things we hear, the things we see and the things we experience.

As I look back, I recognise that I learned little about investing from my parents but a lot from my parents' friends and my friends' parents.

Childhood learnings

Interestingly, while both my parents worked as employees (my father was too afraid to take the "risk" of running his own business), almost all of their friends owned their own businesses and were considerably wealthier than we were. It seemed to me that we were the poorest family in the street and I definitely felt the poorest amongst our friends.

My friends' parents all owned cars — mine couldn't afford one for many years. My friends and their parents went on summer holidays, for many years we didn't. And my friends' parents owned investment properties, mine didn't when I was young.

So, while my friends' parents owned their own businesses and invested in property to grow their wealth, I remember my father's financial "plan". Every Saturday morning he would sit at the kitchen table smoking his cigarettes, drinking his black coffee and daydreaming. He would make a list of how he would spend the winnings when his lottery numbers would come up.

Of course, he never won the big jackpot. But occasionally he won a small prize, just enough to encourage him to buy a few more lottery tickets in the hope of getting the big one the following weekend. But we know the lottery is not a financial plan … but it was the only way my father could see himself escaping the rat race.

I learned a lot of very beneficial things from my parents who tried to instil good moral values in me. They wanted me to have a better life than they did. They strongly encouraged me to get a good education, get a secure job, buy a house and pay it off.

On the other hand, when I visited my friends, I heard their parents give them very different advice. They said things like, "If you want to get on in Australia (the 'lucky country' as they would call it, as most were European migrants), you need to go into business and earn money, which you should then invest in property — that's the true path to real wealth".

Through my friends' parents I learned you couldn't count on the lottery or your boss to make you rich. I knew from an early age that I wanted to be rich and successful, and I soon realised that if I was going to achieve those goals it was up to me!

My stock market education

I remember going to my friend Laurie's home one afternoon and his father was sitting at the kitchen table looking at the stock market section of the newspaper, so, being curious, I asked him what all the numbers and figures meant.

When he started explaining bonds, stocks, shares, dividends, yields and price-to-earnings ratio he could see my eyes glaze over, so he told me a little story to try and make it easier for me to understand. Here is what he said:

Once upon a time long before we had all these complicated investment options like shares, bonds and options, there were two farmers, Ernest and Hugh, who lived in neighbouring towns.

Ernest's farm was doing very well. He inherited it from his family many years ago, he had many fields with good irritation growing corn and this year his fields were fruitful so he had more crops stockpiled than his family could possibly eat.

He sold some of his corn at the local market and stored the rest in his barn, but having been through lean years in the past Ernest was really keen to exchange some of his excess crops today for food in the future when he may be hit by a drought or a plague of locusts.

In the next town Hugh was just starting out. He was newly married, bought an old rundown farm which he planted, but knew it would take a number of years before his crops would mature. In the meantime, he was looking to build a barn to store his crops so his future could be as successful as Ernest's. And he found himself in the unfortunate position that after buying seeds to plant his crops he didn't have enough money left over to buy food for his wife and family.

Since Hugh needed extra money or food today in order to produce more crops later, and Ernest had excess food today but would like the security of more food in the future, it would make sense for the two farmers to make a mutually-beneficial trade and satisfy each other's needs.

In the old days this type of deal would have probably been made on a handshake, but it's also likely that at times this type of deal went sour. Sometimes the Hughs of this world would never build successful farms and would not be able repay their debts. And at other times they'd just run away with other people's crops or money.

Interestingly, our modern financial markets evolved to help people and companies with precisely these problems.

Bonds

Laurie's dad went on to explain that one way the two farmers might have struck their deal would have been in a simple "I'll pay you back later" arrangement, where Hugh would agree to take a quantity of corn today and pay back Ernest in a year's time, plus give him three extra bushels as a form of interest.

If Ernest and Hugh had come to this type of arrangement they would have created something similar to what today we call a *bond*.

Bonds are at type of debt that represents an I.O.U. from somebody who receives the money to the provider of the money.

When you purchase a bond, you effectively are lending a company (or a government) money. The bond issuer is the borrower and agrees to pay whoever holds the bond interest on a regular basis, and then to return the principal (the initial loan) when the bond matures. This can make bonds attractive for people looking for a relatively stable investment.

INVESTMENT SUCCESS FACT

The owner of the bond makes a return over the course of the investment because they get the initial investment back at the end of the term and receive interest payments in the meantime.

The rate of interest a bond must pay depends in part on the creditworthiness of the buyer. That's why government bonds typically carry the lowest yields in the bond market. Large, stable corporations pay a slightly higher rate. Bonds from companies with very poor credit ratings are sometimes known as junk bonds and pay high rates to compensate for the risk that they will default.

Another variable is when the bond pays back its principal (the amount lent) — called the bond's maturity date. Generally, the farther away the maturity date, the higher the interest a bond must pay.

Except in cases of default, which is when the company that has borrowed the money goes broke and can't repay it, investors know exactly what they can expect to make on a bond so long as they hold it to maturity.

But bonds can also be bought or sold on the bond market, which means a bond's current value can fluctuate if you decided to sell it. For example, when interest rates rise, the value of existing bonds on the market will fall.

Here's why: Imagine you hold a 2.5 per cent bond and interest rates rise to 3.5 per cent. With a 3.5 per cent yield now available on the market, no one will want to buy your paltry 2.5 per cent bond, unless you cut the price. Likewise, bond prices rise when interest rates fall.

Shares (or stocks as they are called in the USA)

Now Laurie's father went on to explain a bit about shares.

He said the other way the farmers could have structured their deal would be for Hugh to offer Ernest part ownership in his farm in exchange for one hundred bushels of corn.

This way Ernest would be entitled to a fixed proportion of all the future production of Hugh's farm.

If Hugh's new farm was successful, Ernest would earn a great return on his initial investment but if the farm proved to be infertile, Ernest would lose some or all of his investment.

Since this arrangement allows Hugh and Ernest to share both the risks and the rewards of the farming business, it's really like Ernest holding shares in the farm business.

In case you're wondering why they would they come to an arrangement like this, it's because if the novice farmer Hugh was feeling uncertain about the future profitability of his farming venture or if he was worried that maybe the crops wouldn't grow or the market price for his crop would drop, he might prefer to sell shares in his farm rather than borrowing money to build his business.

Sure he'd be giving away a portion of his future profits (if there were any) but he'd have working capital today and eliminate the risk of not being able to remake repayments if his crops failed because in reality he hasn't borrowed any money — he's gained funds by selling shares in his farm.

On the other hand, if Ernest has a different view and felt confident the farm would be fruitful, he'd prefer the share arrangement since it would give him the potential for a greater return on his investment.

The difference is that with a bond (the "I'll lend you some money or corn" deal), Ernest would have the security of knowing he would at least get his money back (assuming that Hugh could pay his bills) plus a small interest payment, however by owning a share of the farm he has the upside potential of earning much more.

Now I don't know if Laurie's father made up this parable or not as I've since read similar stories in a number of books including *A Beginner's Guide To Investing* by Alex Frey, but after hearing this great analogy of how stock markets worked I wanted to learn more, so here are some of the other questions I asked him.

What exactly is a share?

Put simply, a stock is a share in the ownership of a company. Whether you say shares, equity or stock, it all means the same thing.

Shares represent a claim on the company's assets and earnings. As you acquire more shares, your ownership stake in the company becomes greater.

In other words, holding a company's shares means that you are one of the many owners (shareholders) of a company and, as such, you have a claim (albeit usually very small) to everything the company owns. As an owner, you are entitled to your share of the company's earnings as well as any voting rights attached to the stock.

But what if circumstances change?

Imagine shortly after investing in Hugh's corn, Ernest's crop is infected by a plague of worms. Now he'll go short of food. So he asks Hugh for his 100 bushels of corn back. But Hugh has eaten some, traded some for seeds and has stored some in his barn for his own consumption over the next year so he can't return the 100 bushels plus interest.

So what is Ernest to do? He needs his corn now — he can't wait three years until Hugh harvests his crop.

The answer may be to sell his contract with Hugh to another farmer, Ron, who happens to have a surplus of corn this year. Ron would give his corn to Ernest today in exchange for future payments of corn from Hugh, but he may not give him the full 100 bushels — today he may only give him 80 bushels.

This concept of secondary exchange of financial contracts is exactly what happens in stock markets around the world every day.

The price of stocks and bonds that you see quoted on the internet or on the tickers at the bottom of the TV screen are simply the most recent prices at which these exchanges occur between individuals.

But there's a wrinkle in this scenario …

There are many such exchanges happening all the time and sometimes investors just don't have enough time or money to manage a portfolio of shares and that has led to the evolution of *managed funds* (mutual funds) where many investors pull their resources and hand control of their money over to a professional fund manager who invests the funds for them. Each investor in the managed fund owns a proportion of the portfolio and receives a proportion of the income or gain in value.

Meet Mr Market

As I started to understand how the stock market worked, I asked Laurie's father what makes stock prices fluctuate so widely as I'd heard a little about stock market booms and busts.

Laurie's father told me a parable about Mr Market that helped to explain things to me. I was impressed with the story and years later learned that it was an allegory initially written by Warren Buffett's famous mentor Ben Graham in his book *The Intelligent Investor*.

The story went something like this ...

Imagine you are partners in a company with a man named Mr Market. Each day he comes to your office and offers to buy your interest in the company or sell you his — the choice is yours. The catch is, Mr Market is manic depressive — at times he suffers from excessive highs and other times from depressive lows.

Sometimes his idea of the value of your company seems reasonable and justified by the business's prospects as you know them. At other times Mr Market lets his enthusiasm or his fears run away with him and the value he proposes seems a little short or silly to you.

When he is on one of his manic highs, he believes the value of the business is high because everything in his world is rosy at the time. As his outlook for the company is strongly positive, he is only willing to sell you his stake in the company at a premium.

At other times, his mood becomes dark and all he sees is a dismal future for the company. In fact, he is so concerned he is willing to sell you his part of the company for far less than it is worth.

Of course, all the while, the underlying value of the company may not have changed at all — it's just Mr Market's mood.

The best part of this entire arrangement is that you are free to ignore him if you don't like his price. The next day, he'll show up at your door with a new one.

The story helped me understand the reason for the daily change in price of stocks is Mr Market's emotions. The big lesson for me was that a rational investor will sell if the price of the particular stock is high and buy if the price is low. He or she would not sell *because* the price has gone down or buy because the price has gone up.

INVESTMENT SUCCESS FACT

The behaviour of Mr Market allows you as an investor to wait until Mr Market is in a 'pessimistic mood' and offers a low sale price, meaning patience is an important virtue when dealing with Mr Market.

If you think about it, the more manic-depressive Mr Market is, the more opportunity you will have to take advantage of him. And don't worry; he doesn't have feelings or mind being taken advantage of.

Laurie's father told me that this is exactly how an intelligent investor should look at the stock market. The stocks you own are part of a business and each morning, when you turn on your computer, you can find Mr Market's prices. It is your choice whether or not to buy or sell. If you find a company that he is offering stock for less than it is worth, take advantage of him and buy some shares, because as long as the company is fundamentally sound, one day he will come back in one of his manic highs and offer to buy the same company from you for a much higher price.

He explained that thinking of share prices this way — as merely quotes from an emotionally unstable business partner — frees you up from the emotional attachment most investors feel toward rising and falling stock prices and makes you a better investor.

The lesson in all of this is that investment is really an exchange between two parties. One who needs money now in order to build something that will generate more money in the future and another party who has money now, but no real need for it at present, yet wants more of it in the future.

Now let's take a closer look at some of your investment options in more detail in the next chapter.

CHAPTER 19:
THE MANY DIFFERENT
TYPES OF INVESTMENTS

With so many investment options, you need to understand their characteristics and how they may suit your particular investment objectives to help decide which investment vehicle is suitable for you. And these are likely to change throughout your life.

In many poor countries people invest in large families to ensure their old age. In more developed countries many invest in their education and skills hoping their job and pension will safeguard their golden years (it won't!).

And then there are those who invest in precious objects (art works, antiques and collectables) and others who build their Cash Machine by building a business. I'll leave those for others to write about and instead deal with four main types of investments.

1. Property — I've devoted a whole section of this book to real estate, my favoured form of investment.

2. Cash.

3. Fixed interest.

4. Shares and similar investments such as bonds, managed funds, indexed funds, etc.

5. Cryptocurrencies

These investment classes could also be divided into:

1. Defensive investments — which focus on generating regular income as opposed to growing in value over time. These include cash investments, savings accounts, term deposits and bonds.

2. Growth investments — which aim to grow in value over time, as well as pay out income along the way. Two common types of growth investment are shares and property, but just to make things clear, even though your investment intention may be for them to grow in value, their prices can rise and fall significantly.

Investing means different things to different people, no one can be an expert in all the different classes of investments and your needs are likely to change over time. When you're beginning, capital appreciation is likely to be more important to you as you grow your asset base and you're probably going to place a bigger emphasis on income (cash flow) as you reach your retirement years.

Before I go on, maybe I should explain that the income you receive from investing can come in many forms, including profit, interest earnings or appreciation (the increase in value of your asset).

To help you understand a bit more about successful investing here are some of the common questions that investors ask themselves:

1. What do I want to achieve?

Is it money? Wealth? Financial freedom? Maybe all of the above!

2. What is my preferred strategy?

Once you know where you are going, you need to implement an investment strategy that helps you get there.

3. When should I buy?

While there are investment opportunities at most times, I've found that many of my successful investments have been made by going against the crowd and buying when the majority of people are worried about the market and sitting on the sidelines.

4. What can I afford?

Before you start looking at what to buy, you need to know what you can afford to buy.

5. How will I set up my purchase?

Whether you buy in your own name, your super fund or a trust, you need to be aware of what it will mean for you and your family, now and in the future.

6. Who should I ask for help?

Remember, if you are the smartest person in the room, you are in the wrong room!

7. Should I take advice from my friends and family?

In general the answer is — no!

Let's move on to talk about some of the different types of investments available to you.

1. Cash investment

These include:

1. Savings accounts

2. Interest bearing savings accounts, which the banks call various fancy names, and

3. Term deposits, which lock up your money for the duration of the 'term' so you can't be tempted to spend it.

These are generally the least risky types of investment and in the current low interest rate environment offer minimal income through interest payments, and it is possible the value of your investment could decrease over time, even though its dollar figure remains the same. This is because inflation means the cost of goods and services rises too quickly and at the same time taxes on the interest you receive eats away your profits.

2. Bonds

Remember I introduced the concept of bonds (which is a type of interest-bearing loan) in the previous chapter?

These are loans to governments or companies, who sell them to investors for a fixed period of time and pay them a regular rate of interest. At the end of that period, the price of the bond is repaid to the investor.

Although bonds are considered a low-risk investment, some decrease in value over time, so you could potentially get back less money than you initially paid.

However, not all bonds are the same — and they can range from very safe (for example, Australian or US Government bonds) through to very risky (unlikely to repay your money).

In general, however, bonds are less volatile than shares and some can be traded on a secondary market such as the ASX — these are known as 'listed' or 'exchange-traded' bonds, giving you the flexibility to sell your investment if your circumstances change.

Bonds have a *face value,* which is the amount you will get back at maturity and a *coupon amount,* which is the interest paid each year.

3. Shares

Simply, a stock or share is a unit of ownership of a company. For every share you own in a company, you own a small piece of the office furniture, equipment, company cars, and even the tea and coffee in the lunchroom.

More importantly, you are entitled to a portion of the company's profits and any voting rights attached to the stock. The more shares you own, the larger the portion of the company (and profits) you own.

A "public" company is one that has issued shares by selling them to the general public.

What sort of companies issue shares? All different sorts. When you invest in the share market you're investing in real companies who sell real things to real people.

If you're reading this on a Kindle, Amazon issued stocks to fund its growth. If you're reading the book version, the utility company that provides electricity for the light above your head issued shares. As did the company that made your car, your clothes, possibly the furniture in your house, the supermarket where you bought your food and the company that made the refrigerator in which you store it. All these things happened because people invested in companies that started small and grew in size because they delivered a product or service that people required.

And along the way these companies needed funds for expansion and the easiest way to access funds was to issue shares, which were bought and sold on the stock exchange via a broking platform or stockbroker.

The shareholders have the benefit of liquidity — their shares are quickly and easily sold. But this liquidity leads to the price of shares being very volatile, even from day to day, which makes them an investment generally best suited to long-term investors who are comfortable withstanding these ups and downs.

Because of their volatility, shares are often considered one of the riskiest types of investment. By that I mean there is a strong possibility that you will lose money or that the value of your shares won't increase.

How risky your investment is can vary widely depending on the company. Purchasing shares in a well-established and profitable company such as Coca Cola (it's unlikely people will stop drinking Coke) or Procter & Gamble (people will keep using detergent and shampoo) means there is less risk you'll lose your investment, whereas purchasing shares in technology stocks, mining companies or start-ups increases the risks substantially.

Stock market volatility is always temporary and feared by those who don't understand it. But strategic investors expect it and take advantage of share prices when they are on sale, recognising the advance of the general share market is permanent, while the declines are temporary.

Speaking to investors, many are worried about the regular corrections to the share market, but I explain to them the corrections are just a part of investing. I've been investing in shares years for many, many decades and have seen prices decline, drop, rise and throughout that I have remained unphased.

But the average investor says "I don't like it" — but to me it's just part of investing.

It's like saying to your personal trainer I don't like sweating — it's part of getting fit. If you want to create wealth, you need to become a disciplined investor and get your head around the fluctuations of the share market and not become concerned when the media reports the ups and downs of the market. In my mind, the real risk in investing in shares is believing that volatility is a risk.

When you buy shares in a company, you become a co-owner and, in theory, have a right to a piece of the profits that the company (hopefully) generates. But the ways those profits end up in investor's pockets can vary from stock to stock.

How do I receive my profits with shares?

1. The increased share price

You can always sell your shares and if the price goes up you will have made a profit. I've already told you about Mr Market. Sometimes investors (the market) might be optimistic and willing to pay, say, 20 or 30 times a company's per share earnings for a stock. At other times the market will be more bearish (cautious) and investors may only be willing to pay five times earnings.

And then there will be shares that rise in value without their company turning a profit — think about the value versus profit equation of internet-based companies such as Facebook, Twitter and WhatsApp in the early days.

2. Dividends

The other way to profit from the stock market is through sharing part of the company's profit in the form of regular dividend payments, often paid quarterly and occasionally in the form of "one-off" special "bonus" dividends when an extraordinary profit is made.

Another way a company can give profits back to shareholders is by buying back some shares from them. But beware — there is no guarantee that publicly-listed companies will make a profit or pay out dividends. Twitter and Facebook traded for many years without making a profit but, interestingly, speculators kept pushing the price of their shares up in the open market.

Why would they do this? In the anticipation of future earnings and therefore dividends (payments of interest for owning the shares). Sometimes this happens and sometimes it doesn't! We have all heard of companies that have gone bankrupt. Taking a greater risk should demand a greater return on investment but unfortunately things don't always work this way.

INVESTMENT SUCCESS FACT

The more profitable a company is, the more other investors are likely to be willing to pay for it. That's because even if the company isn't paying strong dividends now, higher profits mean the likelihood of higher future dividends.

What is a share certificate?

It used to be a piece of paper that is proof of your ownership. I remember years ago when I wanted to sell my shares, I would have to physically give my certificates to my broker. Now, in the age of electronic trading, this is done by the click of a mouse or a phone call.

What rights and responsibilities does a shareholder have?

Being a shareholder of a public company doesn't mean you have a say in the day-to-day running of the business. Being a Microsoft or Facebook shareholder doesn't allow you to call Bill Gates or Mark Zuckerberg and tell them how you think their companies should be run!

The management of your company is controlled by the board of directors and the full-time employees of the company. And that's generally a good thing because you're probably not an expert in running a supermarket chain or a tech company, are you?

And, after all, the idea of investing is that you don't want to have to work for your money, right?

The company management is meant to work in the interests of the shareholders by increasing the value of their shares and producing a profit. If this doesn't happen, the shareholders can, at least in theory, vote to have the management removed. In reality, individual investors like you and I don't own enough shares to have a material influence on the company. It's really the large institutional investors and major shareholders who make the decisions.

INVESTMENT SUCCESS FACT

An important feature of owning shares is your limited liability — meaning that you're not personally liable if the company goes broke and can't pay its debts.

Think about it this way … if you ran a small business, which went broke but still owed debts to the banks or other creditors, you would be held personally liable and may have to sell off your house or car.

On the other hand, owning shares means that at worst the maximum you can lose is the money you put into purchasing the shares. If the company in which you are a shareholder goes bankrupt, there is no way the creditors can make a claim on your personal assets.

4. Managed or mutual funds

Investors who don't have the time or experience needed to choose a sound investment often turn to professional managers who run *managed funds* and pool your investment with a number of other investors and by a collection of stocks and bonds.

Australians are contributing record amounts of money to professionally managed funds. The *Australian Financial Review* reported that Australians are contributing record amounts of money to professionally managed funds.

Managed funds hoovered up $35.7 billion from Australian investors in 2021. That represents a 162 per cent jump from a steady $13.6 billion in each of the previous two years.

Most managed funds are set up with a specific investment strategy in mind — buying large cap stocks, bonds, growth stocks, shares in certain industries or stocks in certain countries.

The main advantage of investing this way is that it allows you to spread your market bets with a small amount of money. For example, with a minimum initial purchase of around $2,000 to $3,000, you can buy a fund that holds all 500 stocks on the S&P 500 index. You can then build your position with subsequent small incremental investments.

In fact, this is the way most superannuation funds invest.

Interestingly, most mutual funds are "actively" managed, which means the fund's manager chooses the investments that he or she thinks will provide the best return — within the constraints of the fund's style.

How do you know which managed fund to invest in?

The best way of finding out a managed fund's objectives, costs and past performance is to read its prospectus. This is a formal legal document, which is required by law to be given to prospective investors, that provides details about an investment offering for sale to the public. A prospectus should contain the facts that an investor needs to make an informed investment decision.

Although reading a prospectus may cause your eyes to glaze over it's a critical step to understanding what you're investing in.

Some of the advantages of managed funds are:

1. Diversification — the average investor couldn't afford the cost involved in purchasing a diversified portfolio of stocks and bonds, however managed funds invested a large number of stocks, or bonds, or both, and give their investors instant diversification.

2. Professional management — this means you don't have to do all the research, but this comes at a price (management fees) however while in theory your fund is meant to outperform averages, this is not always the case.

3. Liquidity — managed funds don't trade on the stock exchange, but the fund manager will usually buy back your units promptly, however watch out for potentially excessive fees involved in this.

Index funds

There is another type of exchange-traded managed fund out there that doesn't rely on a manager choosing specific stocks in which to invest, but instead holds all of the stocks or bonds on an index.

So what's an index? Basically, it's a group of stocks with something in common. It could be the American S&P 500 (the 500 largest US companies with publicly traded shares) or the top stocks on the Australian Stock Exchange (ASX).

Each stock's weight on the list is usually determined by its overall market value. For example, in early 2014, tech giant Apple Inc. counted for about three per cent of the S&P 500, whereas Avon Products was less than .05 per cent. So, likewise, an S&P 500 index fund would hold three per cent in Apple and .05 per cent in Avon.

But why would you choose an index fund?

Despite all their marketing hype, after they charge their annual management fees, most fund managers can't beat the general benchmark index over a long period. In other words, if you invest in managed funds the fund manager is better off than you are — they get their fees and the share portfolio they manage for you generally underperforms the average rise in share prices and equals it at best.

Index funds, on the other hand, usually carry very low fees (often less than 0.2 per cent annually) and reliably deliver the market's average performance.

Interestingly by aiming for mediocrity (just performing like the average index) you in fact give yourself a good chance of beating most other investors!

Which stocks should you buy?

Let me be clear about this — the most important thing to understand about picking stocks is that if you are buying a share that means that someone else is selling it.

What this means is that no matter the analysis you have done which may tell you that this stock is a good deal at today's price, there is someone else on the other side of the trade who has run the numbers and decided that the smart move is to get out now.

It's much the same with forecasts in the paper or the financial news channels — one so-called expert will predict the market is about to crash, while another who is looking at the same research data will conclude the market is set to rise further.

When it comes to investing in shares, stock picking is a battle of wits against other investors, most of whom, you should assume, are at least as informed and rational as you are. That's why it is difficult for even pros to beat the return they'd get simply from holding an index fund.

I know when I tried my hand at share investing every time I heard a hot stock tip from my broker or in the news, I seemed to buy it at the top of its price range and a few days later it would drop in value. The problem for me was that the professional investors had already made their money in that share — they were in early and got out just around the time I bought in — at the top.

But don't get me wrong, investing in stocks can be exciting and an intellectual challenge. That's why share investing seems to appeal to the analytical types — unfortunately that's not me!

There are generally two types of stock investors and they're called growth or value. The difference between the two is quite self-explanatory.

Growth investors tend to focus their analysis on a company's potential for future profits and gravitate to those whose earnings are rising the fastest. Since growth-oriented investors are interested in big *future* earnings, they are often willing to pay a high price for a stock relative to what it earns right now. The price-to-earnings ratio (or P/E) is a common metric for valuing stocks and growth investors are often willing to pay P/Es of 20 or more.

On the other side of the equation, *value investors* bank less on future potential. They tend to hone in more on the current value of a company's assets (minus its debts), and look for stocks that are cheap compared to those assets. And since they don't want to count on the most optimistic forecasts for profits, they usually buy stocks with lower P/E ratios.

Intuitively, it does sound like using a value strategy is a more conservative approach. But value stocks can go out of style for long stretches of time and buying cheap comes with its own risks. Often when a stock appears to be a bargain, that's only because other investors correctly see that the business has serious problems.

In my experience, there isn't one simple formula that tells you when a stock is a great deal. You have to dig in, do the research and make a judgment call, and that's really why I don't invest in shares — there are too many variables and it's just too hard for the average investor.

So how do you work out the intrinsic value of a share?

You will often hear commentators say a particular stock is overvalued or undervalued so how do you know the fair value of a share?

Economics would teach you that the intrinsic value of any investment is just the future income streams —dividends (or rent if it's a property) plus its increase in value discounted back to the present to account for the time value of money.

This concept of the time value for money (sometimes called an internal rate of return) is complicated but worth spending a few moments understanding because it's fundamental to how you value any investment — stocks, bonds or property.

Here's why … One dollar received today is worth more than $1 received in five years' time. You could:

1. Invest it in the bank and get a fixed rate of return so it would be worth a little bit more in five years' time.

2. Buy more things with a dollar today than you could in five years' time due to inflation.

3. Being human, most of us would rather eat a cake now than wait a week or five years for it.

Thinking about it this way, dividends received in the future are worth less than those received today, so we need to apply a discount rate to them in order to express their intrinsic value to an investor today.

If you do an internet search on calculating intrinsic value you're likely to become very confused. Investopedia (*www.investopedia.com/articles/basics/12/intrinsic-value.asp*) will offer you a number of arithmetic models with symbols that you're not likely to understand — at least I know I don't. However, if you're interested in learning more about this concept I suggest you read the tutorial available on the site.

So let's be honest — it's exceptionally difficult to estimate the intrinsic value of a company since this depends on estimating its future profits and then discounting them back to today's dollar value. How can you really take into account any changes in interest rates, government, consumer demand, the economy, future inflation and technology?

Maybe that's why Mr Market is schizophrenic.

Yet stockbroker's research houses and fund managers spent exorbitant amounts of time and money analysing companies looking for an edge. They look at various ratios to come up with their "fundamental analysis" of the company.

Here are some of the figures looked at by economic commentator Pete Wargent, as outlined in his great book *Get a Financial Grip*:

1. Market capitalisation — this represents the total value of the company on the stock exchange and is the number of ordinary shares on issue multiplied by the current share price. This is an important number as you can then work out whether the company is over or undervalued currently if you have an estimate of its intrinsic value.

2. Return on capital (ROC) = after-tax profits/total assets*100

3. Return on equity (ROE) = after-tax profits/shareholders' equity*100

4. Earnings per share (EPS) = after-tax profits/number of issued ordinary shares

5. Dividend per share (DPS) = total dividend paid/number of issued ordinary shares

6. Payout ratio = dividend per share/earnings per share

7. Dividend yield = dividend per share/share price (in cents)*100

The dividend yield is somewhere between three to eight per cent for profitable companies and nothing for speculative stocks.

8. Price earnings (P/E) ratio = share price in cents/earnings per share

The "Rule of 20" states that fair P/E ratio might be 20 minus the inflation rate per annum, so a fair P/E ratio might be around 17 today, depending on the nature of the company and its industry.

9. Price-earnings growth = PE ratio/earnings growth

10. Total shareholder return (TSR) = sum of capital gains plus dividends received

Fundamental analysts also look at:

1. Interest cover = the company earnings before interest and tax/interest payable on debt

At least three or four times is considered to be good.

2. Debt to equity ratio = debt/equity*100

This should be less than 100 per cent and lower is considered to be better.

3. Current ratio = current assets/current liabilities

Greater than two is good, less than one is dangerous.

Pete explains that if you don't understand these ratios or you are not prepared to learn them, you probably shouldn't risk much money buying individual stocks. Instead, he suggests you make life easier and invest in an indexed fund.

However, Pete also explains that when he tries to identify a healthy company he looks for companies that:

- Are profitable.

- Have a return on capital of more than eight per cent.

- Have a return on equity of more than 10 per cent and preferably rising.

- Provide total shareholder returns of more than 10 per cent (preferably over a period of decades) including the dividends.

- Have a dividend yield of around three to five per cent or more.

- Have interest cover of more than three times and a debt/equity ratio of less than 75 per cent.

- Have a current ratio of more than one.

- Have a P/E ratio of 10 to 20 depending on the industry in which the company operates.

- Have a price-earnings growth of less than one.

Now I know Pete Wargent well. He loves numbers, figures and spreadsheets and that's why he's a successful share investor. If you don't, or can't, carry out this type of due diligence on a company you're planning to invest in, then you're really not an investor — you're a speculator.

By the way … most of these figures can be found relatively easily in a company's annual reports and on stock market data websites.

I'd also recommend educating yourself further by reading Pete's books, subscribing to his blog at *www.PeteWargent.blogspot.com* and his podcast — Low Rates High Returns — that he hosts with Stephen Moriarty.

After finding out about all these numbers figures and ratios you're probably wondering …

Should I just buy a diversified portfolio of shares?

Sure diversification is one of the fundamental models financial planners use — they spread your investment across a wide range of shares (or various asset classes) with the hope of reducing the risk of loss of a large part of your capital. In general this leads to average results — and you'll never become wealthy being average.

Billionaire investor Warren Buffett famously stated that "diversification is protection against ignorance. It makes little sense if you know what you are doing."

On the other hand, most financial advisors recommend that you diversify for your own protection. What they fail to tell you is that it is also for their protection. Since most financial advisors can't tell you exactly which stock or managed fund is a great investment, they tell you to buy a bunch of them.

Which managed fund should you choose?

There are thousands of managed funds you can invest in so choosing the right one can seem a bit confusing — especially to novice investors.

A strategy to use may be to choose a fund that invests in the industries or asset classes you are familiar with or is appropriate for your investment timeframe. It's important to always consider the fund's fees and charges as well.

You've probably heard the disclaimer "past performance is no guarantee of future returns" before and this is especially true of managed funds. That's because past results really are no indicator that a fund will enjoy continued or any future success.

A recent study by Standard & Poor's makes sobering reading because it found that of all funds in the top 25 per cent of their category in one year, fewer than one third made it to the top 25 per cent the next year. And only five per cent managed to stay in the winner's circle three years in a row.

Each year, Money magazine puts together a list of 50 recommended funds and while performance is one of the editor's criteria, it's the least important among many. Money also considers:

Low fees: Remember, you can't count on a fund manager outperforming or even making you money, but you can count on him or her collecting his or her expense ratio! For this reason, the Money 50 list is heavy on low-cost index funds.

Experienced management: A fund is nothing but a pool of money. If performance records matter at all, they belong to the manager not the fund. So, if a fund switched managers last year, you truly can ignore most of its record.

Strong stewardship: Money looks for funds whose managers consistently put shareholders' interests ahead of their own. That means paying incentives aligned to performance, a strong board to represent fund shareholders, and record of avoiding regulatory issues.

Let me be clear: Make sure you pick a fund with a strategy aligned to your goals and your risk appetite. This is because some stock funds focus on big, stable blue-chip companies with the aim of producing relatively steady returns, while others reach for higher returns — with the resulting higher risk profiles — by focusing on smaller companies, or on stocks in volatile but fast-growing industries.

INVESTMENT SUCCESS FACT

In my experience, most stock investors will do relatively well by choosing a low-cost, broadly diversified fund that holds a representative slice of all the stocks on the market.

Are individual stocks or managed funds the best option?

In my opinion most investors should invest in funds rather than individual stocks. That's because smart stock investing takes time and intensive research. It also requires a significant outlay of cash to build a well-diversified portfolio. And I'll explain a lot more about this in the next chapter.

An alternative, which is to hold a highly concentrated position in a handful of stocks, gives you a shot at huge gains (imagine if you bought Apple in 2002 for $7 a share?) but also risks catastrophic losses (imagine you owned stock in Enron or Lehman Brothers, at any price?). Or the many local Australian companies that were once the darlings of the stock exchange but are no longer trading today. A managed fund automatically spreads your bets among dozens or even hundreds of stocks and thus reduces your risk.

What is the right investment mix for you?

It should be fairly obvious by now, my recommended investment class is property but I also believe in diversification if it fits your long-term investing strategy and goals.

Most Australians already have this type of diversification because of compulsory superannuation — their superannuation fund general is heavily invested in the share market.

But I've seen too many ordinary mum and dad investors lose out by trying to trade or invest in shares.

However, if you're keen to do so, one final point to consider is your own psychology so you can clearly understand whether you are emotional or disciplined. This is because you must know whether you can hold your nerve when markets go haywire, which they inevitably do from time to time.

When markets crash, some investors find it very tempting to sell just to make the pain go away. But frequent trading in and out of the market is likely to cost you returns — it's just too hard to correctly time when to buy and when to sell. Take a look at how much money you have in stocks and imagine losing a half of it because stocks fell by about that much in the Global Financial Crisis or when the Australian share market plummeted more than 30% when fears about the Coronavirus became more real in March 2020. If you know you couldn't stand that big a hit, hold less in equities and reduce your stress level at the same time, too!

How big a share portfolio do you need to live comfortably in retirement?

Now this is a great question, and the answer varies widely.

I know many financial planners suggest a portfolio worth $1 million will see you through, but while financial planners try and build you a nest egg that you deplete in your golden years, I advocate building an ongoing Cash Machine so that you have lifetime wealth and leave a legacy.

Also, no one really knows what sort of rollercoaster ride the economy will take between now and your retirement or what rate of inflation will persist through your lifetime. Will a loaf of bread cost $6.00 when you're 65 or will it be closer to $60?

So, how can you possibly know how much money we will need to live on in retirement? In my mind, it will be significantly more than $1 million and that's why most superannuation payouts won't be enough.

Of course, it also depends on how much income you want in retirement. I've found most people are looking for at least $100,000 after tax (in today's dollar value).

Financial independence enthusiasts have come up with two rules:

1. **The 4 Percent Rule:** which states you can sustainably live on four per cent of your investments every year. In other words, $1 million in your portfolio means you can live on $40,000, adjusted for inflation, every year.

2. **The 25 x Rule:** Here you calculate the amount you want to live on, multiply this by 25 and this is the size your portfolio needs to be. Notice the relationship to the 4 percent rule — $40,000 x 25 equals $1 million.

Of course there are heaps of assumptions made if you use this rule, so it may be worth plugging your own figures into one of the many online calculators such as the one at *www.FireCalc.com*.

The bottom line is it's likely your portfolio will need to be much larger than you probably think.

In the next chapter, I'll share some more insights about investing in stocks or shares so you can understand the risks and the potential rewards, too.

CHAPTER 20:
INVESTING IN SHARES

As I've explained, for most of us, the stock market is a game of chance and anyone who claims to know how to predict the future value of the stock market or individual shares is either fooling themselves or lying to you!

The reality is that unforeseen events can change stock prices overnight and even the largest institutions can lose millions in the mere blink of an eye.

While it may seem reasonable that the latest technical software will help you beat the markets, and get an above average return, my many years of watching the markets have concluded that both the chartists and the fundamentalists lose out because the stock market has a mind of its own.

Consider this fact — more than 95 per cent of the gain in the stock market in an average year can occur in just a few days within that year, which means that you'll lose more often than you'll win trying to trade shares.

However, you'll find most stock market newsletters try to time the market, yet their track record has been particularly poor over the past decade.

I've found the stocks recommended in magazines and in internet newsletters — you know, those touted as the latest hottest stocks — while tending to perform well in the short-term, rarely outperform over the long-term.

Look at all the companies that are working on the cutting edge of a new technology, or perhaps the latest internet stocks, and see how they're performed. Sure there is the occasional Google, Facebook or Tesla, but they're the rarity and certainly not the norm.

Let me illustrate this better for you.

The All Ordinaries (XAO) or "All Ords" is considered a total market barometer for the Australian stock market and contains the 500 largest ASX listed companies by way of market capitalisation.

Back in early 2020 we started hearing about this Coronavirus "thingy" that was spreading around the world and as fears of what may lie head spread over just a couple of days in March 2020 the values our share market plummeted erasing over seven years of gains — *poof!*

That's because nervous share investors, including many funds and institutions, sold down their shareholdings, but there was no one willing to buy them other than at a bargain price leading to a market freefall.

Little did these sellers know how strongly the market would rebound in the next 12 months, rising almost 50 per cent as the chart below shows:

All Ordinaries Chart

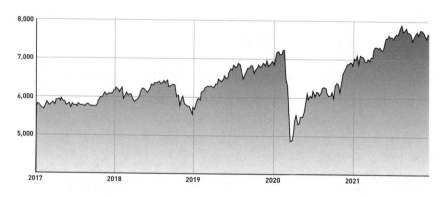

But let me ask you a question: did the value of our banks, our supermarkets, our chemical companies, etc really change that much overnight or from week to week? Of course not!

This is a beautiful example of Mr Market, that I introduced two chapters ago, at work.

One of the problems with investing in the share market is that you can see a minute by minute valuation of your shares and the market in general.

I'm sure when the overall stock market fell significantly in March 2020, many investors sold up in a panic. Of course those investors who didn't panic and held on to their shares were not really affected. And those who were willing to buy into the share market when others were panicking have done really well.

But those investors who listened to the news and sold up their shareholding lost a significant amount of their capital and even if they bought back into the market as it rose, they almost certainly would not have had the nerve to buy at the bottom.

In times of turbulence the market changes, but if you think about it, your goals haven't changed so strategic investors hang tight. So for those who didn't pay attention to Mr Market and held on for the long-term, the value of their shares are worth much more today than they were at the start of the Coronavirus pandemic.

Now let's look at a chart showing what's happened to the All Ords over the past 10 years:

All Ordinaries Chart

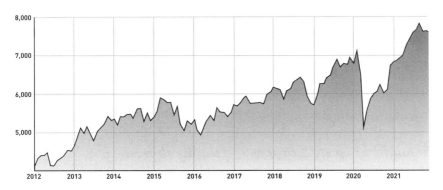

There's Mr Market at work again — up and down, down and up. Even before this time period there was a significant slump in 2008 and 2009 in response to the Global Financial Crisis, but look at the right-hand side of the graph at share values at the end of 2021. All those falls in previous decade weren't really significant for a long-term investor in the stock market.

Of course, this doesn't take into account the dividends they would have received along the way, but owning well-located residential real estate over the same 10-year period would have been a much, much more profitable investment, as the value of most well-located homes more than doubled in value over that period.

Now, to give you more insight into share investing, let me answer some of the common questions you may have:

How many Australians invest in shares?

According to Finder.com.au around half (49 per cent) of Australians, an estimated 9.5 million people, now own shares. Many own them indirectly through their superannuation funds but with the prevailing ultra-low interest rates more and more Australians are shifting money out of their savings accounts and into other investments include direct ownership of shares.

The Australian Stock Exchange (ASX) is the 16th largest in the world, and depending on your broker, you could also have access to some of the largest exchanges in the world, such as the NASDAQ in the United States. Australian brokerages are regulated by the Australian Securities & Investments Commission (ASIC).

Should I use a stockbroker to pick my shares?

Many investors consider using a stockbroker as a way of protecting themselves against the high-risk game of trading shares.

Sure, some are in the business of trying to predict stock prices and, yes, they have large research departments behind them, but you'll often find that your stockbrokers "buy" recommendation is another broker's "sell" recommendation — after all, somebody is on the other side of the transaction with an opposite view to the long-term value of the share that you are considering.

There are two types of stockbroker you can choose from:

1. **Online:** these brokers tend to be the cheapest and most popular option for beginning investors and the brokerage fee usually starts at $20. Online brokers do not provide specific advice on which shares to buy or sell. You are required to place the trade yourself and know exactly which shares you want to buy and what price to pay — the broker just executes the trade. While these brokers provide access to the company's research and recommendations, it's up to you to make the investment decision. The Big Four Australian banks all offer an online broking service, as do many other firms.

2. **Full-service brokers** will provide advice on what shares to buy or sell and place trades on your behalf. Their brokerage fee usually starts at around $80 per trade.

What is a brokerage fee?

A brokerage fee is a fee or commission a stockbroker charges you to execute transactions or provide specialised services such as consultations, negotiations, and delivery. Regardless of whether you're buying shares online or by using a full-service broker, you will pay a brokerage fee so just accept it as a cost of doing business.

The fee is usually calculated based on a percentage of the total transaction, but many be set as a fixed fee.

How do I buy shares?

The most common way to purchase shares is through a stockbroker *"On Market"* — through a stock exchange. In Australia the primary exchange is the ASX and when you place a trade with your broker they will automatically purchase your shares at the best available price.

Other ways to buy shares are through an *Initial Public Offering* (IPO) when a private company initially lists on a stock exchange to raise funds by selling shares in the company to the public.

Another way is through a *Capital Raising* when a listed company looks to raise funds by issuing additional shares to its current shareholders or other investors. The price of these shares is usually at a discount to current market value to entice investors to take part in the raising.

How do I hold my shares?

Remember I mentioned share certificates, well today with electronic trading in Australia there are two choices of how to hold your shares.

1. Hold the Shares via your Stockbroker using a HIN

You are given a 10 digit Holder Identification Number (HIN) that begins with an "X". This number represents all your share holdings at that specific stockbroker and is documented in the CHESS register, which is used by the ASX to confirm holdings.

If you use multiple stockbrokers you will receive a different HIN from each stockbroker.

Don't worry — you maintain full control of your shares — they're just being held on your behalf for your convenience, so they can be sold instantly because your stockbroker can confirm your exact holdings.

2. Hold the Shares directly with a Share Registry (SRN)

If you chose this route you are given a 10 or 11 digit Security Reference Number (SRN) that starts with an "I". This represents your shareholdings in that specific company.

If you own shares in multiple listed companies, each share holding will be represented by a different SRN. To confirm your share holdings you must log into the applicable share registries website (e.g. Computershare, Link Market Services, etc.) using your personal details and SRN.

To sell your shares you must quote the SRN to your stockbroker so they can double-check your holdings with the registry.

In most cases it's easier to hold your shares on a HIN.

How do I sell my shares?

Selling is an identical process to buying shares but in reverse. If you think about it, every time someone buys shares there's someone on the other end of the transaction selling and they've instructed their broker to place their shares for sale at a certain price or for the best price he or she can obtain.

Shares are very liquid, meaning you can usually sell them within minutes and receive proceeds into your bank account in about two days.

Should I consider using a professional fund manager?

If all of this is starting to sound too daunting, you're probably thinking "shouldn't I just hand over my money to a fund manager? Surely there will perform better than I can?"

In truth, if fund managers just cracked the market's averages, they would be happy with their performance, and you pay them a privilege for looking after your money.

Are blue-chips the best?

Gee this is getting complicated. So why not just invest in blue-chip shares? They're the top of the economic food chain and therefore are more likely to make money, right?

History shows us that it's certainly not a bad thing to own shares in a few solid blue-chip companies because they're likely to have increased in value over time and their consistent profit would have paid you regular dividends.

The trick is not to listen to Mr Market but hold your shares for the long-term.

Of course, that's not how most people treat the stock market. Most beginning share investors hope it will become a "get rich quick scheme" but looking at the long performance of our major stock markets you'll realise that's not the case.

Instead, here are some recommendations on making money through investing in shares, if that's the path you choose (even though I'd rather see you invest the majority of your funds in property):

- Buy and hold blue-chip stocks for the long-term. Disciplined behaviour will ensure your financial success.

- Only invest in industry leaders — don't look for the next "hot" stock because it could just as easily be "cold" tomorrow! No one can time the markets, identify in advance a winning sector or winning fund manager. Therefore looking for the "best stocks" is a waste of time — with enough information and $1 million you are likely to go broke very quickly.

- After you have bought a good stock, the next most important factor is discipline — stay in the market through the ups and downs, hibernate and check your portfolio's performance once a year and then leave it alone. The stock market rewards the patient and punishes the rest.

• Reinvest your dividends to buy more shares — this is another form of compounding as we've discussed in previous chapters.

• Only invest in profitable companies — ones that have had a strong and long earning history — a company that is not making money for itself can't make money for you. Sure, occasionally companies that don't make a profit, like Twitter, rocket up the charts, but don't count on them in the long-term.

• Buy companies with well-known brands that have been in business for a long time but perhaps are innovating and doing something new.

• Never rely on a hunch tip from a friend or that internet newsletter from a self-proclaimed "expert".

• The media do not have your financial futures in mind. It moves from crisis to panic and back to crisis. There will always be negative news to report, so learn to ignore it. Don't make investment decisions based on what you read or hear from a publication built for the sole purpose of grabbing your attention and selling advertising. What bearing will today's crisis have on your retirement plans for 30 years or so down the track?

• The stock market is volatile, but this is always temporary so expect it, yet it is feared by those who don't understand it. When the markets are down strategic investors take advantage of the "big sale". The advance is permanent, the declines are temporary.

• Successful share investing is about "time in" the markets and certainly not about "timing" the markets. Like all types on investment, success share has very little to do with investment returns, but a lot to do with investor behaviour. Investing is more emotional than intellectual. I explain this in great detail in *Rich Habits, Poor Habits* — the international best selling book I've written with Tom Corley — www.RichHabitsPoorHabits.com.

What's the difference between fundamental and technical analysis?

When it comes to stocks there are two different schools of thought — the fundamental approach and the technical analysis, as I mentioned at the start of this chapter — so let's now take a look at each of these.

Fundamental analysis is a method of evaluating a security that involves attempting to measure its intrinsic (fair) value by examining related economic, financial and other qualitative and quantitative factors, like I explained in the previous chapter.

One of the most famous and successful fundamental analysts is the Oracle of Omaha, Warren Buffett, who is well known for successfully employing fundamental analysis to pick securities. His abilities have turned him into a billionaire. I'll have more about his investing philosophy later in this chapter.

The "Holy Grail" of books on fundamental analysis is called *The Intelligent Investor* by Benjamin Graham who was one of Buffet's mentors.

The other camp are the *technical analysts,* who take a completely different approach using charts and computer programs to determine whether stocks are under price or are overpriced. They don't care one bit about the "value" of a company or a commodity. Often called "chartists" they're only interested in the price movements in the market.

They study past market data (primarily share price and volume) to predict future price movements. The theory is that share prices establish repetitive patterns and these can be found by overlaying indicators and trend lines to a chart.

My good friends Louise Bedford and Chris Tate are Australia's leading educators in technical analysis and work on these three assumptions:

1. The market discounts everything.

In other words, at any given time, a stock's price reflects everything that has or could affect the company — including all the fundamental factors the fundamentalists agonise over.

2. Price moves in trends.

This means that after a trend has been established (the share price moves up or down) the future price movement is more likely to be in the same direction as the trend than to be against it.

3. History tends to repeat itself.

Crowd psychology is a major factor behind the repetitive nature of share price movements; in other words, market participants tend to provide a consistent reaction to similar market stimuli over time. Technical analysis uses chart patterns to analyse market movements and understand these trends.

A quick disclaimer: many years ago I tried my hand at technical trading and failed miserably. Despite the fancy computer programs and all the assistance I received from my mentors, my head just didn't work that way — I guess I'm not analytical enough. I made some money, I lost some money, I lost some more and I got out.

If you're interested in going down this route, get some good mentors, get a first class education and start small — tippy toe steps into the market to minimise your risk.

INVESTMENT SUCCESS FACT

The journey to financial freedom is a long one, and you won't arrive at your destination any sooner by rushing, looking for the next "get rich quick scheme" or cutting corners.

The secrets of success

As I've already mentioned, many people consider Warren Buffet to be the world's greatest investor and clearly he's one of the world's wealthiest men. He's also one of the most studied men around — everyone wants to know how he does it and to learn his secret.

An interview with Warren Buffett in 2011 shared some of his secrets so we can all learn to invest with success like him. Here is a brief excerpt:

> *The good news I can tell you is that to be a great investor you don't have to have a terrific IQ.*
>
> *What you do need is the right temperament. You need to be able to detach yourself from the views of others or the opinions of others.*
>
> *You need to be able to look at the facts about a business, about an industry, and evaluate a business unaffected by what other people think. That is very difficult for most people.*
>
> *Most people have, sometimes, a herd mentality which can, under certain circumstances, develop into delusional behaviour. You saw that in the internet craze and so on. I'm sure everybody in this room has the intelligence to do extremely well in investments.*
>
> *You have to come to your own conclusions, and you have to do it based on facts that are available. If you don't have enough facts to reach a conclusion, you forget it. You go on to the next one. You have to also have the willingness to walk away from things that other people think are very simple.*

A lot of people don't have that. I don't know why it is. I've been asked a lot of times whether that was something that you're born with or something you learn. I'm not sure I know the answer. Temperament's important.

Don't do anything in life where, if somebody asks you the reason why you are doing it, the answer is "everybody else is doing it." I mean, if you cancel that as a rationale for doing an activity in life, you'll live a better life whether it's in the stock market or any place else.

INVESTMENT SUCCESS FACT

"You have to do what works, what you understand, and if you don't understand it and somebody else is doing it, don't get envious or anything of the sort. Just go on and wait until you find something you understand."
Warren Buffett

More on picking stocks

So, according to Warren Buffett, you need to be in control of your own investment destiny and a big part of that is your research and education about the companies in which you're considering investing. Of course, this philosophy is the same for property, too.

To further help with your education, I've collated some top tips that are designed as much to avoid losers as to pick winners!

1. Can you explain to a 10-year-old what this business does and how it makes money? You'll make fewer mistakes if you stay within your circle of competence. Pick businesses where you understand how it makes money.

2. Is the company still selling what it did 10 or 20 years ago? Industries characterised by rapid technological change are harder to value and face a greater risk of obsolescence.

3. Is it a high-quality business? Look for companies earning high returns on capital and those with a sustainable competitive advantage. Companies that enjoy economies of scale, brand recognition or network effects, whose customers face high switching costs and whose business models are backed by patents or government/regulatory permits tend to be better investments. The more boxes a company ticks on this list the better.

4. Is management acting in the interest of shareholders? Look for high insider ownership and executive compensation based on performance and earnings per share growth. Beware of companies that regularly issue shares to raise capital and those with overly promotional managements.

5. Is the company's future dependent on factors outside its control? Examples include commodity prices, interest rates and regulatory changes. Aim to own businesses where major external forces are minimised.

6. Does the company have a conservative balance sheet? Companies with net debt-to-equity ratios have 50 per cent or interest coverage ratios below 5.0 are more likely to get into trouble in times of crisis. The less debt the better.

7. Do profits turn into cash available to shareholders? If free cash flow consistently trails net profit, it may suggest a capital-intensive or low-quality business.

8. Are you confident that earnings will be materially higher five or 10 years from now? Ideally, you want to own businesses whose intrinsic value marches upwards over the years and whose earnings are protected against inflation and competition.

9. It's important to consider why others are selling this stock. Can you articulate the "bear" case better than the sellers and explain why they're wrong?

10. Are you being adequately compensated for the risk? All equities carry risks. For all but the safest stocks, you should seek a total return of 10 per cent or more, including dividends and growth in the intrinsic value of the business.

11. Are you overexposing yourself to a single sector or set of risks if you add this stock to your portfolio? Those investments with the least downside should be your biggest positions and speculative investments should only ever make up a small part of your portfolio.

12. What's the worst-case scenario? What errors in judgment could you be making and what uncertainties could hurt this investment? Always seek a margin of safety in your assumptions.

Can you really beat the share market averages?

How can you or I sitting at home with our computer and an online brokerage account possibly get better returns than an institutional fund manager — you know the pension funds, insurance companies, banks, managed and hedge funds?

These institutional investors have significant resources that do extensive research on a wide range of investment options. They have portfolio managers who meet with the company executives of listed companies. They have specialists in every industry and "experts" to evaluate individual companies for investment.

Remember, because of the size of their portfolios, institutional buying and selling greatly influences the price of an individual share as the majority of stock market activity is controlled by these institutions.

And basically, they're a whole bunch of really smart people with a bunch of money under their management looking for investment opportunities.

So how can an individual investor like you or me possibly expect to get better returns that these institutional investors in the share market?

Well … I know some investors can over the long-term. This is partly because institutional investment funds have a short-term focus, because they are typically measured on their short-term performance. Investors looking for a place to place their money regularly compare their recent performance to that of other institutions.

Therefore, they don't have the luxury of time to pick undervalued shares that may take years to show results. It is simply too risky for professional investors to stake their career on a value pick over the long term.

As individual investors we do have time to buy the value shares, when they're cheap, and wait for them to revert to their intrinsic value and provide great returns.

I love Warren Buffett's great quote: "I will tell you the secret to getting rich on Wall Street. You try to be greedy when others are fearful. And you try to be fearful when others are greedy."

In reality, even when fund managers know which stocks have the best opportunity to outperform in the long-term, they often have you make choices that are palatable to the majority of their investors in the short-term, even if it means mediocre returns. And as I've already explained most funds just track the market averages at best.

The lesson from all this is that investing in the share market is complicated, and while for some investors it can be a useful addition to their overall investment portfolio, it's not an easy route to riches.

Don't forget to register your book at <u>www.InvestingSuccessfully.today</u> to access extra resources to help you on your path to investment success.

CHAPTER 21: PROPERTY INVESTMENT VERSUS SHARES

What makes a better investment — property or shares?

Ask Donald Trump and he would say property. Ask Warren Buffet and he'd tell you shares.

When I invest, I look for an asset class that is strong (grows at wealth-producing rates of return) and stable (has minimal volatility — it's price doesn't fluctuate widely). So it should be fairly obvious by now that I believe income-producing residential property is the best option for the average person to develop financial independence.

In essence, while it's really hard to outperform the long-term averages in the share market (that's why many managed funds just try to track the averages), I believe it's very easy to outperform the averages when investing in property.

You do this by buying well and buying the right type of property — one which is in a high growth area and one to which you can add value.

Now just to be clear … I believe there is a place for both property and shares in every investor's portfolio, but there are a number of reasons why I strongly favour property as the main asset class to grow your wealth.

To help you understand why, let me walk you through an example for which I must give credit to Bill Zheng of Investors Direct Financial Services. He showed me this almost 20 years ago.

Imagine you have two assets both worth $500,000. Asset A grows in value by eight per cent each year and give you a four per cent cash return. Asset B grows by 10 per cent per annum and yields five per cent.

Which is a better investment?

On the face of it, Asset B looks much better, doesn't it?

With those sorts of returns Asset A could well be investment grade residential real estate, while Asset B could be a blue-chip share.

	Asset A	Asset B
Value	$500,000	$500,000
Growth % + Yield %	8% + 4%	10% + 5%
Growth + Yield	$40,000 + $20,000	$50,000 + $30,000
Profit	$60,000	$80,000

But it's unlikely you would put $500,000 cash down to buy either asset. To buy a $500,000 property you'd probably borrow 80 per cent of that sum, putting in say $100,000 of your own money (20 per cent).

But the banks may only lend you up to 50 per cent of the value of shares (even in their own stock) meaning you have to find $250,000 of your own money to buy $500,000 with the shares.

Let's imagine you could borrow the money to buy either of these assets at five per cent per annum. This is what the sums would look like:

	Asset A	Asset B
Value	$500,000	$500,000
Growth % + Yield%	8% + 4%	10% + 5%
Growth + Yield	$40,000 + $20,000	$50,000 + $30,000
Profit	$60,000	$80,000
Leverage Capacity	80%	50%
My Money	$100,000	$250,000
Finance	$400,000	$250,000

Interest Rate	5%	5%
Interest Cost	$20,000	$12,500
Net Profit	$40,000	$67,500

It still looks like Asset B (the shares) comes out a clear winner, until you look at the **return on your money invested** — you only needed $100,000 to buy your half million property, but needed two and a half times that amount to buy an equivalent amount of shares.

	Asset A	Asset B
Value	$500,000	$500,000
Growth % + Yield%	8% + 4%	10% + 5%
Growth + Yield	$40,000 + $20,000	$50,000 + $30,000
Profit	$60,000	$80,000
Leverage Capacity	80%	50%
My Money	$100,000	$250,000
Finance	$400,000	$250,000
Interest Rate	5%	5%
Interest Cost	$20,000	$12,500
Net Profit	$40,000	$67,500
Return on my moncy	**40%**	**27%**

So when you look at the return on your own funds — it's 40 per cent if you buy a property compared with 27 per cent on shares — it's easy to see how you get much more bang for your buck's buying real estate.

And it's much the same with commercial property where banks will require you to put in a bigger deposit — usually 30 per cent or more. By the way

… I think commercial property is a great investment for sophisticated investors. In fact, I hold a significant portfolio of shops, offices and industrial properties.

INVESTMENT SUCCESS FACT

The ability to use leverage with real estate significantly increases the amount of profit you can make and, importantly, it allows you to purchase a significantly larger investment than you would otherwise be able to.

Another eight reasons why I prefer property as an investment

1. Property is an imperfect market

When I look to invest, I want to invest in an imperfect market, one where I'm more likely to be able to buy an investment below its true value or sell it above its true value and I've already explained why this is the case in a previous chapter.

INVESTMENT SUCCESS FACT

You can get a good deal in the property market because information, contacts and expertise help you get an insider's edge in an imperfect market.

---

2. You can add value to your properties

By adding value to your property, through buying well or through renovations, you can accelerate its rate of capital growth. On the other hand, the fate of the value of your shares is completely out of your hands — it depends on how well the company, and the directors who run it, perform.

3. Property is a fundamental human requirement, but companies (and their shares) come and go

Unlike a business or corporation in which you can buy shares, property is a fundamental necessity. Everyone needs a roof over their head, whether they rent or own their own home, but let's face it — companies come and go all the time.

As a basic necessity, housing will always be in demand — it will always have value because we simply can't live without it, which gives property the advantage over shares with less risk and greater stability over time — in other words, property is as "safe as houses".

4. We all love property

We all love property — this is partly because property, unlike shares, is a tangible commodity. You can touch it, see it and, yes, live in it, and people like the security associated with property.

INVESTMENT SUCCESS FACT

It is easier to become an expert in property — there are fewer unknowns than with shares.

While you might like to think that you can master the world of shares, online trading and corporate legalities and structures, the simple fact is that it is much easier to gain a sound comprehension of property investment than it is of shares.

Sure, it will require some learning to become an expert in property, but this is far less daunting for the beginning investor than trying to comprehend how the corporate world or the share market works.

5. Property can be leveraged

I've just explained that no other investment vehicle provides you with the opportunity to leverage 80 per cent of its value in order to acquire more of it as a part of your portfolio.

Not only that, if the value of your property investment falls (as may happen in the downward phase of the cycle), the bank doesn't come knocking on your door asking for their money back as they do with margin calls on shares (unless of course you can't meet the repayments).

Even better, once you own property, you can leverage off the growing equity you have in it to buy even more property.

6. Property has a proven rate of return

Property is a proven stable strong investment. When you can look back over 10, 20, 30, even 50 years, you get a picture of exactly how strongly property has increased in value over time.

7. Property values are less volatile than shares

Think about it … residential property is the only investment market not dominated by investors and this effectively gives investors a built-in safety net. Even if all the investors were to leave the market at once, it would not totally collapse.

8. Property is more tax-effective than shares for investment

When you set up your property investment business in Australia there are a raft of legal tax deductions open to you.

Still need convincing?

If you look at the results others have achieved, you have to say that property makes pretty good investment sense.

According to the *Australian Financial Review* annual Rich 200 List, property has consistently been the major source of wealth for Australia's multi-millionaires.

And it's the same all over the world. Those that haven't made their money in property generally invest their surplus funds in real estate.

The property market is now in a more mature phase of its cycle so be careful — not all properties make good investments, however now may be a good time for you to get into the property game.

The right strategy for the right asset

To become a successful investor, you've got to follow the right strategy and then use it on the right investment class.

In my mind residential real estate in Australia is a high growth relatively low yield investment. Investors who try and use a cash flow strategy for properties won't develop financial freedom, but those who invest for capital growth are more likely to do so.

On the other hand, those who've done well in shares generally treat them as an income asset and derive benefit from the ever-increasing tax-advantaged dividends with franking credits. Because, let's face it, the overall value of the share market has gone nowhere over the past decade.

But those who trade shares, try to find the next hot stock or indulge themselves in the endless and fruitless conjecture of market commentary, trying to somehow miraculously divine which direction the market will move in next, are using the wrong strategy and are unlikely to build the asset base they require for financial freedom.

Want some more reasons to choose property?

Think of it this way ... when you own an investment property the tenants go to work to earn a living and then pay you for the use of your property to live in.

Property is also a great investment because you make all the decisions and have direct control over the returns from your property. If your property is not producing good returns, then you can add value through refurbishment or renovations or adding furniture to make it more desirable to tenants. In other words, you can directly influence your returns by taking an interest in your property and by understanding and then meeting the needs of prospective tenants.

There are hundreds of ways you can add value to your property, which will increase your income and your property's worth.

Unlike other investments, when real estate goes up in value you don't need to sell in order to capitalise on that increased value. You simply get your lender to increase your loan.

Another factor that adds to the security of residential property as an investment is that you can insure it against most risks. You can insure the building against fire or damage and you can insure yourself against the tenant leaving and breaking a lease.

Isn't property hard to sell?

I know some people like the liquidity of shares — they're quick and easy to sell, while offloading a property takes time.

If I had the choice (and I do), I'll take stability (lack of big swings in price) over liquidity every time.

I would also avoid "when-to" investments, the type where you have to know when to buy and when to sell. Timing is crucial with these investments, if you buy low and sell high, you do well. If you get your timing wrong, though, your money can be wiped out. Shares, commodities and futures all tend to be "when-to" investments.

I would rather put my money into a "how-to" investment such as real estate, which increases steadily in value and doesn't have the wild variations in price, yet is still powerful enough to generate wealth-producing rates of return through the benefits of leverage.

While timing is still important in "how-to" investments, it's nowhere near as important as how you buy them and how you add value. "How-to" investments are rarely liquid, but produce real wealth. Most "when-to" investment vehicles (like the stock market) produce only a handful of large winners (the millionaires), but there tends to be millions of losers. On the other hand, real estate produces millions of wealthy people and only a handful of losers.

So that's my argument for property over shares as a wealth creation and investment success strategy. It has worked for me and millions of other investors over hundreds of years.

And a way to help with the success of your portfolio is to understand how taxes impact property and the best ways that you can benefit from the system. Let's move on to the next chapter, which is about investing in a tax-sheltered environment.

CHAPTER 22:
WHAT ABOUT INVESTING IN CRYPTOCURRENCY AND BITCOIN?

If you're confused about cryptocurrencies, like Bitcoin and Ethereum as an investment you're not alone.

What you're about to read is a property expert's take on crypto, so I'm not sure if it's worth more than your hairdresser's take on physical fitness. I don't profess to be an expert but let me give you some insights into crypto assets (crypto) also known as cryptocurrencies, coins or tokens which are digital assets that don't have a physical form.

In my mind crypto is a high-risk investment. This is because it is so volatile, often fluctuating by huge amounts within a short period. And I'll declare upfront I don't own any crypto as I'm not prepared to invest in anything I don't understand — and neither should you.

For the first time in history — outside of a widespread markets collapse — a major so-called asset class has lost more than $US1 trillion (A $1.4 trillion) in three months. But that's what happened at the time of writing this chapter in February 2022 as the cryptocurrency market led by bitcoin has fallen more than 45 per cent since its October peak.

Despite this, over the last few years cryptocurrency had made a cultural turn, the price ballooned (and then fell again), crypto buzz had nearly reached societal ubiquity and there has been a sharp 180-degree turn as what was once deemed "fringe" now has long time doubters beginning to embrace it and more investors are becoming concerned if they don't have any crypto exposure. In fact at the end of 2021 more than 2 million Australians held crypto investments.

What is cryptocurrency?

Crypto-assets (crypto) also known as cryptocurrency, virtual or digital assets, is an emerging type of asset class that generally only exists electronically — it does not exist physically as coins or notes, but as digital tokens stored in a digital "wallet". You usually exchange cryptocurrency with someone online, with your phone or computer, without using an intermediary like a bank. Bitcoin and Ether are well-known cryptocurrencies, but there are many different cryptocurrency brands, and new ones are continuously being created.

Anyone can create a crypto-asset, so at any given time there can be thousands in circulation.

People use cryptocurrency for quick payments, to avoid transaction fees that regular banks charge, or because it offers some anonymity. But more and more investors (or really speculators) hold cryptocurrency as an "investment", hoping the value goes up.

While some stores accept crypto as payment for goods and services, and some ATMs let you withdraw it as physical money, crypto is not legal tender in Australia and is not widely accepted as payment. Instead, as I said, it is commonly used as a speculative, longer-term investment, as most people don't access their balance for everyday transactions.

One of the problems for me is that the price of crypto is very volatile as it is not backed by assets and is only worth what people are willing to pay for it meaning the price fluctuates considerably solely based on market speculation. Factors that can influence the price of crypto include, media focus, public announcements, social media and the public actions of individuals who hold large amounts of a crypto or who influence the price through social media (sometimes for a fee).

A major reason for the price volatility of crypto is that some investors and many funds enter the crypto markets with highly leveraged margin deals. Their equity is often geared up to 10 times. This means that they can made huge fortunes when prices rise but they are savaged when prices fall.

However a collective insanity seems to have sprouted around bitcoin over the last decade and it's hard to predict whether this cryptocurrency will become the global reserve currency or a store of value as widely accepted as gold or if it will be just another fad. But the thrill of potential riches has made many investors want to chase the chance for massive profits from investing in bitcoin.

How is cryptocurrency different from normal Dollars?

At its core, money is a token or symbol built on trust, that facilitates an exchange of one's products or services for that token or symbol. Historically, that trust has been forged by virtue of the backing of government entities.

On the other hand, cryptocurrency accounts are not backed by a government or insured by a government like Australian dollars deposited into a bank account. If you store cryptocurrency with a third-party company, and the company goes out of business or is hacked, the government has no obligation to step in and help get your money back.

All this stems back to the 2008 Global Financial Crisis which took down the global financial system and the flow of money came to a standstill. The libertarian cryptocurrency underground took notice and their response to the world's seemingly flawed centralised financial system, was Bitcoin.

Bitcoin runs over a network of computers that belong to many people, spread out across the globe, who are collectively charged with maintaining and validating its ledger of accounts. No government, no banks, no financial institutions, no middlemen. Just like-minded people with computers, glued together with a common purpose — to create a financial system that was independent and decentralised.

The mechanism for validating that ledger is something called Blockchain. Blockchain is encrypted software, or an algorithm. Thousands of individual computer systems must all validate each transaction that occurs on the Bitcoin Blockchain ledger. Because that validation process is foolproof, meaning always 100% accurate, it has slowly built trust for those who use it.

This trust in Bitcoin represents a counterweight to the need for traditional currencies backed or guaranteed by a government entity and run by a complex labyrinth of financial partners that, together, represent the current global financial system.

Slowly, Bitcoin has become a new token or symbol built on trust to facilitate an exchange of one's products or services for that token or symbol. In other words, thanks to Blockchain technology, crypto currencies, like Bitcoin, are quickly evolving from a crypto asset to a form of currency that can be used just like money.

There are now a lot of cryptocurrencies modelled after bitcoin. At the time of writing in early 2022, there are more than 8000 cryptocurrencies in existence, and though some of these currencies may have some impressive features that bitcoin does not, matching the level of security of bitcoins network has yet to be seen. Though many of these cryptos have little to no following or trading volume, some enjoy immense popularity among dedicated communities of backers and investors.

Another major difference to normal currencies is that, as I've explained, cryptocurrency values change constantly and often rapidly, even changing by the hour. This means your investment that's worth thousands of dollars today might be worth only hundreds tomorrow. And, if the value goes down, there's no guarantee it will go up again.

Buying and storing crypto

You can buy or sell crypto through one of the many online exchange platform using traditional money or even PayPal. Some people earn cryptocurrency through a complex process called "mining", which requires advanced computer equipment to solve highly complicated math puzzles.

Cryptocurrency is stored in a unique digital wallet, which can be online, on your computer, or on an external hard drive. But if something unexpected happens — your online exchange platform goes out of business, you send cryptocurrency to the wrong person, you lose the password to your digital wallet, or your digital wallet is stolen or compromised — you're likely to find that no one can step in to help you recover your funds.

And, because you typically transfer cryptocurrency directly without an intermediary like a bank, there is often no one to turn to if you encounter a problem.

Watch out for Crypto scams

The stunning growth of cryptocurrency markets from bitcoin to dogecoin also came with another risk — the steep rise in illicit activity and scams.

In 2021, crypto-based crimes hit a new all-time high with illicit addresses receiving $14 billion, nearly 80% higher compared to the $7.8 billion seen in 2020. These crimes included the ongoing threat of ransomware and NFT (non-fungible token) related frauds. But two rising trends are scamming and stealing funds, with decentralised finance being the common denominator.

This led the Australian Securities and Investments Commission to warn that retail investors face potentially large losses on risky crypto assets and dodgy managed investment schemes and recommend people should seek financial advice before allocating money into riskier assets that they don't understand.

As for avoiding scams, watch out for:

1. Phishing attacks. This is where someone will send you a message, most likely through email, pretending to be someone you are familiar with to gain your trust and ask for your details. If you give your details, either through email or on a website that the message has directed you to watch out — your funds will be removed very quickly! What happens is malware (computer viruses) will look through your device to find your cryptocurrency wallet details and will attempt to drain any wallets that you have of their contents.

2. Imposter websites that have been set up to resemble original, valid startup companies. If there isn't a small lock icon indicating security near the URL bar and no "https" in the site address think twice.

3. Fake Mobile Apps set up by scammers and available for download through Google Play and the Apple Appstore.

4. Bad Tweets and other Social Media Updates. If you're following celebrities and executives on social media, you can't be sure that you're not following impostor accounts. If someone on these platforms asks for even a small amount of your cryptocurrency, it's likely you can never get it back. Just because others are replying to the offer, don't assume they aren't bots, either. You have to be extra careful.

Unfortunately, there are many ways that scammers exploit unsecure the internet to mine or steal cryptocurrency.

The bottom line:

If you don't understand a financial product, don't invest in it. Investing in cryptocurrency is like buying a very expensive lottery ticket; there's no guarantee of a huge payoff.

I recommend you research carefully and learn more about staying safe and protecting yourself in this emerging market before you start investing in cryptocurrency.

CHAPTER 23 : 15 INVESTMENT LESSONS I LEARNED FROM COVID

It would be a shame to allow a cataclysmic event such as the financial disruption of COVID-19 go by without taking some lessons from it — 2020 and 2021 have been among the most tumultuous in living memory, and yet Australia looks set to emerge better placed than almost any other country and our property markets have surprised just about every commentator.

So let's take a look at what home truths can be taken from Covid to make us better investors.

1. The Australian property market is too big to fail

The naysayers and property pessimists were proven wrong. Despite prolonged lockdowns, no immigration, no international students, the threat of high unemployment and all the negative forecasting for Australian housing markets, the value of many homes around the country grew by more than 20% — or by as much as 30% in some locations — in 2021.

The government and banks have a vested interest in keeping the housing market propped up. They are invested with us and when things got tough in the thick of the pandemic, they stepped in to help those in need.

Given the incredible circumstances the past couple of years has thrown our way, the resilience of our banking system is also clear — it is also too big and too strong to fail.

2. The supply of money is important

As I've already explained, property investment is a game of finance with houses thrown onto centre stage. When cash is plentiful (and cheap like it's been in recent years) property values rise.

Now, however, the financial landscape is beginning to change as lenders start to slowly move up their fixed rates and APRA steps in to ensure sound lending practices.

3. The wealth effect is key to consumer confidence

The government knows the best way to guide a population out of a recession is for people to spend their way out. When we feel wealthy, we are more likely to spend money which in turn makes the wheels of industry go around.

Those who held assets and particularly property , be it their homes or investments, have benefited from government stimulus and therefore have been keen to reinvest in the market.

4. Knowledge-based workers have job security

Anyone who could do their work remotely was at an advantage during the pandemic. These Australians were able to "sell" their knowledge, rather than rely on their hands to make money, which meant not only could they work from anywhere, but they were less impacted by lockdowns.

One take away lesson if you are looking to future-proof your career is to consider pivoting to a knowledge-based job if you're not in one already. It means your skills are likely to be in strong demand moving forward, you'll attract higher wages and won't be disrupted in the event of another pandemic meaning you'll have the money to invest in assets.

5. You can't rely on one income stream

Whether it's one job or one business, you need multiple sources of income for financial security — but the rich have always known this.

Next time it may not be another pandemic, it could be a personal health issue or other unique circumstance. If you have an additional passive income from an investment property then you could live off the rent or even sell a property if needed.

The pandemic was a wakeup call for many Australians to save and invests as they realised they were really only a few weeks of lost income away from being broke.

6. Cashflow buffers are important

Having plenty of cash savings provides a safety net in case your income unexpectedly falls, or a large expense crops up.

This doesn't necessarily need to be in cash — it could be in an offset account. Ideally, you would want to hold between 6–12 months of living expenses in cash savings but depending on your financial position and risk appetite it might make sense to hold more. That cash buffer just reduces unnecessary stress and anxiety plus ensures you have sufficient time to make whatever adjustments are prudent, including selling assets.

And clearly this is a lesson many Australians learned as it is estimated we have amassed a war chest of over $200 billion in pandemic saving and an estimated 80% of homeowners overpaying on their monthly mortgage payments.

7. Financial security lets you a sleep at night

Many people have been working hard for years (or decades) and have very little to show for it other than their own home and compulsory super. So building a nest egg outside of these main assets provides greater financial strength to weather any storms — pandemic or not.

If, for example, you lose your job and have liquid investments such as shares, then you know you have a fallback position that doesn't involve selling the roof over your head.

If you haven't been regularly investing, perhaps Covid is your reason to start.

8. Markets will always correct

Property market corrections are not uncommon, in fact major corrections seem to occur every 8–12 years. On the other hand the share market is more volatile and corrections occur much more frequently.

But I don't try to time them, and neither should you.

- I expect there will be another recession in the next decade, but I don't know when.

- I expect the property market will boom over the next few years followed by falling prices, but I don't know when.

- I expect that some investments I make won't do well, but I can't be sure which ones.

- I expect interest rates will rise, but when that will happen, I'm not sure.

- And I also expect there will be another global financial crisis, but I don't have a crystal ball to know when that will occur.

There is a big difference between expectations and a forecast. An expectation is the anticipation of how things are likely to play out in the future based on how I see things have unfolded in the past. A forecast is putting a timeframe on that expectation.

In an ideal world we would be able to forecast what's ahead for our property markets with a level of accuracy, but we can't because there are just too many moving parts.

The lesson is to be ready for times of very high uncertainty so you can stay the course.

9. The importance of investing in resilient large cities

My hometown of Melbourne survived six lockdowns and a total of 260 days of locals confined to their homes during 2020 and 2021. Rather than collapse, Melbourne's property market has shown its resilience and bouncing back strongly. And so has its economy.

The fact that the Victorian capital has a range of different industries is living proof that it makes great financial sense to invest in large cities. The key is to invest in diverse economies that can easily rebound — one reason why I believe you shouldn't invest in regional Australia. No small country town could survive a lockdown the length that Melbourne did.

10. The importance of neighbourhood

One thing I know many of our Melbourne friends missed during the prolonged lockdowns is their "third place".

If our first place is home and our second place is work or the office, then that third place — whether it is the homes of extended family and friends, a favourite café, gym, place of worship, the shops or the local pub — was temporarily taken away from millions of people.

They missed that connection to others and an outlet to take a break from family or colleagues for a short period to reset. All these amenities will be in demand moving forward and have come to be what some refer to as the 20-minute neighbourhood.

Location does about 80% of the heavy lifting when it comes to your property's price performance and some locations will outperform others by 50–100% over the next decade.

So, how do we identify these locations?

It's well known that the wealthier people get, the less they want to be commuting or moving around their city in traffic so they are prepared to (and can afford to) pay for the privilege of living in lifestyle suburbs with a high walk score.

Therefore, lifestyle and destination suburbs where there are loads of amenities within a 20-minute walk or drive are likely to perform well in the future. Many of these suburbs will be undergoing some form of gentrification and will see incomes growing, which will in turn increase people's ability to afford higher prices.

11. The importance of owning the right assets

A-grade property assets held their own during the downturn of 2020. They either maintained their values, or if they did see falls they quickly clawed back any losses in both value and rents.

In a post-pandemic world A-grade homes and investment grade properties will continue to outperform inferior properties. Owning top shelf assets means you can harvest that wealth when the current cycle ends.

12. Houses tend to outperform apartments

While it's nothing new, the price gap between houses and units has never been so large as space became a top commodity throughout lockdowns. Many established apartments are now selling below their intrinsic value or replacement cost because units largely fell out of favour during Covid.

This upward property cycle was led by home buyers, but they weren't all driven by pandemic panic. Millions of Millennials are moving into the family formation stage and are seeking to move out of their apartments and into houses. This shift just shows that the Great Australian dream is still alive.

In addition, pre-downsizers are buying homes for future retirement but are not selling their current homes.

Although I have praised the power of houses over units, I still believe apartments can be great choice for investors on a tight budget.

Well-considered family-friendly apartments in medium- and low-density complexes that are located in desirable lifestyle suburbs may still make good returns.

13. A two-speed property market is on the horizon

Unfortunately, the pandemic has left some members of society struggling financially. There has been a fragmentation in society — those who have been adversely affected by Covid, and those who have not (or have even soared ahead financially).

Moving forward many potential buyers will be priced out of the market as property values have grown by over 20% at a time when their wages have hardly grown at all. This means homes in median and lower priced suburbs are likely to languish at a time when those Australians who are still doing well financially fight of the few properties available in the higher price bracket.

On the other hand, prices at the upper end of the market and in aspirational suburbs will keep growing this year.

14. Immigration is not as important as we thought

Despite our borders being shut for over two years, property values not only kept rising but they have increased at their fastest pace in decades. This was mainly due to the fact Australians are upgrading 'en masse', are making Covid-induced lifestyle changes and are also taking advantage of historically low interest rates.

Simultaneously, markets are undersupplied and so when borders open up completely housing availability will be tight, therefore underpinning property price growth.

We have, however, discovered that immigration is very important for our CBD apartment markets. Without students and overseas tourists, these inner-city suburbs have taken an enormous hit.

15. Building costs will rise

The Cordell Construction Cost Index shows that the costs of building and renovating a home have surged by 7.1 per cent nationwide over 2021 — more than double the rate of inflation. And this is likely to continue as the surge in new construction and renovation coincides with the disruptions to supply chains and a shortage of materials and labour.

This means the cost of new dwelling will have to rise as builders and developers pass on these costs and, in turn, this will pull up the price of established properties.

The Bottom Line:

During the period of financial uncertainty caused by COVID-19 strategic investors took advantage of our property and share markets while others sat on the sidelines over the last few years waiting for the picture to become clear.

It's likely that we'll continue to experience financial uncertainty in the future, so the first step towards your financial freedom is to gain knowledge to take control of your situation. But that's why you're reading this book — isn't it?

And you'll need to have the serenity to accept what you can't control, the courage to control what you can and the wisdom to know the difference .

My suggestion is to get a good team around you and invest in your future — after all you'll be spending a lot of time there.

CHAPTER 24:
THE IMPORTANCE OF INVESTING IN A TAX-SHELTERED ENVIRONMENT

Investing in a tax-efficient way is essential to maximising your investment returns. Otherwise the tax man eats away too much of your profit.

However, due to the complexities of both investing and our tax laws, many investors just don't understand how to manage their portfolio to minimise their tax burden and they end up losing out.

Of course, I don't in any way profess to be an expert on taxation and I strongly advise that you seek professional advice from a good accountant who has extensive knowledge of the tax system and specifically how it relates to investment.

So it's not my intention to give you specific instruction on how to formulate and structure your portfolio in order to maximise the tax benefits, yet I simply want to point out a few of the strategies that the rich and successful use in order to legally reduce their tax bill.

Current tax rates in Australia

If you're an Australian resident these are the tax rates at the time of writing.

Income thresholds	Rate	Tax payable on this income
0 - $18,200	0%	Nil
$18,201 - $45,000	19%	19c for each $1 over $18,200
$45,001 - $120,000	32.5%	$5,092 plus 32.5c for each $1 over $ $45,000
$120,001 - $180,000	37%	$29,467 plus 37c for each $1 over $120,000
$180,001 and over	45%	$51,667 plus 45c for each $1 over $180,000

On top of this the government will charge you a Medicare levy of two per cent.

Add to this compulsory superannuation at the rate of 10 per cent per annum (increasing over the years to 12 per cent) and you can see why I suggest you will never get rich from your salary.

Once you start earning a decent wage the government takes around half before you even see it. That hurts!

One of the big differences between the rich and the average Australian is how they use tax-effective systems and structures to accumulate their wealth. This dramatically enhances the strategies that I've already outlined in this book.

Strategic investors don't just earn compound returns, but accumulate their wealth in a tax-deferred, or tax-free, environment, making their property portfolio grow even faster.

Different strokes for different folks

In Australia, the average salary earner makes their money, hands some over to the government and then gets to spend whatever is left over. The rich, however, have worked out how to make their money, spend the amount they choose on legitimate expenses and then pay tax on whatever is left over.

Have a look at the following figures to see what I mean:

Salary earner		Successful investor	
Income	$100,000	Income	$100,000
		Spend on legitimate expenses	$40,000
		Taxable income	$60,000
Tax paid	$32,000	Tax paid (approx.)	$14,800
Net income	$68,000	Net income	$45,200
Spending capacity	$68,000	Spending capacity	$85,200

You can see by this example that simply by being able to spend money on legitimate, claimable expenses (such as investment-related expenses) the strategic investor has pocketed an extra $17,200 from the same initial income as the salary earner (who handed that $17,200 over to the tax man).

The two main tax types

When you invest, there are two main types of tax that have the potential to affect your profits.

The first type, and one that we all know about because we pay it whenever we earn money, is *income tax*. That is a portion of the income you derive from employment, or investment or any other form of taxable payment you receive from any source. As an investor you are liable to pay income tax on the rental returns of your investment property and on the dividends you receive from your shares.

If you become a share trader, then you will pay tax on any profits you make from your trades in the form of *income tax* as well as the transaction costs and this can considerably reduce the profit you keep in your pocket.

The second tax that impacts property investors is *Capital Gains Tax* (CGT).

When you hold an asset for a period of time and sell it you pay tax (Capital Gains Tax) on the profit, which is the amount it has increased by since you bought it.

CGT is payable on any property you sell where the capital gain itself is more than $30,000, except when it's your own home. The applicable rate of CGT is the same as income tax, however if you own the investment property for more than 12 months, you get a 50 per cent discount on the capital gain. In other words, if you sold a property after achieving a capital gain of $50,000 more than 12 months after the initial purchase, the applicable CGT would be calculated on a capital gain of $25,000.

Of course my property investment strategy entails rarely selling your assets. By holding onto your properties for as long as possible, you will minimise your CGT obligations, as it's only when you sell that this tax is payable.

Similarly, if you invest in shares you're likely to hold them in the long-term, but if you do sell some or all of your share portfolio you will become liable for CGT.

Structuring your portfolio in the correct way can greatly reduce the amount of income tax and CGT you might have to hand over to the government. I won't be discussing the various structures in this book, but there's a whole section on this topic in my book — *What Every Property Investor Needs to Know about Finance, Tax and the Law* (*www.FinancialFluency.com.au*). But there's lots of other tax stuff I'm going to discuss so let's start with …

Leverage and compounding

I've already explained how important leverage and compounding are to growing your asset base.

While some investors are keen to make a fast buck and sell their properties when the market peaks, those who hold on to their assets for the long-term don't have to pay tax on their capital gain. Yet they can access their funds by borrowing against the increased value of their property and use the money as a deposit to buy more property — leveraging.

In other words, you can have your cake and eat it, too. You maximise the profit-generating potential of your properties by using their increasing value to buy even more investments, and you never have to pay tax on any of those profits, unless you sell.

Now here's the thing ... investing in property offers a special type of compounding — the **capital growth** (increase in value of your property) that you achieve is **not taxed**, which means you are left with a larger asset on which to base your compounding the following year.

Let's look at this principle in more detail by reviewing three examples:

Example 1: Your investment dollar doubles in value every year and no tax is payable

Let's see what would happen if you found an investment that could double in value every year. As the table below indicates, after doubling every year for 20 years with no tax payable, your dollar has compounded to more than $1,000,000.

Year	Value
0 (i.e. now)	$1
At end of year 1	$2
At end of year 2	$4
At end of year 3	$8
At end of year 4	$16
At end of year 5	$32
At end of year 6	$64
At end of year 7	$128
At end of year 8	$256
At end of year 9	$512
At end of year 10	$1,024
At end of year 11	$2,048
At end of year 12	$4,096
At end of year 13	$8,192
At end of year 14	$16,384
At end of year 15	$32,768
At end of year 16	$65,536
At end of year 17	$131,072
At end of year 18	$262,144
At end of year 19	$524,288
At end of year 20	**$1,048,576**

After doubling every year for 20 years with no tax payable, your dollar has compounded to more than $1,000,000

It's also a great illustration of how compounding works — look at the exponential growth in the last few years in the graph below. This is another reason my preferred holding time for good investments is forever.

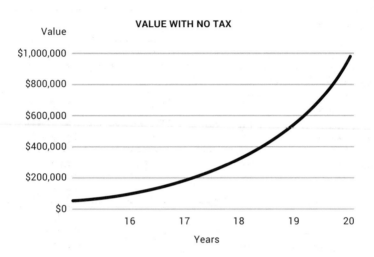

VALUE WITH NO TAX

Example 2: Your investment dollar doubles in value every year and you pay 35 per cent tax annually

Of course the example above doesn't take income tax into account and usually when you earn income, the government expects you to pay tax. So let's see what would happen with the same investment return if you had to pay tax at the rate of 35 per cent of your earnings each year.

As you can see from the table below, after 20 years your dollar has only compounded to around $22,370 because of the effects of income tax, and it takes another seven years for you to accumulate the $1,000,000 you made in the first example.

Year	Pre-Tax Value	Tax Paid	Post-Tax Value
0 (i.e. now)	1		1
At end of year 1	2	0	2
At end of year 2	3	1	3
At end of year 3	5	1	4
At end of year 4	9	2	7
At end of year 5	15	3	12
At end of year 6	24	4	20
At end of year 7	40	7	33
At end of year 8	67	12	55
At end of year 9	110	19	91
At end of year 10	181	32	150
At end of year 11	299	52	247
At end of year 12	494	86	407
At end of year 13	814	143	672
At end of year 14	1,344	235	1,109
At end of year 15	2,217	388	1,829
At end of year 16	3,658	640	3,018
At end of year 17	6,036	1,056	4,980
At end of year 18	9,960	1,743	8,217
At end of year 19	16,434	2,876	13,558
At end of year 20	**27,116**	**4,746**	**22,371**
After 20 Years, your dollar has only compounded to around $22,370			

Boy, does taxing your profits make a difference! Without paying tax (as in the first example) your investments grow much, much faster.

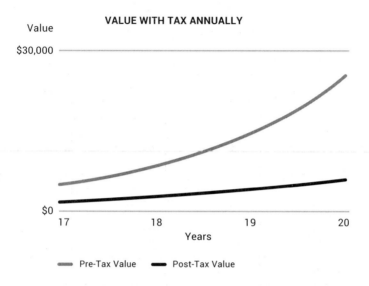

This means that if you can find a type of investment that increases in value (compounds) and on which you don't have to pay tax on this compounding profit, you will be way ahead of the pack. That's the beauty of residential property investment — you don't pay tax on the increasing value of your property unless you sell it. But what if you did want to sell your properties down the track? Let's look at another example to highlight this scenario.

Example 3: Your investment dollar doubles in value every year, but your 35 per cent tax is payable only in the final year

If you buy an investment property, your capital growth isn't taxed unless you sell that property. Using this principle and assuming you won't sell your property until the final year of the exercise, this means you will only pay tax in the final year and in the meantime (as your property's value has been increasing) your dollar's compounding has been uninhibited.

Look at the table below and then compare it to the previous one. Between years 27 and 28, your dollar value has compounded past $200 million. After 35 per cent tax is paid on this amount, the after-tax value equates to a whopping $130 million compared to just over $1 million in the previous example.

Year	Pre-Tax Value	Tax Paid	Post-Tax Value
0 (i.e. now)	$1	0	
At end of year 1	$2	0	$2.00
At end of year 2	$4	0	$4.00
At end of year 3	$8	0	$8.00
At end of year 4	$16	0	$16.00
At end of year 5	$32	0	$32.00
At end of year 6	$64	0	$64.00
At end of year 7	$128	0	$128.00
At end of year 8	$256	0	$256.00
At end of year 9	$512	0	$512.00
At end of year 10	$1,024	0	$1,024.00
At end of year 11	$2,048	0	$2,048.00
At end of year 12	$4,096	0	$4,096.00
At end of year 13	$8,192	0	$8,192.00
At end of year 14	$16,384	0	$16,384.00
At end of year 15	$32,768	0	$32,768.00
At end of year 16	$65,536	0	$65,536.00
At end of year 17	$131,072	0	$131,072.00
At end of year 18	$262,144	0	$262,144.00
At end of year 19	$524,288	0	$524,288.00
At end of year 20	**$1,048,576**	**$367,001.60**	**$681,574.40**

With tax only paid in the final year, your dollar's compounding is uninhibited. Between the 27th & 28th years, your dollar value has compounded past $200 million. After 35% tax is paid on this amount, the after-tax value equates to $173 million.

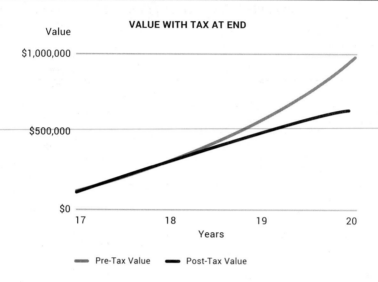

These examples clearly illustrate the benefits of using residential property to grow your Cash Machine. It highlights the fact than not only is compounding a powerful tool in the sense that it allows you to leverage into even more high-growth assets, it also represents tax-free profits that can accelerate your wealth accumulation to breakneck speeds.

How much tax do the rich pay?

Well, we keep reading that most big companies like Google and Apple only pay a fraction of the tax that they should by structuring themselves correctly.

But let's get things straight — while these companies pay a very low tax rate, it's not because they somehow illegally avoid paying corporate income tax. It's just that they use the tax laws to their advantage, and so should you.

One of Australia's wealthiest men in his time, the late Kerry Packer, told a Senate hearing that anyone who didn't minimise their tax "need their heads read" because governments tend to waste a lot of taxpayer money.

Warren Buffett minimises his tax in two ways. Firstly, his company Berkshire Hathaway has only ever paid one dividend. Maybe that's because dividends from company profits in the USA are effectively taxed twice — once at the company level and once in the hands of the shareholders when they receive dividends. This doesn't occur in Australia due to franked dividends.

The second way he reduces the impact of tax is by not selling. Buffett's preferred timescale for holding a quality investment is *forever*. I was interested to read that Buffett, one of the most famous investors of recent history, has been able to defer $61.9 billion of corporate taxes by holding onto his investments for the long-term.

This figure is apparently about eight years' worth of taxes at Berkshire's current rate and a reminder that Mr Buffett understands how putting off the moment when taxes are due gives him more money today to invest elsewhere.

The taxation pros of property

One of the many reasons I prefer property as an investment is because it's privileged with many legitimate tax deductions that allow you to boost your portfolio without any tax penalties. In fact, I've devoted the whole next chapter to these.

The one piece of advice I want you to heed is that you should never make an investment to save tax. I would also like to stress that all of the tax reduction strategies you employ must be legitimate. There are so many ways to legally reduce your tax and it's very difficult to spend your money from a prison cell.

So with these words of warning in mind let's have a look at how investors can minimise their tax obligations and maximise their tax benefits.

Minimising tax as a share investor

The simplest way to minimise your tax as a share investor is to hold your shares for the long-term — just like Warren Buffett does.

In effect this gives you an interest-free loan from the tax department.

Another way is to avoid managed funds who seem to pay a lot of tax because they're continuously buying and selling shares to try and beat the market and racking up Capital Gains Tax and brokerage costs along the way. Instead I would recommend buying indexed funds and holding them for the long-term as these generally have much lower costs of management.

What does it mean for you?

The buy and hold for the long-term strategy offers the average investor the best chance they have of not being average.

But as they say in the ads, there's more …

For Australian property investors there are whole range of tax loopholes that make investing in real estate a very favourable investment. So let's look at these in the next chapter.

CHAPTER 25:
HOW TAXES AFFECT
PROPERTY INVESTING

As the saying goes, there are only two certainties in life — death and taxes. And while none of us can do anything about death, as I started showing you in the last chapter — there are definitely things you can do to legally minimise your taxes.

And this is especially true for property investors, which is the focus of this chapter.

Property and taxes

Just in case you need any further incentive to embrace property investing, how about this: the Australian Government historically wants you to be a real estate investor! Could there be a more powerful ally?

Despite the political discussion about housing affordability and property investors, luckily for us the government recognises that private property investors play an important role in the housing market and economy — that's why there are so many tax advantages available to property investors.

INVESTMENT SUCCESS FACT

My property investment strategy entails rarely selling your assets because by holding on to your properties for as long as possible, you will minimise your CGT obligations.

Structuring your portfolio in the correct way can greatly reduce the amount of income tax that you might have to hand over to the government, which I'll cover a little later on.

Legal tax loopholes

These legal tax 'loopholes" — some would call them benefits of owning investment properties in Australia, largely fit into four main categories:

1. Tax deductions

There is a vast array of legitimate deductions an investor can make in the course of running their property investment business.

2. Depreciation allowances

Many investors don't fully understand these benefits, but depreciation allowances can deliver up to one-third of your rental income tax-free.

3. Negative gearing

Often investors subsidise their loss-making properties, gaining tax breaks while capital growth works its magic.

4. Special benefits

Even more perfectly legal advanced strategies that allow serious real estate investors to get the most from their property investments.

Let's take a brief look at some of these:

1. Tax deductions

If you are in the business of owning investment properties that earns you taxable income, you are able to claim legitimate costs necessary for earning that income. These include, but are not limited to:

Rental expenses

You can claim a deduction for some of the expenses you incur for the period your property is rented or available for rent. These include:

- Advertising costs to find tenants

- Body corporate fees

- Cleaning costs

- Council rates

- Electricity and gas not paid by the tenant

- Gardening and lawn mowing

- Insurance — including the building, contents and public liability

- Interest on your loans

- Land tax

- Legal expenses

- Managing agent's fees and commissions

- Pest control costs

- Quantity surveyor's fees

- Repairs and maintenance

- Secretarial and book-keeping costs

- Stationery and postage expenses

- Telephone bills

- Tax-related expenses

- Travel and car expenses for rent collection

- Costs incurred in inspecting or maintaining your property

- Water charges

- You can also claim your mortgage interest and borrowing costs as a tax deduction.

The expenses incurred in the process of generating your property income are deductible against your total income including your wages for tax purposes and may reduce the amount of tax you pay on the income you earn in your day job through what is called negative gearing. More on that in a moment.

2. Building depreciation

Even though the value of property tends to go up over time, the Australian Tax Office lets us pretend that it actually goes down. In fact, it says that if you own a property it will be worthless in 40 years!

This applies to the building shell, which will age and wear out over time. The fixtures and fittings inside the building can be depreciated over an even shorter timeframe.

What this means is that any residential property in Australia that was built after July 17, 1985, and is owned by an investor for rental purposes, qualifies for an annual building depreciation allowance of 2.5 per cent of the original construction cost and this can be offset against other income on your tax return.

Recently these rules were changed and for second hand (really established — not new) residential rental properties purchased on or after 7.30pm on 9 May 2017, property investors can no longer claim depreciation for previously used plant and equipment. The changes mean that depreciation is not allowed on such assets as floor coverings, air-conditioning and appliances within the property at the time of purchase.

The rules do not change depreciation claims allowed for properties purchased prior to 9 May 2017 and importantly the new rules do not apply to capital works so the deduction for structural (such as the building shell) and fixed items contained within an investment property are still allowed.

Most property investors don't fully understand the impact of these tax breaks. The figure of 2.5 per cent of the cost of construction doesn't sound that much, but it can amount to up to one-third of the income from your investment property being tax-free.

Not many investments can boast that advantage!

Let's look at how this works in more detail: Assume you bought a new house as an investment and, of its $700,000 purchase price, let's say 50 per cent is the actual cost of construction, with the balance being the land value.

Of the $350,000 building cost, 2.5 per cent can be taken as a tax deduction each year. This amounts to a $5,000 deduction every year for 40 years.

Purchase price	$700,000
Construction cost	$350,000
2.5 per cent depreciation	$8,750 per annum

Now you could expect a rental income of say $28,000 each year. Of that $28,000, through the 2.5 per cent building depreciation allowance, $8,750 or **one-third** of your rental income, is **TAX-FREE**.

Rent at $540 per week	$28,000 per annum
Building depreciation allowance (2.5 per cent of $350,000)	$8,750 per annum
Per cent of gross income tax-free	31 per cent

This tax break creates a real distinction between older and newer properties for investment purposes.

Newer is just clearly better from a taxation standpoint. Having said that, as many new properties are bought at a premium or in outer suburbs with lower capital growth, this negates some of the tax benefits.

INVESTMENT SUCCESS FACT

Remember … you should never buy a property just for tax benefits; it's only one of the many factors to consider when making your decision.

And there are likely to be many thousands of dollars of depreciation benefits in established properties also because of depreciation on the fixtures and fittings in the dwelling: items such as the carpets, blinds or hot water systems.

Don't underestimate the value of these depreciation benefits for your investment property. Remember that when you claim depreciation allowances, it doesn't really cost you any money — you are not out of pocket one cent.

Quantifying these amounts is complicated and I suggest you employ a quantity surveyor to prepare a schedule of depreciable items for your investment properties.

3. Negative gearing

Negative gearing is when your rental income doesn't cover the property expenses, such as interest payments, agent's commission, maintenance, etc. This negative result — your shortfall after all deductions including interest that come off your rental income — can be applied to other income, such as your salary, to reduce your total tax liability.

This tax deduction has enticed many high-income earners into property because when coupled with leveraged growth, it can have dazzling results and is currently on the political radar because of this.

But I suggest you be cautious about using negative gearing because it involves producing a loss, and even though after-tax this loss is minimised, it's still a loss and is only recaptured if the value of your property grows.

INVESTMENT SUCCESS FACT

If your property doesn't increase in value, no amount of tax deductions will overcome the fact that you are subsidising the investment.

Negative gearing isn't really a property investment strategy; it's a result of how you finance your properties and occurs when you have a high LVR. It's a typical part of the growth stage for property investors and means they have to cover the cash flow shortfall each month.

One way of doing this is to use some of your surplus income (what's left over after your living expenses) to cover the cash flow shortfall. Or you could set up a Line of Credit when you purchase your property — a loan facility that you won't use immediately but will draw down over time to cover the shortfall for a number of years, until the property's value grows sufficiently to refinance the loan. This buys an investor time.

What you can learn from the rich and successful

I've shown how the rich have more to invest than the average person because they earn their income, spend and invest their money and only pay tax on what is left, as opposed to the average person who earns their income, pays tax and spend what is left.

Of course, your property business doesn't have to be your full-time occupation in order to claim these benefits. You could still be growing your property business in your spare time, while holding down your regular day job.

These deductions work for me because I own a number of companies that earn considerable income through property investment and my property business is clearly my main source of income. Some of these deductions may not be available to investors who only have one property and hand out management of that property to an agent.

MICHAEL YARDNEY'S GUIDE TO INVESTING SUCCESSFULLY

However, as your property portfolio becomes larger, then more deductions will apply to you. Before you consider these, you must consult your tax advisor for clarification on which of the following deductions could apply to you.

A question of structure

All of the sophisticated property investors I know hold no assets in their own name, but control everything through correctly established business and investment structures. This allows them to legally reduce their tax, protect their assets and pass them on to future generations, because they are owned in companies, trusts or a combination of both.

While the main reason investors form business entities to own their properties has nothing to do with tax, how you own your property investments, or more to the point, who owns your investment properties, will affect how much tax you pay.

The main ownership options fall into two broad categories: owning your properties in your own name or owning them through a business structure.

Most first-time investors usually just buy their properties in their own names, rarely considering their property ownership structure, but this is one of the critical aspects of building your property investment business.

INVESTMENT SUCCESS FACT
Even if you're just starting to build your asset base, it's important to begin with the end in mind.

Decide what your property investment business will look like in five or 10 years' time and set up the right structures in advance, before you've created significant wealth. This will save the expense of accountants and lawyers unravelling a maze of incorrectly structured assets.

When considering which structures to use to own your assets, you need to think about the following issues:

1. Liability protection — minimise the risks of being sued.

2. Asset protection — protecting your assets if you do get sued.

3. Legally maximising your tax minimisation opportunities.

4. Accelerating your wealth creation — different structures will have different cash flow outcomes and will help you sustain and grow your property portfolio.

5. Optimising your opportunities.

6. Estate planning — how your assets will be transferred to your beneficiaries after your death.

Common types of investment entities

There are five basic ways you can own your assets in Australia, each with its own benefits and disadvantages. Let's consider them in a bit more detail:

1. Your personal name

The majority of people own their home and investment properties in their own name. When you own investments in your own name, you are taxed at the personal income tax rate, which varies depending upon how much of that you earn. Add the Medicare levy to the equation and it could mean losing close to 50 per cent of your income to the ATO.

There are some *advantages* of investing in your own name including:

• It's a simple and cheap way to operate with minimal accounting and no set up costs.

- If you are a high income earner, you could get income tax benefits through negative gearing.

- Capital Gains Tax concessions are greater for individuals than for companies.

The *disadvantages* include:

- You deny yourself the tax loopholes available to companies and trusts.

- You cannot distribute any income to your partner or children, which means that once you enter the top tax bracket you pay a punitive rate of tax.

- All of your assets are exposed to creditors if you fall into debt or are sued.

- Upon death, your assets are distributed according to your will, rather than continuing on in perpetuity as they would if owned by a company or trust.

2. Partnerships

If you own your investments with another person in both of your names, you are acting as a partnership. Legally, the individuals within a partnership are not treated as separate entities, meaning each person is jointly and severally liable for all of the actions of the other partners. That's fancy legal talk to say that if one of the partners enters into a commitment, you and the other partners are equally responsible.

Partnerships are treated in a special way for tax purposes. They have their own tax file number and their own separate tax return. The partnership doesn't actually pay tax, but the taxable profit is split between the partners and disclosed in their own personal tax returns. This means that partners within this type of structure pay tax at their personal tax rate, which may not be an ideal situation. The advantages and disadvantages of a partnership are similar to that of owning assets in your own name.

3. Companies

The first thing you need to know about a company is that it is a completely separate legal entity. Even if you are a director and own shares in the company, in the eyes of the law and the tax department, it is a separate entity from the owners (who are called shareholders).

But it is not treated like a person, as it is subject to different tax laws and a Commonwealth law called the Corporations Act. Companies lodge tax returns and currently pay tax at preferential rate. In May 2017, the Australian government passed the first phase of the Enterprise Tax Plan, cutting the company tax rate to 27.5 per cent for smaller enterprises and this rate will in time apply to larger companies (with a turnover of over $25 million). Once the company has paid its tax, shareholders receive part or all of the remaining profit by way of dividends.

The *advantages* of a company owning your investments include:

- A high degree of asset protection compared with other structures.

- Tax benefits — companies pay a flat tax rate of 30 per cent, which is significantly less than the highest personal tax rate.

- A number of other tax benefits gained by running a business or holding your investments in a company structure, including tax deductions you wouldn't otherwise be entitled to claim.

- Companies continue until they're wound up, even after the death or retirement of the directors or shareholders.

Some of the *disadvantages* are:

- Companies are generally more complex to operate than owning assets in your own name; there are obligations under corporation law to maintain proper records and lodge certain documents with ASIC and they can be a little expensive to set up (often a couple of thousand dollars). There are also ongoing annual compliance fees involved.

- The extra responsibilities that company directors have under corporation law.

- A company doesn't get the benefit of the 50 per cent CGT (Capital Gains Tax) discount that is available to an individual.

- You can't leave the assets in a company to the beneficiaries of your will — only the shares in the company.

4. Trusts

Most rich people in Australia use trusts to own their wealth. Now I don't know about you, but I think that if the rich and successful are all doing something, it makes sense to understand what it is they're doing and why!

Now the concept of a trust isn't that easy to understand at first, but it's basically where a person or company agrees to hold assets for the benefit of another. The one who holds the assets is called the *trustee* and those who benefit are called *beneficiaries*.

You should never set up a trust for the dominant purpose of reducing your tax. The ATO looks carefully at the reasons why people choose trusts as an investment-owning vehicle and if it is for tax avoidance, then the tax could still be payable. However, there are many legitimate and very valid reasons sophisticated investors own nothing in their own name and everything in trusts.

These include:

- Better asset protection, as properties held within the trust cannot be claimed as compensation if someone tries to sue you.

- Estate planning — you have more control when it comes to determining how your portfolio is divvied up among family members.

- The trust doesn't pay tax on any income it earns. Instead, it distributes the net income to the trust beneficiaries, who then pay tax on their portion of the income at their own personal tax rate.

- The trustee can distribute income in any way they see fit, provided distributions are made to people who qualify as beneficiaries. They do not have to make trust distributions in any particular proportion or in the same proportions as they did in previous years.

- Owning your assets in a trust will allow you (the trustee) to distribute the trust income to the beneficiary who benefits the most in terms of their income tax — those at the top taxable income tier would derive less benefit than those at a lower taxable income bracket.

- You can decide whom to distribute any sales profits to if you sell a property within your trust. Naturally, it would make sense to choose the beneficiary based on their marginal tax rate, in order to minimise the CGT payable.

Some of the *disadvantages* of trusts include:

- They must be prepared by lawyers and require a corporate trustee, so they are a little expensive to establish. But having said that, in the long-term, this structure could save you lots of money.

- The same obligations and responsibilities apply to the trustee as those of company directors.

I haven't included information about Self-Managed Superannuation Funds (SMSF), which are in fact a special form of trust, because this requires specialised advice from your accountant or a financial planner, however I currently own both properties and shares in my SMSF and have done so for many years.

The rules about what you can and cannot do in a SMSF are strict but worth exploring if you have substantial sums stashed away in your super.

What is the right structure for you?

The bottom line is that every investor's situation is different, so there is no one-rule-fits-all approach and you should seek the advice of an accountant or tax solicitor who understands your needs.

Remember how I said to begin with the end in mind? This means that you should imagine what your investment portfolio would look like in the future and have the right structures in place to account for that.

And as there are so many options and the various taxation and ownership structures are complex, it's important that you access expert advice on these matters to help you on our investment journey.

But now let's move away from the numbers and look at something you may find more interesting – the 20 common traits of successful investors.

CHAPTER 26:
THE 20 TRAITS OF
SUCCESSFUL INVESTORS

If you cornered me and asked me to come up with the traits that I have found among the most successful investors that I've ever come across … what would those attributes be?

Obviously, there are a number of important factors underpinning success, but I've come to the conclusion that there really are about 20 traits of successful investors.

I've also discovered that there is one critical attribute that stands above virtually everything else when it comes to creating success in your investing, in wealth creation and, in fact in all areas of your life.

You see … a man once came up to me after attending one of my seminars and thanked me. He said he learned a lot and was inspired.

He then shared with me that he'd been to almost all of the seminars that I'd conducted in his home town over the past 10 years. When I asked him how many properties he owned he told me he was still getting ready to buy his first investment. He was waiting for everything to be *"just right"*.

Of course, I couldn't help but explain he'd be much wealthier today if he had bought almost any property when he first considered investing 10 years ago, even if he had made a terrible mistake in his property selection.

So what is this characteristic all successful investors share?

It's that they make decisions and take appropriate action.

In his classic book *Think and Grow Rich*, Napoleon Hill outlined 17 principles that he found to be responsible for the success of the world's top business leaders of his day. Way back in the 1930s Hill discovered that all of the most successful people had the habit of making swift and committed decisions.

This principle, which is just as relevant today as it was almost a century ago, holds the key to determining the level of success you will achieve.

INVESTMENT SUCCESS FACT

I've found successful investors gather the necessary information quickly, make an informed decision and then take appropriate action. They are able to see the big picture and don't get caught up in the detail.

And even when they don't have all the information they need, they believe it is better to make a decision with some information, than to not make a decision at all. They then take action and gather the balance of the information as they move on.

Of course, they don't always make the right choices. However, over time, the number of correct decisions they make far outweigh the incorrect ones and this propels them to investment success.

It should come as no surprise that others who procrastinate and avoid taking action rarely achieve much success in their lives.

Why is it that taking action is so daunting for many people?

One of the big things that hold back so many potential investors is fear, especially fear of making an incorrect decision or fear of failure.

The problem is that as human beings we like to feel in control. We like to have choices. However, when you take action you've made a commitment towards one choice, thereby eliminating a number of other choices that you could have made. So subconsciously we procrastinate, thinking it has left us with options.

The trouble is we've really made a decision to not make a decision — and that decision has its own consequences.

Do you find it easy to make decisions? Currently the world is riddled with uncertainty and unpredictability. This makes it difficult to be sure of what actions we should take and leads to procrastination.

However, if your life isn't where you want it to be right now, it's likely that you are not making the right decisions or taking the appropriate actions to move forward.

How do successful investors manage to take decisive action?

The fact is that successful investors are faced with just as much uncertainty in their lives as the rest of us however they manage to take action because they have focus. They have clarity about where they want to be.

INVESTMENT SUCCESS FACT

Successful investors follow a plan. They know exactly why they are investing in property. They have a property strategy, a finance strategy and a tax and asset protection strategy.

Every time they have to make an investment decision, they evaluate their actions and the potential consequences in light of their plan and their goals. If the action will move them closer to their goals, they go for it. This makes their investing more predictable, their decisions less emotional and their results more consistent.

It was no coincidence that when I became clear in my goals I began associating with other successful investors who were already very clear in every aspect of their property investing. I don't know who said it … but *"to become successful, hang around successful people"* seems to be a very good piece of advice.

The interesting thing is that when you start associating with successful people, you begin to change without knowing it — you act, talk, think and dress like them. You begin to see things in a positive new way.

The 20 traits of successful investors

Apart from the ability to take decisive action I've found that successful investors have mastered other skills that make it easier and faster for them to achieve financial prosperity. Let's now go through them one by one.

1. Creating and controlling capital

Successful investors understand the importance of building a substantial asset base while the majority of investors look for cash flow.

So it's no coincidence that they control as big an asset base as they safely can by leveraging and borrowing against appreciating assets.

Sophisticated investors also force the appreciation of their assets — in effect "manufacturing" capital growth by adding value to their properties using techniques like renovations and development. They also add value through their expertise or through smart negotiations and buying well.

2. Transforming capital into passive residual income

Successful investors grow money trees and recognise that cash flow is the fruit. This means that once they have built a substantial asset base, they transition into the cash flow stage of their investment life by lowering their Loan to Value ratios and then borrowing against and living off their equity.

Strategic successful investors also follow these four rules of capital:

1. They concentrate it — rather than diversifying, they focus their energy and efforts on their area of expertise.

2. They don't risk it — once they've built a substantial capital base the wealthy invest rather than speculate. They are prepared to forgo a "potential" future profit so as to not risk their current assets.

3. They protect it — by owning their assets in the correct structures to safeguard their capital and by having financial buffers in place.

4. They value it — professional investors don't eat away their capital. Instead they convert their capital into cash flow and live off the fruits of their money tree.

3. They are financially fluent

Smart investors learn how the finance, tax and legal systems work and how they favour investors who treat their investments like a business.

They understand the language of accounting and know how to read balance sheets and income statements, understand how to calculate the Internal Rate of Return on their investments and how to assess their different investment options.

4. They understand the importance of building a great team around them

Successful investors know they can't do it alone; so they recruit, direct and refine a team of finance, tax, legal and property professionals. They know that if they're the smartest person in their team they're in trouble.

While I believe it important to "outsource" the implementation of your investment business to your property strategists, stockbrokers and accountants, you should never "outsource" the knowledge — you can't rely on others for that.

As CEO of their investment business, the wealthy don't abdicate control of their money to others. Instead they set up systems to evaluate the performance of their investments and their advisors.

5. They understand the true importance of money

They recognise that to be truly prosperous, they need a lot more than money — the time to enjoy it, the relationships to share it with, the sense of purpose and passion with which to direct it. And they understand the importance of contribution to the community, which brings meaning to their lives.

On the other hand, I've found that most people who don't have money spend so much time struggling to make money that they lose out on the quality of life they deserve. It's only when you have enough money that you can go about creating real wealth.

6. They have the capacity for growth

Great investors are usually voracious learners. They know the fastest way to wealth is through consistently investing in their personal development.

They read books, attend seminars and cultivate relationships with mentors who can advise and guide them. They also network with other positive wealth-builders with whom they can mastermind and bounce ideas off. It's no surprise that the more they grow, the more their wealth grows.

7. They have a strategy

Successful investors have defined goals and devised a wealth creation plan to help them achieve those goals, allowing them to visualise the big picture yet maintain their focus.

INVESTMENT SUCCESS FACT

Every property purchase they make, or share they invest in, is based on proven investment criteria rather than emotions.

This allows them to say "no" more often, bypassing the mediocre investments to take advantage of great investments.

8. Treat their investments like a business

Smart investors treat their investments like a business, they get the right type of finance and set up financial buffers to buy themselves time through the ups and downs. They establish the correct ownership and asset protection structures and know how to legally use the taxation system to their advantage.

9. They think big

While the average Australian is content on buying a home and slowly paying it off, those who become financially free paint a much bigger picture for themselves. They see themselves building a substantial property or share portfolio that will one day replace the income from their day job.

10. They understand that property is an imperfect market

Successful property investors gain an unfair advantage by acquiring an in-depth knowledge of their selected market because they recognise that real estate is an imperfect market.

11. They understand and accept the risks

Prudent investors understand that there are inherent risks associated with any type of investment, so they educate themselves around the risks associated with the business of property, including fluctuating cycles and interest rates and the inevitable "x factors" that come out of the blue to undo their best laid plans. They take precautions and make the necessary adjustments to their business plan in order to mitigate their risks.

12. They take full responsibility

Successful people are the pilots of their lives, not a passenger going along for a journey. I believe everything that happens to you is a result of your thoughts, feelings and actions — or your lack of action.

INVESTMENT SUCCESS FACT

By taking responsibility for both the good and bad things that happen in your life, you will reduce the number of bad situations that occur and increase the number of good things.

---

13. They find opportunities where others see problems

Some people see the cup as half full, while others see it as half empty. When confronted with opportunities, the average person will find reasons not to do something, yet successful people look for reasons to take action. They find ways to make the situation work.

14. They embrace change

It's often said that "the only constant in life is change". So you may as well see change as an opportunity and take advantage of the prospects that can change the present.

Property markets, the share market, interest rates, market sentiment and supply and demand all change, but whenever change occurs it opens up fantastic possibilities. If you are committed to moving forward, you'll have to step out of your comfort zone, embracing and adapting to the variables that will inevitably come your way.

15. They invest instead of speculating

Speculation is based on hope. Investment is based on facts. Speculators look for the next "hotspot", big thing, latest fad or the next Facebook and *hope* that things will work out. Whereas successful investors take the less sexy, more certain road; recognising that it's not very exciting to buy property and waiting for it to increase in value or shares in a proven business and reap the rewards of steady dividends.

They don't seek excitement from their investments, and they don't speculate.

Rather than trying to pick the next hotspot, successful investors ask questions like *"What has worked well over the past 20 to 30 years?"* and follow a strong longstanding trend.

16. They have learned to use debt wisely

Successful investors are not scared of taking on debt. They have learned how to use other people's money to grow their own substantial property portfolio. While beginning investors use finance to buy properties, sophisticated investors understand that once they have a property portfolio they can borrow against it and use the subsequent finance to fund their lifestyle.

17. They act with integrity

If you commit to do something, always make sure that you do it.

I have seen many people in the investment business tell you that they will do something and then create all sorts of excuses as to why it hasn't happened. Some of them are acting as honestly as they can. Some of them never had any intention of keeping their commitments.

INVESTMENT SUCCESS FACT

To stand out from the crowd you must do what you commit to do.

---

18. *They see the big picture*

Successful investors think of the big picture, recognising that the value of their property, if well-positioned, will double in value every seven to 10 years. Similarly, successful share investors buy into companies with an established product or service with proven long-term demand, knowing the company will still be around making money in one or two decades.

Yet the average investor will worry about fluctuations in interest rates, market confidence, a change in government, land tax changes or other minor details; they become paralysed when analysing the situation, failing to act.

Of course, part of the reason successful investors look at the big picture is that they have a plan and know where they're heading.

19. *They belong to a Mastermind Group*

Successful investors have learned to hang out with "winners" not "whingers". Find a group of like-minded people and meet with them regularly to help you in your investment endeavours. Learn what makes winners and copy their habits.

20. *They think differently to average investors*

I once read that if you want to be successful, you should look at what everybody else is doing and then do the opposite. It's much the same with investment.

You already know most investors fail to reach their objective of financial independence. This means that in order to become successful, you must do the opposite to what the vast majority of investors are doing.

The truth about investment success

Success is not a miracle. Nor is it a matter of luck.

And it's the same with success in property investment, which is clearly what I'm advocating that you consider. While real estate is generally considered a sound investment, by now you know that only a small number of those who get involved in the property game ever manage to eventually develop financial independence.

It probably won't come as a surprise that when you study those who have achieved financial freedom through property investment, you will find they come from a variety of backgrounds, walks of life and educational standards, but there are certain traits shared by all of these successful investors as I've outlined above.

Despite abundant advertisements claiming that property investing is an easy way to wealth, it is in fact a challenging business requiring expertise, planning and focus.

Though it may be relatively simple to enjoy short-lived profits from property, developing a viable, long-term investment business that provides you and your family with financial independence requires additional skill and effort.

Successful investors all share these 20 essential habits. Embrace them and you are already one step closer to the top of the property ladder!

Thank you for staying with me because now we're almost at the end of the book, but first I'd share some final words of wisdom from some of the most successful investors of all time.

But first off, let's take a look at some of the most common investment mistakes.

CHAPTER 27:
COMMON INVESTMENT
MISTAKES TO AVOID

All investors make mistakes — otherwise we'd all be millionaires.

It has nothing to do with their intelligence; I've seen some very intelligent investors make costly investment blunders. And it has nothing to do with the amount of time spent researching the markets or even their level of expertise.

If you can learn quickly from your own mistakes, you're ahead of the game, but if you can learn quickly from other's mistakes, you've won the game. Since all of the investment mistakes you could possibly make have already been made by someone else, let's look at some of the common investing mistakes so you can avoid them.

General Investment Mistakes

Wanting it all right now

In my mind, two of the big killers of an investment career are fear and greed. While fear can stop you from investing, greed can lead you to make poor investment choices, often ignoring the associated risks.

I've seen seemingly intelligent people driven by greed do foolish things because they have succumbed to their emotions rather than analysing their investment position from a place of impartial objectivity.

Of course, it's this greed that infamous spruikers pray on to sell their next flash in the pan, moneymaking system. But the only people who make money from these fly-by-night operations are the operators themselves.

Rather than become a victim of your emotions, work on formulating a sensibly balanced investment strategy that accounts for your long-term goals and outlines the steps you need to reach them, all the while thinking about how you can maximise your time and money in the market while also minimising risk.

Sure, if you take this approach you won't make a million dollars overnight, but you will reach your goals sooner without having to suffer any significant financial losses along the way. Remember, if it sounds too good to be true, it probably is.

Not getting an education

Getting an education is a critical part of becoming a successful investor. It's much easier and less costly to educate yourself than to make mistakes in the real world. We are lucky to live at a time when educational opportunities abound — this is very different to when I first started investing when there were only a few books to read and the occasional tape set to buy.

INVESTMENT SUCCESS FACT

Great investing is taking action while average investing is about reacting.

Surprisingly, though, not everyone takes the initiative to learn before they invest, which exposes them to costly mistakes that may have easily been avoided. It amazes me how some beginners complain that the books, courses or seminars are too expensive. I understand how a novice with limited funds may think this way but as the saying goes, "If you think education is expensive, try ignorance."

Not getting an education from the right people

On the other hand, while the internet is a great tool, it's saturated with too much information, both good and bad, and unfortunately novice investors don't have the perspective to sift through the clutter nor to separate the noise from the quality. Just because someone has a blog or podcast, doesn't mean they necessarily know what they're talking about and the misinformation you read may be costly.

Paralysis by analysis

Some would-be investors get so caught up in researching for the right areas to invest in property or the best share investments — to the point where they can rattle off historical prices in their sleep — but then scare themselves out of the game and never end up buying anything.

We call this roadblock *paralysis by analysis*, which is usually grounded in the fear of making a mistake.

After all, it's human nature not to want to fail, and with the potential to make an investment mistake and lose money, it is often easier to do nothing because at least you won't be any worse off than you already are.

But maybe that's not really true … while not investing can prevent you from making a loss it often costs you significantly in terms of lost opportunity — which is the profit you could have made if you had invested.

Let's look at what might happen if you do nothing. In 10 years' time, rather than having built the foundations of a successful, wealth-generating property or share portfolio, you will be in the same position you are today … worrying about the uncertainty of your financial future and probably with less spending power because of the damage done by inflation.

INVESTMENT SUCCESS FACT

Not doing anything is really a loss — it's an opportunity cost that in itself is very expensive.

Reading books, subscribing to blogs, listening to podcasts and dreaming about your future fortune isn't going to make you any money. Knowledge is only power once you begin to apply it. Acting and making a mistake is better than not taking action, because you can learn from your mistakes and get it right the next time. And once you've already done it, the next time is far less daunting.

Put simply, while some beginners put off taking action because they're still searching for that magical "secret" that is going to make a fortune without risk, not taking action is a sure way to fail.

Having unrealistic expectations

Most beginning investors have unrealistic expectations. This is loosely related to overconfidence. Ask people if they have the ability to pick stocks or properties that will deliver above average returns and you may be surprised by how many think they can.

Investments rarely go exactly as planned. When you're unreasonably optimistic you are just readying yourself for a disaster. Experienced investors understand the importance of planning for the unexpected. This way, when things don't go as planned, it's not the end of the world.

Not being patient

When starting out it can take a while for investors to see positive results and it takes years for your investments to grow to a significant size where you'll start to feel a level of financial security.

But then again, there aren't too many businesses that become profitable immediately. It often takes several years for businesses to get to a point where they make steady and reliable profits and it's the same with your investment business. Remember Warren Buffet once said: *"Wealth is the transfer of money from the impatient to the patient."*

Bad money management skills

Another common mistake I see is spending too much time finding out all you can about property or shares, without first learning the fundamentals of budgeting, money and finance. Building and managing a successful investment portfolio comes about by recognising that you need to be equally good at managing your money as you are at managing property or a share portfolio.

Getting caught in the income trap

Most people are caught in a rat race — they're trapped on that little mouse wheel chasing the cheese, because they are under the false impression that the way to become rich is to increase their active (working) income.

It goes like this … the majority of people start their working life earning $60,000 to $80,000 a year and manage to survive. They rent a small place or continue to live at home with mum and dad. Eventually they get a bit of a raise, and what do they do as soon as they get that bit of extra money? They buy their first car.

All of a sudden, that extra income is spent, plus a bit more because they usually haven't budgeted for all the costs associated with car ownership like petrol, insurance and maintenance. So they work a little bit harder and turn up the speed on the treadmill just that little bit more.

Sometimes they take on a part-time job in order to afford the luxuries they now expect. Then they advance into a higher paying position and earn a little bit more. When that happens, they want to replace their second-hand furniture or their old car. And on it goes — as they earn more they spend more and tend to hit that button on the treadmill to make it go just a bit faster in order to try and keep up.

Then they find a partner or significant other and the expenses increase again. Sure their partner might bring in some extra income, but there just never seems to be any money left over at the end of each week. They buy a house then have to furnish it and the outgoings keep increasing. Once again, the speed of the treadmill increases. They have to earn more just to break even.

Fast forward a little and our typical couple have a baby, which usually means that one income disappears for a time.

Others decide to start their own business, rather than work for a boss. Sometimes this works out, but more often than not the business doesn't advance as expected and their income declines. Alternatively, the business goes well and the business owner buys themself a flashier car or moves into a bigger house as their family grows up. More income rolls in, but more expenses drain that extra income out. It's interesting how the treadmill just seems to be getting faster and faster.

When you focus on income, you tend to fall into the trap of spending all the money you earn (and then some) in an attempt to support your increasingly expensive lifestyle. You're effectively stuck in the rat race. The problem is when you focus on income you can't get off the treadmill. More income, without the right financial understanding, habits and skills, is every bit as dangerous to your financial success as too little income.

INVESTMENT SUCCESS FACT

The solution is to get off the treadmill and create passive recurring income, which is money that comes in even if you don't go to work.

Learning to save like middle income people

Many of us have been taught to set aside five to 10 per cent of our income to build a nest egg for retirement and/or put our money into superannuation.

"What's wrong with this?" you ask, "Isn't saving a nest egg to fund my retirement a smart move?"

It is if your goal is to be middle income. But this approach will never get you beyond Level 1 or 2 on the Wealth Pyramid. Let me explain why …

Most people try and save their "after tax" dollars in wealth vehicles they have no real understanding of, or control over, handing their money over to financial planners hoping they will do all the work for them. I've already explained this rarely works well.

More importantly, the concept of "building a nest egg" is inherently flawed. Your goal should not be to accumulate a lump sum of money to retire on and slowly spend, hoping you don't outlive your money.Z

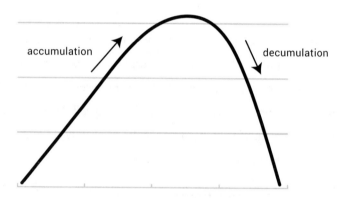

Rather I want you to build an asset base that will generate ongoing passive income. This is the Cash Machine I spoke of earlier — a self-perpetuating money machine that won't run out over time like the traditional "nest egg".

NEW LIFE CYCLE CONSUMPTION THEORY

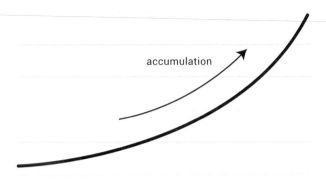

Thinking investing is too difficult

Many people feel that they just can't do it or are too busy to invest, so they take the path of least resistance and don't do anything about their financial independence. How many people have you met who did nothing for 40 years and ended up wealthy? Not many.

INVESTMENT SUCCESS FACT

Wealthy people planned, invested, took action, learned from their mistakes (and the mistakes of others), consulted with experts and took charge of their own financial affairs.

Notice I said that they consulted with experts? The sad reality is that most people aren't prepared to pay for good financial advice. They'll go to a "cheap" accountant or financial planner, but usually find the cheap advice they receive is very expensive in the long run because it won't help them to achieve Level 4 wealth.

Others commence the climb up the Wealth Pyramid but get tired and give up along the way, because they're running on that treadmill and can't see the light at the end of the tunnel. They can't see themselves getting anywhere; they just know they are working too hard so they give up.

Getting "free" advice

Look, I'm sure your friends mean well, and just about everybody has an opinion on investing in property or shares. Yet few of them have actually made money investing. It's much the same when taking advice from sales people pretending to be advisors — if they're being paid by the property developer who's project they're recommending or the investment product they're suggesting your put your money into — that's not independent advice.

The most expensive advice is free advice that is wrong! Be prepared to pay for good independent and unbiased advice — that's what successful investors do.

Property investment mistakes

Learning to invest in real estate is one of the best decisions I've made for my financial health. However, it can be a minefield that has derailed many an investor over the years because it can be risky if you don't know what you're doing. Knowing the most common mistakes and how to avoid them can help you limit your risk and maximise your chances of a good return.

So, let's look at some of the common property investment mistakes:

Heart over head

When buying a home, often 90 per cent of your purchasing decision will be based on emotion and only 10 per cent on logic. This is understandable, as your home is your sanctuary.

However, when it comes to investing in real estate, don't let emotion drive your decision.

INVESTMENT SUCCESS FACT

As an investor, the only good reasons for falling in love with a property are that it fits your strategic property plan, the numbers are right, it has more upside potential than issues and it will help you meet your financial goals.

I've found many people buy their investments close to where they live, where they like to holiday or where they hope to retire — all emotional decisions and not necessarily good places to invest.

With less than four per cent of all properties on the market being what I call "investment grade", you can't allow your emotions to cloud your judgment. You should always buy an investment property based on analytical research.

When you fail to plan you plan to fail

It's an old adage but very true. The main reason most people don't get what they want is that they don't *know* what they want. Setting yourself goals and then planning to achieve them is a crucial aspect of financial success.

Fast forward 10 or 15 years: How much income do you want your property portfolio to give you? How many properties will you need to achieve this? What type of property do you need to buy in order to meet your goals? How are you going to finance them? What skills are you going to need to learn? Who do you need in your team to help you achieve your goals?

Plan your action and then action your plan.

Speculation over patience

I've seen so many people get into property investment hoping to become overnight millionaires. They think property will be a quick fix to their financial problems, but the truth is expecting a short-term gain in real estate is really speculation rather than strategic investing.

To me, real estate is a long-term play, not something you can easily buy and sell at a profit — even after you've improved it with renovations.

INVESTMENT SUCCESS FACT

Rather than trying to profit from buying and selling, the way to make money in property is to use the equity you earn from the tax-free capital growth of your property as the deposit for your next purchase.

Not doing your homework

Many people think they understand property because they live in a house or apartment, but they don't really understand the fundamentals of property investment.

Firstly, you need to become familiar with the big picture — things like the economy, the property cycle, finance, tax and the law. Then you've got to become an area expert by developing an "investment comfort zone" — a territory you become familiar with.

Buying the wrong property

One of the most common questions I'm asked is, "What is the best investment property?"

Of course, there is no simple answer — but the short answer is that you have to own the sort of property that will be in continuous strong demand by a wide range of owner-occupiers (who will push up the value of similar properties) and tenants (who will pay you rent to help meet your mortgage payments).

But I've already explained this in the chapters on property investment.

Poor cash flow management

Make sure that you can afford to hold onto any property that you buy. In other words, how much income will your investment generate and if it won't be enough to cover your outgoings how will you manage the shortfall?

Don't forget to account for any contingencies, such as vacancy periods or unexpected maintenance costs. A good rule of thumb is to allow close to 20 per cent of the property's gross rental for costs such as rates, land taxes, insurance, maintenance and management fees.

INVESTMENT SUCCESS FACT

Strategic real estate investors not only buy a property but also buy time allowing their property to increase in value. They do this by having financial buffers in place.

Financing faux pas

By the way … low interest rates are the least important reason to choose a particular type of loan. There are so many finance considerations when buying an investment property that I recommend that you engage an investment-savvy finance broker to help you through the maze of banks and lending institutions.

Don't even think about self-managing

I know some investors think that by self-managing their properties themselves — that is, finding their tenants and acting as their own property managers, collecting rents, organising maintenance and so forth — they will save a packet and have better control. Wrong, wrong, wrong!

It's just too hard and time consuming. You have to find and qualify suitable tenants, know the laws pertaining to renting, have a firm grip on the value of your rental, conduct regular inspections to ensure your tenants are looking after your asset, collect the rent, represent yourself at tribunal should things go awry, deal with all the maintenance issues that crop up and be on call 24/7 for your tenants. Sound appealing? I didn't think so.

Paying a professional property manager to handle all of these things on your behalf will not only mean you get the best outcome for your rental property, it will also give you something just as valuable as money when it comes to investing — time.

The time spent managing your properties could be put to far better use … finding more investments to add to your portfolio and generating even greater wealth.

Not having a plan

Lack of a good plan is the biggest mistake made by new investors. Many make the mistake of buying a property because they think it's a great deal, and then trying to see how it fits into their plan, or creating a plan around the property. Putting the cart before the horse, so to speak, is always a bad idea.

Good property investment involves developing a strategic plan and sticking to it over the long-term.

Thinking you can do it all on your own

It's imperative that you have some key team members in place before you start investing.

As I've mentioned in previous chapters, the rich and successful have a team of people around them, including mentors, who help him achieve their goals. Importantly, they're not afraid of paying for sound advice that is ultimately going to make them money.

Believing the hype

We've all seen those ads. You know, the ones that say it's easy to become a multi-millionaire overnight with real estate or how to buy 10 properties in ten years or seven properties in seven minutes.

The truth about property investing is that it's a long-term wealth creation strategy. The real capital growth usually only starts kicking in when you've owned a property for seven to 10 years and then exponentially increases from that time on, which is when your wealth really starts to grow.

Patience is a virtue for many reasons but especially in property investment.

Shopping without getting finance preapproval

Having financial pre-approval does several things for you when it comes to property investment. It gives you a general idea of how much you can afford, allows sellers to take you and your offer seriously, limits how much risk you take and gives you the confidence to make a decision.

Without understanding your true borrowing capacity, it really is a waste of time to search for property that you have no idea whether you can afford or not.

Paying too much

Once again, don't let your ego or your emotions drive what you pay for a property. Get to know your investment patch so you'll know what top dollar you can pay and still have a good investment. Don't go over that amount — walk away — there is another deal out there waiting for you and it's probably just around the corner.

Looking for the one big deal

Unfortunately, I've met a number of would-be investors in my time who have been researching the market forever looking for the "perfect deal". Sometimes their search goes on for years and years and they never end up buying anything at all because they're foolishly looking for the ideal deal.

Meanwhile, those investors who took the plunge on properties that met their fundamentals, or which they could improve through renovations and the like, saw their wealth grow and grow.

The perfect deal doesn't exist, but there are plenty of investment grade properties out there if you know what to look for.

Under-estimating the cost of renovating

Many novice renovators underestimate the true cost of renovating. They over-pay for materials or perhaps think they are saving themselves money by attempting to do the majority of it themselves.

Using experienced tradespersons may cost money, but they're experts and can get the job done quickly and well, which means the property can get back on the rental or sales market sooner.

Stock Market Mistakes

Trying to outsmart the market

A lot of people try and time the market — buying low and selling high but the reality is that you really can't "pick the market". Certainly you can get lucky and it can happen once or twice for you, but you can't build a successful investment strategy on this because it's not something you can replicate.

Not having a system to track investments

Beginner investors may think that after buying shares or investing in their superannuation they can settle back and let the money roll in. You need to have a system, a strategy that works for you and regularly review the performance of your investments.

Following "hot stock tips"

From the taxi driver to the financial talking heads on TV, it seems everyone is an expert. Most stock tips have no substance and if somehow you get a tip that is based on accurate information from someone close to the company, you may be found guilty of insider trading.

Overtrading

This book is about investing and that's very different to trading shares, selling your holdings and buying new shares trying to make a small profit along the way. Frequent trading, chasing the quick dollar or the next hot stock is generally associated with lower returns. Put bluntly — *trading is hazardous to your wealth.*

Day trading stocks is like smoking. It's amazing that we let people do it on their own but require manicurists to do a three-month course.

Blindly following a strategy

Look around and you'll see people peddling all sorts of supposedly sure-fire investments and investing regimens. Recently, for example, some advisors have touted "The Warren Buffett Portfolio," essentially a mix of 90 per cent stocks and 10 per cent bonds, designed to ensure that you don't outlive your nest egg in retirement.

But just because the name of a well-known investor or investment firm is attached to a strategy or because a strategy has generated impressive results in the past doesn't mean you should hop aboard.

INVESTMENT SUCCESS FACT

You need to develop an investing strategy that's right for your particular situation and goals.

Investing in the wrong asset

This applies equally to shares and property. The quality of the assets you invest in has the greatest impact on our investment returns.

You need to select the most appropriate class of asset, in terms of risk and return, for your personal situation and then find the highest quality investment within that asset class.

A good quality asset means an investment asset that is expected to provide strong returns driven by sound, logical and proven investment fundamentals.

For example, if you're still at the asset growth stage of your investment journey, it would make no sense to invest the majority of your money in term deposits as you'll get no capital growth. Similarly, if you're nearing retirement and transitioning to the cash flow stage of your journey, you shouldn't be embarking on a highly geared property investment.

Cutting out the costly mistakes

No matter how hard you try, you won't avoid mistakes. The key, though, is to recognise when you've made a mistake and to minimise its impact on your portfolio. If you can do that, you'll have come a long way towards creating the perfect investing strategy.

Of course, you can minimise them by putting together a well-formulated investment strategy and action plan based on your clearly defined financial goals and, most importantly, the reality of your situation.

Planning is key with everything really and investment is no different. You wouldn't build a house without a set of plans or drive to a destination without first thinking about the best route to get you there. The same applies to investing.

Embarking on the planning process makes you consider certain things that you might otherwise neglect to account for if you just jump in, feet first, such as the most appropriate assets for your risk profile and anticipated rewards.

In turn, you are more likely to devise a very clear and concise roadmap to take you safely to your financial destination — hopefully without too many diversions along the way.

You should also build a system around the investment decisions you make, applying rules to the process in order to maintain that objective step-by-step mentality you will need to succeed.

This might be something like only investing in property in gentrified suburbs in the three big capital cities of Australia. Or you may only invest in shares in companies who's dividends are "x" per cent.

You see how in applying these types of rules and systems, there is less chance for you to get caught up in emotional, reactionary investing because you are basing your decisions on proven axioms that are the very foundation of the property market itself and, in turn, maintaining a disciplined investment approach.

Never stop learning and don't be afraid to ask

Wall Street's Gordon Gekko infamously coined the saying, "Greed is good" in the now widely-quoted eighties movie starring Michael Douglas. He also said, "the most valuable commodity I know of is information."

What I'm trying to say is that you should invest in your learning to the point where you are a confidently "informed" and "aware" investor. Being informed means you are less likely to find yourself derailed by those "get rich quick schemes" I mentioned earlier and ensures that you maintain control of your investment journey.

You don't need to know it all, but you do need to know enough so that you can apply your own logical, objective thought process to any decision-making that happens around your investment portfolio. One of the worst things you can do is hand the reins to an advisor and just expect them to act on your behalf without any further input. Remember, it is your journey and your destination.

Educated investors will then wisely seek counsel that is appropriate for them at any given time. They know the value of an independent opinion, and importantly, possess the knowledge to objectively seek out the right advice from the most credible source and then evaluate the information they receive in line with their overall investment plan.

From this point, they can confidently make a decision and then action it accordingly.

CHAPTER 28:
100 INVESTMENT LESSONS I'VE
LEARNED FROM THE EXPERTS

Everything I know today I've learned from someone, and I guess they also learned their craft from their teachers and mentors.

As we're reaching the final pages of my book, I thought I'd leave you with 100 of the best lessons, ideas and words of wisdom I've learned from a small handful of my many teachers and mentors.

Great quotes from Robert Kiyosaki

Many investors I know got started by reading one of Robert Kiyosaki's books and I've certainly learned a lot from him. While his "cash flow" real estate concepts don't work well in Australia and his predictions of economic Armageddon have been wrong for the last decade or so, his early investment philosophy is based around encouraging people to become financially educated and to take an active role in investing for their financial future.

Here are 19 great quotes from Robert Kiyosaki:

1. "It's not how much money you make, but how much money you keep, how hard it works for you, and how many generations you keep it for."

Kiyosaki hits the nail on the head on making sound investment choices. He reminds us to focus on the long-term capital gain and making that investment work hard so that you'll have something left to hand over to your loved ones.

2. "Losers are people who are afraid of losing."

3. *"If you are the kind of person who is waiting for the 'right' thing to happen, you might wait for a long time. It's like waiting for all the traffic lights to be green before starting the trip."*

4. *"People think that working hard for money and then buying things that make them look rich will make them rich. In most cases it doesn't. It only makes them more tired. They call it 'keeping up with the Joneses' and if you notice, the Joneses are exhausted."*

5. *"The wealthy buy luxuries last, while the poor and middle-class tend to buy luxuries first. Why? Emotional discipline."*

6. *"Jobs are a centuries-old concept created during the Industrial Revolution. Despite the reality that we're now deep in the Information Age, many people are studying for, or working at, or clinging to the Industrial Age idea of a safe, secure job."*

7. *"The only difference between a rich person and a poor person is what they do in their spare time."*

8. *"The poor and middle-class work for money. The rich have money work for them. The rich buy or create assets that work for them so they don't have to."*

9. *"Critics only make you stronger. You have to look at what they are saying as feedback. Sometimes the feedback helps and other times it's just noise that can be a distraction."*

10. *"You need to understand the difference between an asset and a liability. An asset puts money in your pocket and a liability takes money from your pocket. The rich understand the difference and buy assets, not liabilities."*

11. *"The rich focus on their asset columns while the poor and middle-class focus on their income columns."*

12. "Often, in the real world, it's not the smart that get ahead but the bold."

13. "The size of your success is measured by the strength of your desire, the size of your dream, and how you handle disappointment along the way."

14. "Most people never get wealthy simply because they are not trained financially to recognise opportunities right in front of them. The rich have learned to recognise opportunities as well as how to create them."

15. "There are three very important money skills that everyone should possess: how to earn money, how to manage it and how to invest it."

16. "Financial freedom is available to those who learn about it and work for it."

17. "Your future is created by what you do today, not tomorrow."

18. "The richest people in the world look for and build networks; everyone else looks for work."

19. "People say 'I want to be rich'. The question is, 'Are you willing to do what it takes?'"

Savvy insights from Morgan Housel

Morgan Housel was a columnist with Motley Fool (*www.Fool.com*). He now writes for the Collaborative Fund www.CollaberativeFund.com. He has an economics degree so you could say that he knows his stuff. I love reading his insights, so here are some of his best quotes followed by his musings:

20. Nine out of 10 people in finance don't have your best interest at heart

Housel explains: Wall Street is a magnet for some of the nation's smartest students hailing from the best universities. And let me tell you, few of them go into finance because they want to help the world allocate capital efficiently. They do it because they want to get rich.

And the fastest and most reliable way to get rich on Wall Street isn't to become the next Warren Buffett. It's to find people gullible enough to pay outrageous fees and commissions on products that rarely beat a basic index fund.

21. Tune out the majority of news

A 24-hour news cycle is built for people who can't see more than 24 hours ahead. That's why a long, slow, but very important rise in domestic energy production is rarely mentioned, but when the Dow falls 20 points it is "breaking news".

Atlantic writer Derek Thompson wrote: "I've written hundreds of articles about the economy in the last two years. But I think I can reduce those thousands of words to one sentence. Things got better, slowly." That's all you needed to know. The rest was noise.

22. Emotional intelligence is more important than classroom intelligence

Take two investors, for example. One is an MIT rocket scientist who aced his SATs and can recite pi out to 50 decimal places. He uses leverage and trades several times a week, tapping his intellect in attempt to outsmart the market by jumping in and out when he's determined it's right.

The other is a country bumpkin who didn't attend college. He saves and invests every month in a low-cost index fund come hell or high water. He doesn't care about beating the market. He just wants it to be his faithful companion.

Who's going to do better in the long run? I'd bet on the latter all day long.

INVESTMENT SUCCESS FACT

Successful investors are those who know their limitations, keep their heads cool and act with discipline. You can't measure that.

23. Talk about your money

Investing isn't easy. It can get emotional. It can make you angry, nervous, scared, excited and confused. Most of the time you make a decision under the fog of these emotions, you'll do something regrettable.

So talk to someone before making a big money move. A friend. An advisor. A fellow investor. Just discuss what you're doing with other people.

24. Forget about past performance

Whether it's a stock or mutual fund, one of the worst (but most common) ways to size up an investment's potential is by looking at past returns.

A stock that's gone up a lot in recent years doesn't say anything about where it might go over the next few years. In fact, investments that have done exceptionally well in the recent past should be a red flag, as they have a higher likelihood of being overhyped and overvalued.

You should buy stocks that:

- You understand.
- Have a competitive advantage.
- Sell for attractive valuations.

Past performance should have nothing to do with the decision.

25. The perfect investment doesn't exist

Gold, often touted as the bastion of stability, fell nearly 70 per cent from the 1980s through the early 2000s. Treasury bonds lost 40 per cent of their inflation-adjusted value from the end of World War II through the early

1980s. Stocks, nearly unquestioned as the greatest investments in 2000, fell 40 per cent by March 2009. And real estate … well, you know.

Housel says: Investing is risky. Bad things happen eventually to *all* assets. Valuations get out of whack, industries change, managers screw up, politicians make terrible decisions and things don't always work out as expected. Diversification is key. As are patience, an open mind, and an ability to ignore crowds and hype.

26. "There will be seven to 10 recessions over the next 50 years. Don't act surprised when they come."

27. "Not a single person in the world knows what the market will do in the short run. End of story."

28. "However much money you think you'll need for retirement, double it. Now you're closer to reality."

29. "The most boring companies — toothpaste, food, bolts — can make some of the best long-term investments. The most innovative, some of the worst."

What Charlie learned from George

Charlie Munger is Berkshire Hathaway's visionary vice chairman and Warren Buffett's indispensable financial partner, and he's outperformed market indexes again and again.

His notion of "elementary, worldly wisdom" — a set of interdisciplinary mental models involving economics, business, psychology, ethics and management — allows him to keep his emotions out of his investments and avoid the common pitfalls of bad judgment.

Here are seven lessons Charlie learned from George Soros, who is the chairman of Soros Fund Management and one of the richest men in the world with a net worth of about $25 billion.

30. "Money is made by discounting the obvious and betting on the unexpected."

George Soros, like other great investors, is very focused on "expected value". Expected value is equal to the weighted-average value for the distribution of possible outcomes (the payoff for a given outcome is multiplied by the probability that this outcome will occur). A bet which is unexpected by the crowd is only wise when the expected value of the bet is positive. Yes, Soros can make huge macro bets that others do not. No, his approach to investing is not fundamentally different from other great investors when it comes to process.

31. "The financial markets generally are unpredictable, so one has to have different scenarios."

Just because markets are often predictable doesn't mean that they are always unpredictable. If an investor is patient and waits for the rare instance when they successfully spot a mispriced bet, they can beat the market and generate alpha.

32. "The hardest thing to judge is what level of risk is safe."

Risk is the possibility that you may suffer harm or loss. Three situations must be faced: (1) sometimes you know the nature of the risky event and the probability (as in a coin flip); (2) sometimes you know the nature of the event, but don't know the probability (which is uncertainty as in the price of a given stock in 20 years); and (3) sometimes you don't even know the nature of what future states might hurt you.

The best thing you can do to be "safe" given risk, uncertainty and ignorance, is to have a "margin of safety".

33. "It's not whether you're right or wrong that's important, but how much money you make when you're right and how much you lose when you're wrong."

It is "magnitude of correctness" that matters for an investor not "frequency of correctness". This is the "Babe Ruth" effect at work (strike outs in baseball and in investing can be acceptable as long as you hit enough home runs).

34. "There is no point in being confident and having a small position."

If the odds are substantially in your favour on a given wager, bet big.

35. "If investing is entertaining, if you're having fun, you're probably not making any money. Good investing is boring."

Your investments should be boring so that the rest of your life is exciting.

36. "Economic history is a never-ending series of episodes based on falsehoods and lies, not truths."

The ability to create a narrative explanation of the past does not mean that the explanation is correct or the basis for a thesis which can predict the future. This human dysfunction is "hindsight bias" at work.

37. "I'm only rich because I know when I'm wrong ... I basically have survived by recognizing my mistakes" and **"Once we realise that imperfect understanding is the human condition there is no shame in being wrong, only in failing to correct our mistakes."**

This speaks for itself.

Housel's top four tips about investing

Morgan Housel has so many great tips for investors, but here are four you should head:

38. *"Compound interest is what will make you rich — and it takes time."*

Warren Buffett is a great investor, but what makes him rich is that he's been a great investor for two thirds of a century. Of his $60 billion net worth, $59.7 billion was added after his 50th birthday, and $57 billion came after his 60th. If Buffett started saving in his 30s and retired in his 60s, you would have never heard of him. His secret is time.

Most people don't start saving in meaningful amounts until a decade or two before retirement, which severely limits the power of compounding.

39. *"Simple is usually better than smart."*

Someone who bought a low-cost S&P 500 index fund in 2003 earned a 97 per cent return by the end of 2012. That's great! And they didn't need to know a thing about portfolio management or technical analysis.

Meanwhile, the average equity market neutral fancy-pants hedge fund lost 4.7 per cent of its value over the same period, according to data from Dow Jones Credit Suisse Hedge Fund Indices. The average long-short equity hedge fund produced a 96 per cent total return — still short of an index fund.

Investing is not like a computer. Simple and basic can be more powerful than complex and cutting-edge. And it's not like golf because the spectators have a pretty good chance of humbling the pros.

40. *"The odds of the stock market experiencing high volatility are 100 per cent."*

Most investors understand that stocks produce superior long-term returns, but at the cost of higher volatility.

Yet every time — every single time — there's even a hint of volatility, the same cry is heard from the investing public: *"What is going on?!"*

Nine times out of 10, the correct answer is the same — nothing is going on because this is just what stocks do.

41. *"The (financial) industry is dominated by cranks, charlatans and salesman."*

The vast majority of financial products are sold by people whose only interest in your wealth is the amount of fees they can sucker out of you.

You need no experience, credentials, or even common sense to be a financial pundit. Sadly, the louder and more bombastic a pundit is, the more attention he or she will receive, even though it makes him or her more likely to be wrong.

This is perhaps the most important theory in finance. Until it is understood you stand a high chance of being bamboozled and misled at every corner.

More brilliant quotes from Charlie Munger

Charlie Munger is a college-dropout who served as a meteorologist in the US Army Air Corps before graduating from Harvard Law. And then he met Warren Buffett.

The rest is history. Here is a list of his most insightful quotes about investing, business and life.

42. *"I constantly see people rise in life who are not the smartest, sometimes not even the most diligent, but they are learning machines. They go to bed every night a little wiser than they were when they got up*

and boy does that help, particularly when you have a long run ahead of you."

43. *"When any guy offers you a chance to earn lots of money without risk, don't listen to the rest of his sentence. Follow this and you'll save yourself a lot of misery."*

44. *"Everywhere there is a large commission, there is a high probability of a rip-off."*

45. *"There's only one way to the top — hard work."*

46. *"If you're lazy and unreliable, it doesn't even matter what you're good at."*

47. *"Someone will always be getting richer faster than you. This is not a tragedy."*

48. *"Self-pity doesn't solve anything."*

"Generally speaking, envy, resentment, revenge and self-pity are disastrous modes of thought. Self-pity gets fairly close to paranoia and paranoia is one of the very hardest things to reverse. You do not want to drift into self-pity … Self-pity will not improve the situation."

49. *"The greatest minds are in books, not classrooms."*

50. *"If Mozart couldn't get away with it, then neither can you."*

"Another thing that does one in, of course, is the self-serving bias to which we're all subject. You think the 'True Little Me' is entitled to do what it wants to do. And, for instance, why shouldn't the True Little Me overspend my income. There once was a man who became the most famous composer in the world but was utterly miserable most of the time, and one of the reasons was because he always overspent his income. That was Mozart. If

Mozart can't get by with this kind of asinine conduct, I don't think you should try."

51. "In the future, someone will come along and do even better."

52. "If you stop learning in this world, the world rushes right by you."

That's why I keep reading the works of all the experts I'm quoting here.

Some random lessons I've learned by reading Motley Fool

While *www.Fool.com* should be on the regular reading list of all stock investors, there are always some great lessons there for investors in every asset class and all stages of their career.

Some lessons from Sean Williams:

53. You don't have to look at your share portfolio every single day — you'll tend to sleep better if you don't. This doesn't mean ignore your shares, but it's a reminder that if you buy for the long-term you don't have to sit on the edge of your chair watching your shares tick up or down two cents throughout the day.

54. Contrary to the fact, history does not always repeat itself. If it did, we'd all be rich by now! It's yet another reminder that timing the market is a hopeless proposition.

55. Analysts are right about as often as the average investor, so stop placing them on a pedestal and start trusting your own analysis.

56. You'll rarely see the next crisis coming. In 2006, I didn't hear a single person talking about subprime loans. Just accept the fact that market downturns are inevitable and invest accordingly.

57. Losing money is a learning experience, not a reason to crawl back under the bed sheets. Chances are you're going to lose money on a stock at some point in the future. The idea is to take what you've learned and not make the same blatant mistakes again.

Some thoughts from Anand Chokkavelu, the managing editor of _Fool.com_:

58. The more we learn about investing, the more we want to start doing exotic things (naked straddle options, anyone?) and buying stock in obscure companies no one has heard of. Maybe it's boredom, maybe arrogance, or maybe the desire to impress people at parties. Or perhaps it's seeking the glory of being right when few saw it coming. I'm guilty as charged on all counts. When I'm at risk of going off the deep end, I try to remember that stock picking isn't diving. As Buffett has noted, there are no extra points (or returns) for degree of difficulty.

59. Don't waste time mastering things that simply don't work:

Example No. 1: _Day trading_. Like playing roulette, you'll have some victories and you may be able to fool yourself into thinking you're skilful. The house just hopes you keep playing.

Example No. 2: _Technical analysis._ The only chart pattern worth noting is the jagged, but likely downward-sloping line of your savings if you follow this technique.

60. If you don't understand it, don't buy it until you do.

61. It is twice as easy to sound intelligent being pessimistic about the future as it is being optimistic.

62. Diversification doesn't entail making a whole bunch of dangerous investments and hoping they cancel out. That's the financial equivalent of stabbing your leg to cure your flu.

Some more great investment lessons

63. *"The stock market is filled with individuals who know the price of everything, but the value of nothing." — Phillip Fisher*

64. *"How many millionaires do you know who have become wealthy by investing in savings accounts? I rest my case." — Robert G. Allen*

65. *"Investing should be more like watching paint dry or watching grass grow. If you want excitement, take $800 and go to Las Vegas." — Paul Samuelson*

66. *"October: This is one of the peculiarly dangerous months to speculate in stocks. The others are July, January, September, April, November, May, March, June, December, August and February." — Mark Twain*

67. *"The broker said the stock was 'poised to move'. Silly me, I thought he meant up." — Randy Thurman*

68. *"The four most expensive words in the English language are 'This time it's different'." — John Templeton*

69. *"Saving is a great habit but without investing and tracking, it just sleeps" — Manoj Arora*

70. *"When I was young I thought that money was the most important thing in life; now that I am old I know that it is." — Oscar Wilde*

71. *"Markets can remain irrational longer than you can remain solvent. — John Maynard Keynes*

Investment lessons from Donald Trump

Love him or loathe him, Donald Trump is undoubtedly a successful businessman who staged a comeback after going bankrupt twice.

He's made his mark on the world by achieving extraordinary wealth and success aand then becoming one of the most controversial US presidents. Here are some of the best Trump quotes and investment lessons.

72. *"Experience taught me a few things. One is to listen to your gut no matter how good something sounds on paper. The second is that you are generally better off sticking with what you know and the third is that sometimes your best investments are the ones you don't make."*

73. *"I try to learn from the past, but I plan for the future by focusing exclusively on the present. That's where the fun is."*

74. *"If you are interested in balancing work and pleasure, stop trying to balance them. Instead make your work more pleasurable."*

75. *"In the end, you are measured not by how much you undertake but by what you finally accomplished."*

76. *"Money was never a big motivation for me except as a way to keep score. The real excitement is playing the game."*

77. *"Part of being a winner is knowing when enough is enough. Sometimes you have to give up the fight and walk away. Move on to something else that's more productive. Sometimes by losing a battle, you will find a new way to win the war."*

78. *"I don't believe you can ever get hurt by buying a good location at a low price."*

79. *"If you want to buy something; it's obviously in your best interest to convince the seller that what he's got isn't worth very much."*

80. *"If you don't have major problems, you're probably not doing something major."*

81. *"Adversity is a fact of life. Accept that and you will be prepared."*

82. *"When you are confronted with a problem, ask yourself this question: Is this a blip or is it a catastrophe? That will align your thoughts and your reactions to where they should be."*

83. *"Reaping and sowing are directly related, but you need to know which comes first."*

84. *"Resilience is part of the survival of the fittest formula — make sure you remain adaptable."*

85. *"Don't depend on anyone else for providing your financial security."*

Final lessons from Warren Buffett

I have mentioned and quoted from Warren Buffett quite liberally in this book because Buffett really is the best investor of the past 100 years. He is also happy to share his strategies with anyone who is keen to learn so I thought the final investment thoughts should come from the man himself.

86. *Buffet's only two rules for investing are: "Rule Nº 1: Never lose money. Rule Nº 2: Never forget rule Nº 1."*

87. *"Tell me who your heroes are, and I'll tell you who you'll turn out to be."*

88. *"It's nice to have a lot of money, but you know, you don't want to keep it around forever. I prefer buying things. Otherwise, it's a little like saving sex for your old age."*

89. *"The best investment you can make is in your own abilities. Anything you can do to develop your own abilities or business is likely to be more productive than investing in foreign currencies."*

90. *"If you aren't thinking about owning a stock for 10 years, don't even think about owning it for 10 minutes."*

91. *"Diversification is protection against ignorance. It makes little sense if you know what you are doing."*

My thoughts: in the beginning, diversification is important but once you have confidence in your investments you can adjust your portfolio accordingly and specialise rather than diversify.

92. *"I will tell you how to become rich. Close the doors. Be fearful when others are greedy. Be greedy when others are fearful."*

93. *"If you're in the luckiest 1% of humanity, you owe it to the rest of humanity to think about the other 99%."*

In other words — give back to society.

94. *"Forecasts may tell you a great deal about the forecaster; they tell you nothing about the future."*

95. *"Risk comes from not knowing what you are doing."*

96. *"If past history was all that is needed to play the game of money, the richest people would be librarians."*

97. *"In the business world, the rear-view mirror is always clearer than the windshield."*

98. *"Honesty is a very expensive gift. Don't expect it from cheap people."*

99. *"We'll never risk what we have for what we don't have and don't need."*

A great Buffett reason not to fudge your taxes.

100. *And the final message is doing nothing is often the right thing to do:* **"You do things when the opportunities come along. I've had periods in my life when I've had a bundle of ideas come along and I've had long dry spells. If I get an idea next week, I'll do something. If not, I won't do a damn thing."**

SOME FINAL WORDS

One of my assumptions behind writing this book was the big question on many people's minds: "How do I get rich?" And I wanted to provide readers with some answers.

When you look at the richest people in the world — what's the common link? Apart from deep pockets, most have grown their wealth through running a business. Mark Zukerberg, Elon Musk, Rupert Murdoch, Gina Rinehart, Warren Buffett and their ilk have become rich from business.

However, if you don't feel adventurous enough to join the other 2.35 million small businesses in Australia, you at least should adopt some business practices to build your wealth.

That's why I've tried to teach you to treat your investments like a business. This means you should create a wealth plan, just as a business should start with a business plan. This requires you to work out your goals and then piece together the strategy to make it happen.

Of course, everyone already has a wealth plan that they are following. And *your* wealth plan will either lead you to financial riches or financial ruin.

Now here's the most shocking part: for more than 96 per cent of people their wealth plan is designed for financial mediocrity at best and for financial failure at worst!

It's true. According to analysis of ABS statistics, currently most Australians who reach age 65 wind up dependent on the government, their family, or a job as one of the main sources to fund their "golden years". And more Australians than ever before intend to work beyond 70, as Generation Xers and Baby Boomers fear they lack the financial security needed to retire any sooner.

That's why I have a problem with the traditional wealth plan of: *"Get a good education so that you can land a good job (as determined by its security and salary); then work for 40 or 50 years saving as you go; invest your leftover money in conventional investments such as superannuation or managed funds so that you can retire at age 65 or 70; then hope that your money doesn't run out while you're still alive."*

Not a very inspiring plan, is it? Especially considering that this plan fails nine out of 10 people who end up finding their later years full of economic uncertainty and anxiety.

Why would anyone choose to follow a plan that at best leads to financial sufficiency but not real freedom, and also has such an astronomically high failure rate? Sadly, it's because the average person doesn't know any better.

But now that you've been introduced to the world of investing this doesn't have to be that way for you. You can take charge of your financial life and secure your financial future.

Yet if you're like many people I share these ideas with, you'll find yourself torn. Part of you wants to run and hide under the covers. All this talk of financial matters intimidates you. Maybe you'd rather not know, yet you know that this route is a recipe for financial disaster.

And part of you knows the ideas I shared with you in this book are right.

Of course it's okay that part of you finds this stuff scary. Fear is a normal, often healthy, reaction to the unknown. It's how you act in the presence of your fear that will determine what your ultimate economic rewards will be.

Have you ever seen a frightened toddler? You go to put him or her to bed and they cling to you because they're scared of the monsters under the bed. Toddlers deal with their fear by covering their eyes and hiding under the covers. Why? Because they believe that if they can't see those monsters then those monsters won't be able to see them.

Well, what's adorable in a toddler isn't so cute in our adult lives. We know that just because we close our eyes doesn't mean the "monsters" in our financial lives will disappear.

So don't let yourself fall prey to this all-too-common way the average person plans out their financial life — by hiding.

It can be different for you; you can become rich and successful. But it's up to you to make it happen!

And don't fall into the trap of blindly turning your investments over to a "professional" manager to do your investing for you. Sure the temptation is there to simply invest in a "diversified portfolio of professionally managed securities" and hope for the best.

As for me, I'm not comfortable passively allowing other people, most of who are still financially struggling employees themselves, to be in control of my financial destiny.

Since I've invested the time and energy to cultivate my investing skills, today I can consistently outperform the market. Passing on these skills to others (to you) is the reason I wrote this book — so that *you* can take control of *your* financial destiny.

You will be the one in control. You will be the one securing your financial results; you will be the one who can make sure you reach your financial dreams.

Not someone else … you!

Does this take more effort? Of course it does. But remember that the stakes are incredibly high and the price of not making the investment could be financially fatal for you and your family.

Plus, the rewards dwarf the investment, and are quite literally 1,000 times greater than the investment of time and money it will take you to master these skills.

As you build your investing skills, you'll reduce your risks

While the mass media is going to tell you to reduce risk by diversifying, I've already taught you that risk cannot be isolated from the investor. In fact, I went one step further and explained that the root cause of investment risk has more to do with the investor than it does with the investment.

What's risky for one investor may be a bread and butter investment for another investor.

For example, I'm very good at investing in real estate. That is my main passive wealth vehicle. When I invest in property I'm able to outperform the average returns two to three times.

But I'm not an expert in investing in commodities. Virtually any investment I make in commodities will be quite risky for me.

As Warren Buffet says, *"Risk comes from not knowing what you are doing."*

Where do you start?

Early in this book I taught you my model of the various levels of investor, now let me remind you how they approach money differently.

Level 0 and 1 people don't build wealth. Their focus is narrowed on getting through today. Unless they do something radically different they will end up financially dependent and struggling their entire lives.

Level 2 investors build wealth out of their income. What this means is that they see investing as a process of scrimping and saving to squirrel away a small amount of their after tax "left over" money to build their "nest egg" bit by bit over 40-plus years.

Level 2 people tend to just hand their money over to a "professional" manager to invest for them. Never mind that this professional manager is usually a salesperson working on commission.

Level 3 investors build their income out of their wealth. They use their wealth as a powerful tool to build more wealth. They don't limit their investments to using just their own limited "nest egg". Instead, they realise that they can leverage their time, their talents, their assets and their other advantages to magnify their returns.

They focus on their skill as an investor because they realise that the better they get — the more informed, the more educated, the more savvy — the greater their investment returns will be and the lower their investment risk will be.

Shouldn't your first wealth priority be to learn what you are doing? Of course it should be, which is the reason why I wrote this book.

The advantages you need to reach your financial goals

If you take just one thing away with you after reading this book I hope it is this — you can learn the skills and develop the advantages that you need to reach your financial dreams.

For many readers this book will be an introduction to the world of investing, for others it will be a refresher, but it was never meant to be the "silver bullet" or a concrete system for you. What I really wanted to do is teach you what the right choices for your money are; how to profitably invest; and to entice you to make the commitment to continue your learning as well as further cultivate your investment skills.

Everyone has the same potential to take charge of their financial situation, irrespective of their current circumstances, level of education, business or investment experience.

Internal obstacles — like limiting beliefs, false perceptions and myths from the past — thwart success more than any external obstacles ever could. I've written a whole book on this in *Michael Yardney's Guide To Getting Rich* (*www.MichaelYardneyBooks.com.au*).

In this book I explain how your mind is the only thing that stands in the way of you and your ultimate wealth and fulfilment. Now that's great news, because it means *you* can break through those self-imposed barriers.

Interestingly as you earn more money, you will realise that money doesn't bring you happiness. It may give you some short-term satisfaction, especially if you are financially insecure, but as you work your way up the Wealth Pyramid you will find that relationships and contributions will mean more to you than money.

Money by itself is empty and meaningless — you have to give it a meaning. Money can be earned, grown, invested, fought over, won, lost, watched over, exchanged, given away or buried. But the nicest thing you can do with money is share it.

Contribution has become an important part of life for Pam and me. Every dollar we have shared with someone less able to gain prosperity has doubled in value — maybe not as cold hard cash but in many other ways.

Now I'm not trying to browbeat you. It's just that I've noticed that really successful, happy wealthy people enjoy sharing their wealth and therein lies a lesson for all of us.

What now?

The trouble with so many books is that when you've finished them, you're finished with what they have to tell you. What happens after that? Readers are often left to their own devices to try to take the next step and put the theory they have learned into action. This book is going to be a little bit different.

I'm eager for the ideas in this book to work for you, so I've assembled a "tool-kit" of resources for you to help you in your climb up the investment ladder — just go to _www.InvestingSuccessfully.today_ and collect them now. There's special reports, spreadsheets and much more.

I also recommend you subscribe to my daily newsletter at _www.PropertyUpdate.com.au_ and join over 2.7 million readers who visited that site last year alone.

And you must really subscribe to the **Michael Yardney Podcast** on your favourite podcast app, because twice a week I'll teach you so new ideas about money, success and property investing.

So thank you for reading this book — now it's up to you! You now have the knowledge to make more intelligent investment decisions. You are now ready to join the ranks of the financially free. When you do, please email me and let me know about your success. The emails I get from readers of my books who have successfully put my strategies to work energise me and really do make my day.

Spend your time … wisely.

Michael Yardney
michael@metropole.com.au